# MENTORING TEACHERS IN SCOTLAND

This book assists mentors in developing their mentoring skills, offering guidance needed to support the development of beginning teachers in early years, primary and secondary schools in the Scottish education system, as well as supporting all teachers in their career-long professional learning.

Based on research and evidence, *Mentoring Teachers in Scotland* explores and discusses the knowledge, skills and understanding that underpin mentoring that is responsive to individual mentees' needs. The book includes reflective activities to enable mentors to consider the application of mentoring processes in their own practice, as well as case studies and other learning activities. This book is a valuable source of support and inspiration for all those involved in mentoring and sustaining teachers' professional development at all stages of their career. Key topics explored include:

- roles and responsibilities of mentors within the Scottish education system, and the Scottish model of teaching and teacher development;
- developing a mentor-mentee relationship;
- guiding beginning teachers in Scotland through the mentoring processes;
- strategies for observation, analysis and reflection on practice; and
- mentoring for beginning teachers and career-long professional learning.

*Mentoring Teachers in Scotland* offers an accessible and practical guide to mentoring teachers in Scotland that aims to support, inspire and guide mentors and mentees.

**Sandra Eady** is a Senior Lecturer in the Division of Psychology, Sociology and Education at Queen Margaret University, Scotland.

**Jane Essex** is a Senior Lecturer in Chemistry Education at the University of Strathclyde, Scotland.

**Kay Livingston** is a Professor of Educational Research Policy and Practice in the School of Education at the University of Glasgow, Scotland.

**Margaret McColl** is a Senior Lecturer in Museum and Art Education in the School of Education at the University of Glasgow, Scotland.

# MENTORING TRAINEE AND EARLY CAREER TEACHERS

Series edited by: Susan Capel, Trevor Wright, Julia Lawrence and Sarah Younie

The **Mentoring Trainee and Early Career Teachers** Series are subject-specific, practical books designed to reinforce and develop mentors' understanding of the different aspects of their role, as well as exploring issues that mentees encounter in the course of learning to teach. The books have two main foci: first, challenging mentors to reflect critically on theory, research and evidence, on their own knowledge, their approaches to mentoring and how they work with beginning teachers in order to move their practice forward; and second, supporting mentors to effectively facilitate the development of beginning teachers. Although the basic structure of all the subject books is similar, each book is different to reflect the needs of mentors in relation to the unique nature of each subject or age phase. Elements of appropriate theory introduce each topic or issue, with emphasis placed on the practical application of material. The chapter authors in each book have been engaged with mentoring over a long period of time and share research, evidence and their experience.

We hope that this series of books supports you in developing into an effective, reflective mentor as you support the development of the next generation of teachers.

For more information about this series, please visit: https://www.routledge.com/Mentoring-Trainee-and-Early-Career-Teachers/book-series/MTNQT

## Titles in the series

*Mentoring English Teachers in the Secondary School*
Edited by Debbie Hickman

*Mentoring Science Teachers in the Secondary School*
Edited by Saima Salehjee

*Mentoring Teachers in the Primary School*
Edited by Kristy Howells and Julia Lawrence, with Judith Roden

*Mentoring Geography Teachers in the Secondary School*
Edited by Grace Healy, Lauren Hammond, Steve Puttick and Nicola Walshe

*Mentoring Teachers in Scotland*
Edited by Sandra Eady, Jane Essex, Kay Livingston and Margaret McColl

# MENTORING TEACHERS IN SCOTLAND

## A Practical Guide

Edited by Sandra Eady, Jane Essex,
Kay Livingston and Margaret McColl

CB2

04 / 27

Routledge
Taylor & Francis Group

LONDON AND NEW YORK

Cover image: © Peter Unger / Getty Images

First published 2022
by Routledge
2 Park Square, Milton Park, Abingdon, Oxon OX14 4RN

and by Routledge
605 Third Avenue, New York, NY 10158

*Routledge is an imprint of the Taylor & Francis Group, an informa business*

© 2022 Sandra Eady, Jane Essex, Kay Livingston and Margaret McColl

*British Library Cataloguing-in-Publication Data*
A catalogue record for this book is available from the British Library

*Library of Congress Cataloging-in-Publication Data*
A catalog record has been requested for this book

ISBN: 978-0-367-40598-4 (hbk)
ISBN: 978-0-367-40599-1 (pbk)
ISBN: 978-0-429-35695-7 (ebk)

DOI: 10.4324/9780429356957

Typeset in Interstate
by Newgen Publishing UK

# CONTENTS

# AUTHOR BIOGRAPHIES

**Fiona Allen** was a full-time mentor for 10 years for Aberdeenshire Council, mentoring probationary teachers across a range of primary schools. Prior to that she was a primary teacher for 12 years.

**Andrea McIlhatton Cardow** has worked in education for North Lanarkshire Council for 29 years. Currently, she is Probation Manager for North Lanarkshire Council, with joint responsibility for planning, co-ordinating and delivering the probationer programme for North Lanarkshire Council. As a Probation Manager, Andrea has responsibility for tailoring the support given to new cohorts of probationary teachers and the staff who support them. In 2015 she was awarded Professional Recognition with the General Teaching Council for Scotland for work done in supporting new teachers with inclusion. Since 2018 Andrea has worked as an Associate Tutor on the MEd Inclusion, Policy and Practice programme at Glasgow University as course leader for Developing Literacy and supervising master's dissertation students.

**Sandra Clarke** is an Education Officer for Argyll and Bute Council. She has led in small rural schools and in large inner-city schools in Scotland and England. She has developed and led professional learning for support staff, probationers, Middle Leaders, and newly appointed and experienced Head Teachers. Educational interests include leadership, literacy, drama, curriculum development, assessment, developing nurturing approaches, skills development, coaching and mentoring.

**Sandra Eady** [0000-0002-1089-666X] is currently a Senior Lecturer in Education at Queen Margaret University. She has experience teaching across both undergraduate and postgraduate teacher education programmes. Sandra has written on a number of subjects relating to professional education, including mentoring, professional learning and education partnership.

**Jane Essex** [0000-0002-9938-8134] is a Senior Lecturer in Chemistry Education at Strathclyde University, with teaching and supervision responsibilities on the PGDE Chemistry. She has worked in Initial Teacher Education for 20 years and was a teacher prior to that. Her major professional and research interest is the preparation of teachers to teach inclusively, most especially in STEM (science, technology, engineering and mathematics). Her work with teachers has included postgraduate teaching and supervision of research degrees. She has also conducted extensive Continuing Lifelong Professional

Learning work and has pioneered the use of outreach with diverse audiences as a mechanism for professional development by STEM academics.

**Jennifer Farrar** [0000-0002-7128-6355] is a Lecturer at the University of Glasgow in children's literature and literacies, with a background in secondary English teaching. She is Programme Leader of the PGDE Primary and Secondary, a 1-year route into the teaching profession, and also leads the School of Education's online MSc in Education. She is currently researching student teachers' knowledge and use of children's literature and is also working on ways to raise Scottish teacher and policy makers' awareness and understanding of critical literacies in classroom contexts.

**Aileen Kennedy** [0000-0002-2724-6911] is Professor of Practice in Teacher Education at the University of Strathclyde. She is the Director of Teacher Education in the School of Education, working with colleagues and wider stakeholders to enhance and promote work in teacher education policy and pedagogy.

**Kay Livingston** [0000-0002-9831-9575] is Professor of Educational Research, Policy and Practice at the School of Education, University of Glasgow. The focus of her work for over 30 years has been teacher education, including career-long professional learning, from research, policy and practice perspectives. Mentors and mentoring of all teachers have been particular research areas of focus and she has provided mentor training in local authorities and schools in Scotland and internationally.

**Maggie McColl** is Director of Post Graduate Taught Studies in the School of Education at the University of Glasgow and a Senior Lecturer in Museum and Art Education. Maggie led the transition from BEd Honours to Master of Education and co-led the design and development of the innovative new Partnership Model of Teacher Education in the School. In 2017, Maggie developed a MSc in Museum Education, a new degree designed to situate education and learning at the core of the museum and heritage experience. Since the launch of the MSc in Museum Education, Maggie has led a consortium of international partners to build an International Masters in Education, Museums and Heritage.

**Willie McGuire** [000-0002-1323-9702] is a Senior Lecturer in English Language (Pedagogy, Praxis and Faith) at the University of Glasgow. He is a member of the university's Teaching Excellence Network and contributes regularly to Glasgow University Teaching Tips Online (GUSTTO). Willie has been the recipient of teaching excellence awards at both college and university levels. He runs an alumni support initiative that supports graduates' transition from their probationary period in teaching into permanent posts.

**Margery McMahon** [0000-0002-2170-5419] is Head of the School of Education at the University of Glasgow and Professor of Educational Leadership. A former teacher of History and Politics, Margery has been involved in teacher education, career-long professional learning and leadership education since joining the University of Glasgow. She is the author and co-author of a range of books and articles focusing on professional learning and leadership, including Forde, C. and McMahon, M. (2019) *Teacher Quality, Professional Learning and Policy*, London: Palgrave MacMillan. She is UK representative for the International Study Association for Teachers and Teaching (ISATT).

**Lorele Mackie** [0000-0003-0249-0253] is a Lecturer in Education in the Faculty of Social Sciences. She is Director of Placements for Initial Teacher Education, Programme Coordinator for the BA (Hons) Professional Education Primary (with specialism in Modern Languages) degree and works across all Initial Teacher Education programmes, as well as supervising students at Master's and Doctoral levels. As a primary education teacher, she has taught at all stages and has experience of both mainstream and additional support needs (ASN). Prior to commencing her post at the University of Stirling, she was a Teaching Fellow at Moray House School of Education where she developed and ran a range of courses on both the PGDE (Primary) and B.Ed (Primary) programmes. She has particular research interests in mentoring beginner teachers, learning and teaching in second and subsequent languages, and innovative pedagogies.

**Geetha Marcus** [0000-0001-5610-5344] is a Senior Lecturer in the Psychology, Sociology and Education Division and the Academic Lead for Placements on the BA Hons Education Studies (Primary) and PGDE Home Economics programmes. She is also Programme Leader on the BA (Hons) Education Studies programme at Queen Margaret University. Geetha is a sociologist who has extensive professional experience in classroom practice, mentoring and senior management.

**Jacqueline Morley** is a Senior Education Officer for the General Teaching Council for Scotland, with a focus on Career-long Professional Learning and Leadership. She began her career as a primary school teacher and has worked in adult learning and teacher education for over 30 years. She was Continuing Professional Development Manager for Scottish Borders Council, where she built a strong coaching and mentoring culture.

**Elaine Napier** is a Senior Strategic Manager for the General Teaching Council for Scotland (GTC Scotland). Originally a primary teacher, Elaine then became a Probation Manager in a local authority before moving to the Early Career team at GTC Scotland. Her current role relates to student placements, probationers and early career teachers.

**Morag Redford** [0000-0002-6677-7811] is Professor of Teacher Education at the University of the Highlands and Islands, where she has led the development of initial teacher education and master's provision for practising teachers across the region. A key focus of her work has been the joint development of mentoring for leadership with local authority partners.

**Lynne Shiach** concluded her 40-year career in Nursery Primary Education as a mentor working with probationary teachers. Prior to that she worked in a range of urban and rural primary schools as a teacher and school leader before becoming a teacher educator in Higher Education.

**Charlaine Simpson** is a Senior Lecturer and Head of Postgraduate (Taught) and Professional Learning in the School of Education at the University of Aberdeen and formerly a Senior Education Officer for the General Teaching Council for Scotland. She taught in Falkirk Council for 23 years, where she worked both within school and across the local authority supporting teacher learning and aspiring leaders. She has recently completed an EdD with a research focus on the enactment of Professional Standards in the Scottish context.

**Niccy Smith** was a full-time mentor for 4 years for Aberdeenshire Council, mentoring probationary teachers across a range of primary schools. Prior to that she was a primary teacher and acting Head Teacher.

**Pauline Stephen** is Chief Executive and Registrar of the General Teaching Council for Scotland. A primary teacher and educational psychologist, Pauline was previously Principal Psychologist for Aberdeenshire Council and Director of Schools and Learning for Angus Council.

# SECTION 1

# The place of mentoring in Scottish education

# 1 What do we mean by mentoring? The context for mentoring in Scotland

*Kay Livingston*

## Objectives

At the end of this chapter, you should be able to:

- critically reflect on different definitions of a mentor and what these mean for mentoring approaches;
- understand the main elements of mentoring and how they underpin all approaches to mentoring;
- have an awareness of the context for mentoring in Scotland; and
- understand how different approaches to mentoring influence the different roles mentors take to support and challenge teachers at different stages of their career.

## Introduction

The task of teaching is complex and continually changing, whether you are a student teacher, a beginning teacher or a teacher who is already well into your career. Mentoring has been recognised as having a prominent role in supporting the learning and development of student teachers and beginning teachers (Hobson et al., 2009; Ambrosetti et al., 2014). There is also a growing number of research studies that identify the positive outcomes of mentoring for all teachers, regardless of their level of experience, as part of their continuing professional learning (e.g., Bressman et al., 2018). This raises the importance of mentoring in all phases of a teacher's career and increases the need for well-prepared mentors in schools. This book provides an opportunity to reflect on and develop your understanding of mentoring and your practice as a mentor. The aim is to enable you to think about and develop your understanding of mentoring from different perspectives.

This chapter begins by considering the challenges of defining mentoring. Different understandings of what mentoring means and what a mentor does are discussed in relation to the different approaches that mentors take with their mentees. These different approaches highlight the dynamic nature of mentoring relationships according to the learning aims and needs of their mentees. The range of mentor roles and the main underpinning elements of mentoring are discussed in the second section. The context and purpose of mentoring has implications for the choices that mentors make about roles and approaches, so the context for mentoring in Scotland is briefly introduced in the third section. In the final section, the

DOI: 10.4324/9780429356957-2

different models of mentoring identified in the chapter are considered in terms of what and how mentors can draw from them to inform and improve their practice.

## Different definitions of a mentor and different approaches to mentoring

There are different definitions of a mentor, and mentoring is open to many interpretations. This section begins with a task for you to reflect on your definition of a mentor and your understanding of what it means for mentoring in practice.

---

### Task 1.1   Reflecting on your understanding of a mentor and mentoring

- What is your definition of a mentor and what is your understanding of mentoring?
- Take time before you read this section to reflect on and write down how you would define a mentor and mentoring.

---

'Mentor' and 'mentoring' are contested concepts and part of the reason for this is the different beliefs and theories people hold about what a mentor is and the role(s) they undertake. Colley (2003, p.524) argues that mentoring 'is ill-defined, poorly conceptualised and weakly theorised'. However, according to Kemmis et al. (2014, p.155), confusion about mentoring 'is not so much about a lack of theories but rather about a plurality of theories'. They argue, 'Just as "mentoring" does not have one fixed and final meaning, there is not just one aim or purpose for mentoring' (p.156). Bearman et al.'s (2007) view is that because mentoring involves social interactions between mentor and mentee, it will always be difficult to define. Different definitions of what 'mentoring' means arise because people have different ideas about how mentoring should be carried out in a variety of settings, and how mentors and mentees should relate to one another in a mentoring relationship. Within an educational context, Orland-Barak (2010, p.2) argues that practice is embedded in multiple realities, 'at the intersection between ideologies, values, belief systems and behaviours'. These multiple realities mean different understandings of mentors and mentoring can arise (for example, from theories that individual's hold about what knowledge is important or about how people learn best, or from their beliefs about the purpose of and the best approach to mentoring teachers at different stages in their career).

To add to the complication of different definitions, the terms 'mentoring' and 'coaching' are often used synonymously. Some researchers distinguish between the terms, suggesting that mentoring is an overarching term and coaching is one role that a mentor takes up out of many mentoring roles. For example, a coach is someone involved in coaching or training specific skills and/or supporting the replication of actions or behaviours (Kochan and Pascarelli, 2012). These different definitions and terms highlight the challenges of conceptual clarity and the potential for misunderstandings to arise between mentors and mentees when people hold different views and expectations about the roles of mentors and the purposes of mentoring. In this book, we acknowledge that terminology and meaning are contested and that people have different reasons for the terminology they choose. As Editors, we have chosen to use the terms mentor and mentoring. Our view is that mentoring is more complex than coaching, involving deeper and broader interactions between mentors and mentees in order to understand and support individual learning needs and areas for professional development.

---

**Task 1.2   Further reflection on your understanding of a mentor and mentoring**

• A selection of different definitions of mentor and mentoring are discussed below. As you read, think about what ways the definitions below are similar to or different from your own definition in Task 1.1?

---

Crafton and Kaiser (2011, p.106) suggest, 'Traditionally, mentoring has meant a one-to-one relationship between a novice and expert …'. This classic definition of a mentor is rooted in Homer's poem, 'The Odyssey'. Odysseus entrusted the care of his young son to Mentor because of his knowledge and expertise to guide, instruct and protect his novice protégé on his journey to manhood. This traditional definition is most closely aligned with a hierarchical model of mentoring, where a knowledgeable other/more experienced teacher is selected to support the development of novice teachers.

> Mentoring is a practice where a more experienced educator (the mentor) offers support, guidance, advice and encouragement to someone who is a beginner or less experienced educator (the mentee) with the intended purpose of enhancing teaching and learning.
>
> (Bressman et al., 2018, p.163)

This definition of a mentor is often associated with a *master/apprentice approach to mentoring*. This approach is underpinned by a transmission view of imparting knowledge that the mentor believes is important to a novice mentee. The mentor models behaviours which the less knowledgeable and less experienced mentee is expected to follow and replicate. The main roles of the mentor in this approach are instructor and adviser to assist the mentee in what to do. This approach to mentoring has been criticised as perpetuating the status quo as it can serve to socialise individuals into established organisational norms (Ensher et al., 2001). It is also argued that in this traditional description of mentoring, where the mentor assumes a dominant role, the power dimension could create tensions between the mentor and mentee (Awaya et al., 2003) and stifle the potential for the mentee's active involvement in their own development as a teacher.

The master/apprentice approach to mentoring was described to me by a beginning teacher as 'a mini-me approach'. Her perception was that her mentor expected her to follow and attempt to enact what she did in her own classroom. In a mentoring study carried out in Scotland (Livingston and Shiach, 2013, 2014), some of the primary and secondary school mentors working with newly qualified teachers said they deliberately took a master/ apprentice approach because they believed that their role as a mentor was to pass on their knowledge and experience by *telling* and *modelling* their tried and tested learning activities and teaching processes. They said they took this approach in their desire to be the best mentor to their mentee and to help them as much as possible. In the mentor preparation pro-gramme during the study, they said they realised that focusing on transferring their know-ledge and experience based on what they had found worked for them was not necessarily the most helpful way to support beginning teachers in developing their own way of working with their pupils. It did not provide the mentees with opportunities to learn to take decisions for themselves about appropriate approaches to learning and teaching in their own classroom or to develop their own understanding of what it means to be a teacher.

While role-modelling and providing advice may be appropriate at specific times, Kram (1983) argues that to fully understand the nature and impact of the developing relation-ship between a mentor and mentee, it is necessary to examine how it changes over time. She identified different phases in the mentoring process when the types of interactions between mentor and mentee change. This changing relationship between a mentor and mentee is evident in an article written by Kochan and Trimble (2000). Trimble was mentored by Kochan and, at first, they both held the view that mentoring was a one-way approach in which the mentee is moulded by someone of greater age, wisdom or position. However, they realised that their mentoring relationship changed over time, 'the mentor, rather than serving as a font of perfect knowledge, became a co-learner in a process of discovery.' (p.21). The mentoring approach became collaborative with both the mentor and mentee having a role in developing each other's learning. This *co-mentoring* or *peer-mentoring approach* adapts over time according to professional learning needs. It is a non-hierarchical approach, more reciprocal and of mutual benefit to mentor and mentee. It enables both to take an enquiring role in problem-solving, progressing knowledge and practice development in col-laboration. As Le Cornu (2005, p.358) suggests, in 'co-mentoring, both mentor and mentee are positioned as co-learners or co-constructors of knowledge'.

Co-mentoring has extended further with *peer-group mentoring*, which is being advocated as a model for supporting teachers' professional development. Heikkinen, Jokinen and Tynjälä (2012, p.xv) define peer-group mentoring as,

> An activity involving teachers sharing and reflecting on their experiences, discussing problems and challenges they meet in their work, listening, encouraging one another, and above all, learning from each other, and learning together.

This approach shifts mentoring from a one-directional or bi-directional approach to a multi-directional approach. It does not privilege one voice but acknowledges that the voices of all parties involved in peer-group mentoring contribute to transformative possibilities for learning and professional development. This approach highlights the active role of everyone involved in constructing their own meanings and interpretations and in the co-construction of meaning with their peers.

Co-mentoring, peer-mentoring and peer-group mentoring approaches are underpinned by social constructionist theories of learning, based on beliefs that knowledge development is rooted in activity and embodied in social and cultural practices (Bereiter, 2002). In this theoretical perspective, mentor and mentee learning is understood as 'participatory, pro-active, communal, collaborative and given over to the construction of meanings rather than receiving them' (Bruner, 1996, p.84). These collaborative forms of mentoring are recognised as being beneficial to all teachers in the career-long professional learning phase of their career. For example, Hargreaves and Fullan (2000, p.55) call for mentoring to move from 'hierarchical dispensations of wisdom to shared inquiries into practice' and 'from being performed in pairs to becoming an integral part of professional cultures in schools'. They argue that mentoring should be less individualistic, more wide-ranging and more inclusive in its orientation than it has been viewed in the past. The emphasis is on *all* teachers being supported to engage regularly with one another in enquiry and reflection to better under-stand and improve learning and teaching. This approach to mentoring is very different to the traditional hierarchical model of mentoring. Mentors take up a much broader range of roles that may include, but will go beyond, being an advisor, a role model or a guide. For example, the mentor role may be a resource for learning, a facilitator, an observer, a collaborator, an enquiry partner, or problem-solver. This list is not exhaustive. Also, a mentor may move from one role to another in a dynamic way during a mentoring meeting with their mentee and/or over time, according to the purpose of mentoring, and/or as professional learning needs are uncovered and better understood.

---

## Task 1.3   Reflection on mentor roles

- List the roles that you currently take up as a mentor.
- If you are not already a mentor, make a list of the roles that your ideal mentor would have (someone who you would like to mentor you according to the stage of your career).
- Reflect on your expectations of a mentor and how they relate to your views about how people learn best.

---

## Mentor roles and actions

Views on the roles of a mentor and their association to different approaches to mentoring have evolved over time and are still evolving. Anderson and Shannon (1988) voiced concern over the lack of conceptual frameworks for organising the various mentoring functions and behaviours found within the definitions of mentoring. They identified five functions with associated roles of mentoring:

- teaching (role-modelling, confirming, disconfirming, informing, questioning, prescribing);
- sponsoring (supporting, protecting, advocating);
- encouraging (inspiring, affirming, challenging);
- counselling (listening, clarifying, probing, problem-solving, advising); and
- befriending (accepting and relating).

They argued that nurturing and caring underpin all the above functions. While mentor roles such as listening, clarifying, probing, problem-solving, advising and relating are important in all mentor approaches, in the context of mentoring teachers, the question of where the boundaries of mentor functions end arises. How the various roles are understood by mentors may differ. For example, counselling may be understood to include functions that require specific skills, requiring specialised training, not expected of a teacher mentor working with a colleague for the purpose of professional development. As a mentor it is important for you to recognise role boundaries. For example, if mental health issues arise, this may go beyond the expertise of the mentor teacher, in which case the role would be to support the mentee in accessing specialised counselling or other relevant services. In relation to befriending, while socioemotional support is important, Achinstein and Athanases (2006, p.6) argue that mentoring should not be limited to the role of 'buddy' to a teacher. More recently, Ambrosetti and Dekker's (2010) analysis of research on mentoring identified additional mentor functions, including critical friend. This role signals the importance of a mentor also challenging practice in order to support a mentee's reflection and ongoing development as a professional. The final section of this chapter considers support and challenge in mentoring in more detail.

The lists of multiple mentor roles and functions that can be found in the literature (e.g., Ambrossetti et al., 2014; Garza et al., 2019) demonstrate the complexity of mentoring. These lists risk overwhelming a new mentor. Also, definitions of a mentor and lists of mentor roles have been criticised for not giving mentors enough specific direction in terms of *what* they are to do or *how* they are to do it (Anderson and Shannon, 1988). Orland-Barak (2010, p.7) argues that to make sense of the multiple roles of a mentor, the process of learning to mentor should focus on the *actions* of a mentor. She provides the following examples,

- reading a mentoring situation;
- observing and appraising pedagogical practices;
- recording appropriate modes of support;
- mediating persons, context and content;
- assuming diverse supportive roles;
- managing accountabilities;
- establishing and sustaining relationships;
- tuning in [to a mentee's needs and their specific context];
- articulating teaching, learning and subject matter; and
- responding on the 'spot' by connecting experience, beliefs and knowledge.

Underlying different mentoring roles and actions there are three elements identified by Kram (1985) that are relevant to all mentoring processes: connection, needs and context. Ambrosetti et al. (2014) summarise these three inter-related elements as relational, developmental and contextual.

*The relational element* concerns the relationship between the mentor and mentee and their willingness to engage in the mentoring process. Livingston and Shiach (2013, 2014) found that the development of a trusting relationship is fundamental to any mentoring approach at any stage of a teacher's career. Without a trusting relationship the potential of mentoring to develop mentee and mentor learning is undermined. Building trust, reciprocity and responsiveness to each other is central to the relational, developmental and contextual elements of mentoring.

*The developmental element* concerns the purpose of the relationship and the specific professional learning needs and goals of the mentor and mentee. 'One size' does not fit all – each mentoring relationship and purpose is different. All teachers are individual learners with different personal and professional development needs at different stages of their careers. Purposes of mentoring and mentor roles can come into conflict. Kemmis et al. (2014) argue that this can particularly be the case in approaches to mentoring teachers at the start of their career. They suggest that the three different purposes that follow, and their associated roles, can be in tension with one another and limit the success of mentoring processes:

*Mentoring as supervision* – 'assisting newly qualified teachers to pass through the formal juridical requirements for probation'.

*Mentoring as support* – 'supporting new teachers in the development of their professional practices by more experienced teachers'.

*Mentoring as collaborative self-development* – 'assisting new teachers collectively to develop their professional identities'.

(Kemmis et al., 2014, p.155)

Supervision can involve an assessor role requiring judgements about the progress of the mentee towards becoming a teacher. This judgemental requirement can be in tension with the developmental element of mentoring. The mentors in Livingston and Shiach's studies (2013, 2014) who were supporting beginning teachers said that a trusting relationship was crucial for them in order to judge the progress of their mentee and, at the same time, support and collaborate with them in a way that enabled their mentee to share learning and teaching challenges openly and honestly. This required the mentee to engage in reflection and self-assessment, which in turn had to be facilitated and supported by the mentor.

*The contextual element* relates to the conditions of the profession and specific job conditions of the mentee. Teachers work in different social and cultural contexts and, while they have individual learning needs, their professional development also relates to specific contextual requirements and needs of a class, school, local authority or at a national level. The challenge for mentors is understanding what their mentee's individual learning needs are within the context in which they work, as well as giving consideration to the particular stage of their mentee's career.

In summary, the mentor roles and the mentoring strategies you choose as a mentor need to be appropriate to your mentee's needs, concerns, current stage of professional development, and the policy and practice context in which your mentee works. The following section focuses on the context for mentoring in Scotland. If you are working in another context, you could use the next section to reflect on your own mentoring context in comparison with the context in Scotland.

## The context in Scotland for mentoring

In Scotland, mentoring is increasingly recognised at policy and practice levels as important across teachers' careers; from the starting point when they become a student teacher in initial teacher education, through induction as a newly qualified teacher and into their career-long professional learning. In 2010 a comprehensive review of teacher education in

Scotland was carried out. The report of the review, *Teaching Scotland's Future* (Donaldson, 2011), made the importance of mentoring for *all* teachers in Scotland clear and signalled the ambition to develop a culture of mentoring across all stages of a teacher's career. However, this ambition needs to be underpinned by an understanding of *all teachers as learners*. It also requires the conditions to be in place to provide support for teachers' ongoing learning. One such condition is the provision of support for mentoring processes in schools, including ongoing support for mentor preparation. It also requires mentoring to be better understood and recognised as a valued process, embedded within professional development opportunities and as professional learning in its own right. Awareness of the professional learning needs of teachers across their careers and of the conditions needed to support teachers and mentors is evident in the recommendations set out in Donaldson's report (2011). The recommendations propose that mentoring is relevant to the professional development of all teachers at all stages of their careers:

*Mentoring student teachers* – 'They [schools] should provide an effective professional learning environment and the capacity to mentor and assess student teachers' (Donaldson, 2011, p.44).

*Mentoring newly qualified teachers* – 'The quality and impact of mentoring for each new teacher is central to the success of the teacher induction scheme' (Donaldson, 2011, p.51).

*Mentoring at all stages of a teacher's career* – 'Mentoring is central to professional development at all stages in a teacher's career and all teachers should see themselves as mentors not just of students and newly qualified teachers but more generally' (Donaldson, 2011, p.98).

The reality has not yet fully met all the recommendations, particularly the latter concerning all teachers seeing themselves as mentors.

In Scotland there is a suite of Professional Standards that provide a framework for the professional development of teachers at each career stage (see Chapter 3). Mentors of beginning teachers are expected to be familiar with the Professional Standards. The requirements for student teachers to progress to the probation phase as a teacher are outlined in *The Standard for Provisional Registration* (General Teaching Council, 2021a). The competences concerning professional knowledge, skills, values and dispositions required of all student teachers at the end of the Initial Teacher Education phase are outlined. During the induction year, provisionally registered teachers (probationary teachers) are required to work towards the *Standard for Full Registration* (General Teaching Council, 2021b). These probationary teachers, as part of the *Teacher Induction Scheme* in Scotland (see Chapters 2, 3 and 5), have access to a supporter who mentors them towards achieving full registration. The need for teachers in this early phase of their career to meet these Professional Standards in order to teach in Scotland highlights the importance of mentors understanding what these standards are and the values that underpin them. Beyond the first year of teaching, the *Standard for Career-Long Professional Learning* (General Teaching Council, 2021c) sets out a framework for the ongoing professional learning and development of all teachers in Scotland. In addition, the *Standard for Middle Leadership* (General Teaching Council, 2021d) and the *Standard for Headship* (General Teaching Council, 2021e) provide frameworks for professional growth for teachers working towards, or already in, leadership roles.

Lists of standards or predefined competences that lead to a *competence approach of mentoring*, where mentor and mentee are focused only on a model of learning to teach that requires learning and checking-off prescribed competences, has been criticised. Sachs (2012) emphasises that the different ways in which the standards are interpreted and understood depend on the values, principles and assumptions that underpin them. Differences in values and assumptions have the potential to result in divergent interpretations and differences in the values that are attached to standards. The suite of Professional Standards in Scotland should be used to stimulate discussion between mentor and mentee, and/or with other colleagues in school or in a school cluster, about teachers' professional development. Rather than being accepted as understood, the standards should be recognised as a framework for discussion and consideration of their meaning through peer dialogue.

Professional dialogue between peers at all career stages was recognised in the Teaching Scotland's Future Report (Donaldson, 2011, p.73):

> Whether or not a teacher has direct responsibility for mentoring of student teachers and probationers at any particular time, every teacher will be engaged in professional dialogue with peers.

Engaging in professional dialogue is a fundamental element of mentoring (see Chapter 7). However, the complexities of professional dialogue in a mentoring conversation cannot be overlooked or under-estimated. Despite an increasing body of research concerning support for teachers' professional learning through collaboration and dialogue with peers in mentoring conversations, there remain gaps in knowledge and understanding about how to develop teachers' capacities to engage in conversations about learning and teaching (European Commission, 2020). While dialogue is taking place between colleagues who work together on a day-to-day basis, it cannot be assumed that everyone has the expertise to engage in a mentoring conversation with their peers. It is not just *engaging* in dialogue that matters; the *quality of the dialogue* is crucial for meaningful professional learning to occur (Livingston and Hutchinson, 2017). Similarly, it cannot be assumed that by giving all teachers the title of mentor and expecting them to engage in mentoring conversations this will mean they are ready or able to mentor their peers without preparation and specific professional development for mentoring.

Mentor preparation opportunities and support for mentoring differs across Scotland's local authorities and schools. Training is provided by the General Teaching Council for Scotland regarding what is expected of those fulfilling the 'supporter' role for probationary teachers. Mentor preparation for mentoring in the context of career-long professional learning is more variable (see Chapter 6). Local authorities and schools vary in the amount and type of mentor preparation provided – e.g., from one-off training sessions to mentor professional development throughout the academic year, with 4- to 6-day sessions for mentors to come together to learn and share mentoring challenges and opportunities. In some cases, training will be provided through a Local Authority Officer, or a training provider that is commissioned by them. Some schools and/or school clusters commission mentor training themselves. Also, some schools and local authorities work in partnership with universities to develop comprehensive mentoring preparation (Livingston and Shiach, 2013, 2014).

The way that mentoring is organised and implemented in schools across Scotland also varies significantly. In most local authorities the selection of mentors, particularly for early-career teachers, is made by the school leadership team. This usually means the selection of an experienced member of staff or, in some cases, a teacher with time available in their timetable. There are differences between primary and secondary schools in terms of mentor selection. For example, in primary schools, one teacher and a school leader may have identified responsibility for supporting a probationary teacher. A small number of local authorities appointed 'full-release mentors' (teachers released from their teaching to become mentors full-time for a fixed period of time) to mentor up to 12 probationary teachers working in different primary schools (see Chapter 6). In a secondary school, one of the school leaders is usually identified to oversee a number of probationary teachers (and student teachers), as well as in some cases a faculty head, a subject head and a teacher identified as a supporter. All may have some role in providing mentoring support to a probationary teacher. In the context of career-long professional learning, in some schools the school leader will identify pairs of teachers to engage in peer-mentoring. In other cases, teachers will be able to choose the colleague they engage with in mentoring conversations. This section has demonstrated that there are different versions of mentoring in Scotland. Kemmis et al. (2014, p.157) remind us of the following:

> different versions of mentoring not only produce different kinds of learning for the individuals involved, they also develop different kinds of dispositions in mentees and in mentors. They invoke different kinds of shared worlds in which people encounter one another … Mentoring can thus be understood as an educational or pedagogical encounter like any other: an encounter that forms both the individuals who participate in it, and the world we share.

The challenge for any mentor is deciding which approach and which mentor strategies are appropriate at a particular time and context when working with their mentee. This is explored further in the next section.

---

### Task 1.4   Understanding the context in which you mentor

- Ensure that you are aware of and familiar with relevant policies relating to your mentee's specific context and career stage. These may be national, local authority and/or school policies.
- Familiarise yourself with the Professional Standards and reflect on how joint discussion of relevant Professional Standards might help you and your mentee discuss expectations about professional knowledge, skills and dispositions of teachers at different stages of their career.
- Find out what mentor preparation opportunities there are for you in the context in which you are mentoring.

---

## Making decisions about which mentoring approaches to take with your mentee

Different approaches to mentoring have been identified in the literature and summarised briefly in this chapter. These approaches are often categorised as follows:

- master/apprentice approaches;
- competence approaches; and
- collaborative approaches.

While these approaches are distinct, motivated by different intentions and involve different patterns of actions (Kemmis et al., 2014), they should all be considered in order to give you a dynamic view of mentoring that enables you to respond to the changing learning needs of your mentee. Mentoring is an interactive social process and both the mentor and the mentee need to continually 'tune-in' to each other to develop a trusting relationship that enables mentoring practices and approaches to evolve according to specific and changing needs of the mentee.

Mentoring teachers at any stage of their career may require mentors to switch from a facilitative approach to a collaborative approach or to an instructional approach. For example, (i) a pedagogical challenge may arise that the mentor and their beginning teacher mentee may not have come across before, requiring a collaborative problem-solving approach; or (ii) a teacher with many years of experience may engage with a mentor concerning the development of specific new technological skills and at first require an instructional mentoring approach. These examples demonstrate that a mentor should not assume that a specific mentoring approach is only relevant at a particular career stage. Achinstein and Athanases (2006) challenge the view that all beginning teachers are in survival mode, which they believe has been a dominant view in mentoring during induction. For example, Katz (1995) suggested that it is useful to think of teachers as having developmental stages in their professional growth patterns and described four stages: survival, consolidation, renewal and maturity. Her argument is that during the survival stage (which she suggests might last for the first year of teaching), a beginning teacher is self-focussed and just coping from day to day. In the consolidation stage, which Katz suggests is at the beginning of the second year of teaching, her view is that teachers will begin to focus on individual children and problem situations but are unlikely to have grasped how to support the diverse needs of all their pupils. According to Katz, a renewal stage occurs around the third or fourth year as the teacher becomes more self-aware and self-critical, with the final maturity stage occurring around the third to fifth year, when a teacher is able to shift their focus from an inwards perspective to a much broader one. In contrast, Achinstein and Athanases (2006) argue that assumptions about approaches to mentoring beginning teachers built on a model of them being in survival mode restricts mentors' roles in supporting and challenging their development as teachers. While it is acknowledged that some new teachers in the early stages may feel they are just surviving from day to day, Grossman (1990) found that beginning teachers are capable of wrestling with complex content-knowledge development in their students. The message for mentors is that mentees differ in their abilities and needs and that professional learning is unlikely to occur in a smooth linear way. Rather than progressing in clear-cut steps from one stage of professional growth to another, there may be some aspects of their teaching that are challenging and others that are not. Similarly, teachers' professional development beyond the induction phase is unlikely to be linear. The contexts and circumstances in which teachers work are complex, and the challenges and opportunities for learning and teaching are constantly changing. This highlights that for mentoring to be effective, mentors need to be aware of and adapt to the specific needs of their mentee in terms of the approach and roles they take and the level of challenge and support they provide.

Daloz's (2012) mentoring model identifies the importance of support and challenge for optimal learning to occur. He argues that the balance of support and challenge has to be appropriate to the needs and development stage of the mentee to enable them to grow. *Support* involves actively listening to your mentee and facilitating or cooperating with them to find solutions to enable them to develop in their learning and teaching. *Challenge* refers to stretching your mentee and involves asking probing questions to enable them to reflect critically on their own beliefs, values and practice. Daloz argues that high challenge and high support is when development and *'growth'* is most likely to occur. Conversely, Daloz refers to *'stasis'* when a mentee's learning is limited when there is low challenge and low support. When challenge is high but support is low, a mentee may *'retreat'* from development. However, where challenge is low but support is high, a mentee may not move beyond their present situation. Daloz refers to this as *'confirmation'* (see Table 1.1).

It is important to understand that the levels of support or challenge you provide are not fixed. Sometimes more support and less challenge will be needed, and at other times, more challenge and less support will be appropriate. Uncovering what each teacher brings to their professional learning is necessary for you to be able to support and challenge them in developing their learning according to their own and their pupils' needs. As a mentor, you need to continually 'tune-in' to your mentee and read the mentoring situation in order to decide on the appropriate balance of challenge and support that is needed by your mentee at a particular time. Orland-Barak (2010, p.95) describes *'tuning-in'* as 'leaving our preconceived notions, including our shoulds and musts[,] in order to connect to the mentee'. This involves being sensitive to the thoughts, feelings and situation of the mentee from their position. Mentoring is a continual process of collaboration with your mentee and requires active negotiation of meaning.

Tillema et al. (2015) emphasise the importance of understanding the communicative exchange between mentor and mentee. They suggest the exchange is the vehicle for learning and professional development. Tuning-in to the mentee and reading the mentoring situation

*Table 1.1* Effects of support and challenge on development

| **High challenge** | High challenge + low support = **retreat** | High challenge + high support = **growth** |
| --- | --- | --- |
| **Low challenge** | Low challenge + low support = **stasis** | Low challenge + high support = **confirmation** |
| | **Low support** | **High support** |

Adapted from Daloz (2012, p. 207)

involves letting them speak about what is happening in their classroom and about learning and teaching from their perspective. This involves listening actively and asking clarifying questions at the start of the mentoring conversation, and if you are still not sure about what your mentee thinks or understands, or why, you should ask for further clarification in order for you to decide on your mentoring approach for the particular circumstance (e.g., 'tell me more about ...'). This requires a trusting relationship to be established with your mentee. Starting a mentoring conversation by asking 'what is going well?' contributes to creating a positive rapport, enabling you to then support your mentee in identifying challenges and areas for their development. The identification of your mentee's next steps, together with them, will involve you using and blending different mentoring approaches as appropriate. Fundamental to the mentoring process is being responsive to your mentee's professional learning needs and context, as well as being reflexive, as both you and your mentee engage in reflecting on and developing practice. It is ongoing enquiry into learning and teaching that enables you and your mentee to engage in professional development. Mentoring, as has been discussed in this chapter, is complex, but as Hargreaves and Fullan (2000) argue, it is central to transforming the teaching profession as a whole.

---

**Task 1.5    Making decisions about the most appropriate mentoring approach for your mentee**

- If you have been mentoring for some time, reflect on the mentoring approaches you take with your mentee and why?
- How might you improve your mentoring approach?
- If you are new to mentoring, reflect on how you would decide which approach would be most relevant for your mentee.

---

## Summary and key points

Mentoring is a demanding and worthwhile process for both mentors and mentees. The key points discussed in this chapter are:

- there are many different definitions of a mentor and mentoring, and different models of mentoring are associated with different approaches;
- there are many different mentor roles and mentors should understand when to move between roles, and understand their role boundaries in relation to mental health issues;
- there are three elements that underpin all effective mentoring approaches: developing and maintaining a trusting relationship between mentor and mentee; keeping a developmental focus; and being aware of and understanding the context in which your mentee works;
- mentoring in the Scottish context is relevant to all teacher across the career stages; and
- mentoring is a dynamic process and it is necessary to tune-in to your mentee and read the mentoring situation in order to make decisions about the most appropriate mentoring approach at a particular time.

---

### Task 1.6   Mentor reflection: Reflecting on your mentoring practice

After reading this chapter, reflect on how your understanding of definitions of a mentor and mentoring, approaches to mentoring, mentor roles and context impact on your practice as a mentor.

---

The following chapters will enable you to explore further and reflect on mentor roles and mentoring approaches and processes, as well as mentoring across the career stages in different contexts. Chapter 2 focuses on the rationale for mentoring and the role it plays in the professional development of teachers in Scotland. Chapter 3 enables you to reflect on the values that underpin the Professional Standards for teachers and the important role that mentors have in supporting and challenging beginning teachers' practice and growth. Chapters 4, 5, 6 and 7 focus on mentoring across the career-stages, from student-teachers, through induction, to career-long professional learning, including leadership development. The following five chapters explore specific aspects of mentoring: Chapter 8 focuses on supporting sustained professional development through reflection; Chapter 9 on fostering effective dialogue between mentor and mentee; Chapter 10 on the use of observation to support mentee's professional development; Chapter 11 on feedback and feed forward to enable mentee's next steps in learning and teaching; and Chapter 12 on developing inclusive practice. The increased use of digital technology in teaching and learning has opened up new possibilities for remote mentoring to support teachers' professional development. This became even more important when the global pandemic that began in 2020 disrupted many of the approaches to mentoring and supporting teacher learning. The final chapter, Chapter 13, therefore explores effective digital and remote models of mentoring.

## References

Ambrosetti, A., Knight, B. A. & Dekkers, J. (2014). Maximizing the potential of mentoring: A framework for pre-service teacher education. *Mentoring & Tutoring: Partnership in Learning,* 22(3), 224-239.

Ambrosetti, A. & Dekkers, J. (2010). The interconnectedness of the roles of mentors and mentees in pre-service teacher education mentoring relationships. *Australian Journal of Teacher Education,* 35, 42-55.

Anderson, E. M. & Shannon, A. (1988). Toward a conceptualization of mentoring. *Journal of Teacher Education,* January-February, 38-42.

Achinstein, B. & Athanases, S. Z. (2006). *Mentors in the making.* New York: Teachers College Press.

Awaya, A., McEwan, H., Heyler, D., Linsky, S., Lum, D. & Wakukawa, P. (2003). Mentoring as a journey. *Teaching and Teacher Education,* 19, 45-56.

Bearman, S., Blake-Beard, S., Hunt, L. & Crosby, F. J. (2007). New directions in mentoring. In T. D. Allen & L. T. Eby (Eds.), *The Blackwell handbook of mentoring: A multiple perspectives approach* (pp. 375-395). Malden, MA: Blackwell.

Bereiter, C. (2002). *Education and mind in the knowledge society.* Mahwah, NJ: Lawrence Erlbaum Associates Publishers.

Bressman, S., Winter, J. S. & Efron, S. E. (2018). Next generation mentoring: Supporting teachers beyond induction. *Teaching and Teacher Education*, 73, 162-170.

Bruner, J. (1996). *The culture of education*. London: Harvard University Press.

Colley, H. (2003). Engagement mentoring for 'disaffected' youth: A new model of mentoring for social inclusion. *British Educational Research Journal*, 29(4), 521-542.

Crafton, L. & Kaiser, E. (2011). The language of collaboration: Dialogue and identity in teacher professional development. *Improving Schools*, 14(2), 104-116.

Daloz, L. A. (2012). *Mentor: Guiding the journey of adult learners*. New York: Wiley.

Donaldson, G. (2011). *Teaching Scotland's Future: Report of a review of teacher education in Scotland*. Edinburgh, UK: The Scottish Government.

Ensher, E. A., Thomas, C. & Murphy, S. E. (2001). Comparison of traditional, step-ahead, and peer mentoring on protégés' support, satisfaction, and perceptions of career success: A social exchange perspective. *Journal of Business and Psychology*, 15(3), 419-438.

European Commission (2020). *Supporting teacher and school leader careers: A policy guide*. Luxembourg: Publications Office of the European Union.

Garza, R., Reynosa, R., Werner, P., Duchaine, E. & Harter, R. A. (2019). Developing a mentoring framework through the examination of mentoring paradigms in a teacher residency program. *Australian Journal of Teacher Education*, 44(3), 1-22.

General Teaching Council Scotland (2021a). *Standard for Provisional Registration*. Edinburgh: General Teaching Council Scotland.

General Teaching Council Scotland (2021b). *Standard for Full Registration*. Edinburgh: General Teaching Council Scotland.

General Teaching Council Scotland (2021c). *Standard for Career-Long Professional Learning*. Edinburgh: General Teaching Council Scotland.

General Teaching Council Scotland (2021d). *Standard for Middle Leadership*. Edinburgh: General Teaching Council Scotland.

General Teaching Council Scotland (2021e). *Standard for Headship*. Edinburgh: General Teaching Council Scotland.

Grossman, P. L. (1990). *The making of a teacher: Teacher knowledge and teacher education*. New York: Teachers College Press.

Hargreaves, A. & Fullan, M. (2000). Mentoring in the new millennium. *Theory into Practice*, 39(1), 50-56.

Heikkinen, H., Jokinen, H. & Tynjälä, P. (2012). *Peer-group mentoring for teacher development*. Abingdon, UK: Routledge

Hobson, A. J., Ashby, P., Malderez, A. & Tomlinson, P. D. (2009). Mentoring beginning teachers: What we know and what we don't. *Teaching and Teacher Education*, 25(1), 207-216.

Katz, L. (1995). *The developmental stages of teachers in talks with teachers of young children: A collection*. Stamford, CT: Ablex.

Kemmis. S., Heikkinen, H., Fransson, G., Aspfors, J. & Edwards-Groves, C. (2014). Mentoring of new teachers as a contested practice: Supervision, support and collaborative self-development. *Teaching and Teacher Education*, 43(2014), 154-164.

Kochan, F. K. & Trimble, S. B. (2000). From mentoring to co-mentoring: Establishing collaborative relationships. *Theory into Practice*, 39(1: New Visions of Mentoring), 20-28.

Kochan, F. & Pascarelli, J. (2012). Perspectives on culture and mentoring in the global age. In S. J. Fletcher & C. A. Mullen (Eds.), *The Sage handbook of mentoring and coaching* (pp. 184-198). Thousand Oaks, CA: Sage Publications.

Kram, K. (1983). Phases of the mentor relationship. *Academy of Management Journal*, 26(4), 608-625.

Kram, K. (1985). *Mentoring at work: Developmental relationships in organizational life*. Glenview, IL: Scott Foresman.

Le Cornu, R. (2005). Peer mentoring: Engaging pre-service teachers in mentoring one another. *Mentoring & Tutoring: Partnership in Learning*, 13(3), 355–366.

Livingston, K. & Hutchinson, C. (2017). Developing teachers' capacities in assessment through career-long professional learning. *Assessment in Education: Principles, Policy and Practice*, 24(2), 290–307.

Livingston, K. & Shiach, L. (2013). *Teaching Scotland's Future: Mentoring Pilot Partnership Project – Final Report*. November, Education Scotland.

Livingston, K. & Shiach, L. (2014). *Teaching Scotland's Future: Further Developing and Sustaining a Strengthened Model of Professional Learning through Mentoring Processes in the Context of Career-long Professional Learning – Final Report*. Education Scotland.

Orland-Barak, L. (2010). *Learning to mentor-as-praxis*. New York: Springer.

Sachs, J. (2012). *Teacher professionalism: Why are we still talking about it?* Keynote address presented at the Association of Teacher Education in Europe annual conference, Anadalou University, Turkey, 29 August.

Tillema, H., van der Westhuizen, G. & van der Merwe, P. (2015). Knowledge building through conversation. In H. Tillema, G. J. van der Westhuizen & K. Smith (Eds.), *Mentoring for learning*. Rotterdam, Netherlands: Sense Publishers.

# 2 The Scottish approach to mentoring in early phase teacher education

## An overview and critique

*Aileen Kennedy*

## Objectives

At the end of this chapter, you should be able to:

- understand the rationale for mentoring within Scotland;
- understand the mentoring approach within the wider policy context, which has conceived of learning to teach as an intellectually engaged and socially practiced activity;
- critically reflect on the Teacher Induction Scheme and the role of mentoring in achieving its aims; and
- critically reflect on the 'Scottish approach' to early phase mentoring in relation to literature and practice in other countries, identifying strengths and possible areas for development.

## Introduction

This chapter explores the rationale for mentoring in Scotland, tracing its development in early phase teacher education (initial teacher education and the induction year). The chapter aims to show how these Scottish developments can be understood in relation to the wider discourse on 'learning to teach' both within and beyond Scotland. This is done through an analysis of the development of the world-renowned 'Teacher Induction Scheme' (TIS) as well as through discussion of contemporary research findings on mentors' and new teachers' views of their mentoring experiences from the 'Measuring Quality in Initial Teacher Education' (MQuITE) project. The chapter concludes by raising a number of challenges, and making some suggestions about how Scotland might move to the next stage of its development regarding early phase mentoring. It is hoped that this chapter will help all of those involved in mentoring processes in Scotland to better understand why things are the way they are, and to be able to take a proactively critical stance on their future engagement in mentoring and towards their contribution to wider mentoring policy going forward.

DOI: 10.4324/9780429356957-3

---

**Task 2.1    What do you already know about early phase mentoring in Scotland?**

- Before engaging with this chapter, think about what you already know about early phase mentoring in Scotland, drawing on your experiences of both mentoring others and being mentored yourself (if relevant).
- What do you think works well and what do you think are the challenges?

---

## Conceptualising mentoring in initial teacher education in Scotland

Mentoring has been an enduring feature of early phase teacher education, particularly in relation to the school-based element of initial teacher education (ITE). While this might seem like an obvious statement to make, it is not necessarily the case globally, where the school-based component of ITE varies considerably (see, for example, European Commission, 2015); it is worth stepping back and looking more analytically at how learning to teach is conceptualised in Scotland vis-à-vis how it might be conceptualised in other places. This analysis helps to reveal how mentoring is positioned in the Scottish context.

ITE in Scotland has long been higher education-led, initially in colleges of education, and then becoming entirely university-based in the 1990s as former colleges of education merged with local universities (Hulme & Kennedy, 2016). While led by the university, it has always comprised both university study and practical experience in schools, with 'placement' being a requirement of all programmes in order to satisfy the General Teaching Council for Scotland (GTCS) accreditation process (GTCS, 2019), and subsequently entitle graduates to become provisionally registered as teachers.

However, while the inclusion of placement in ITE is accepted as 'common sense' in Scotland, it is calibrated in terms of time, i.e., days/weeks, rather than in terms of quality, or with any clearly defined articulation of its purpose within a wider pedagogical framework. Thus, when we talk of 'placement' we may well be talking about a range of very different experiences, varying from programme to programme and school to school. Related to this, MacDonald and Rae (2018) note the influence of the 'practical turn' in teacher education: 'a move toward models which elevate "practical" knowledge over theoretical or pedagogical knowledge' (p.837). This policy movement is a global phenomenon, with, amongst others, Zeichner (2012) warning of the dangers in the US context, Reid (2011) considering the issue from an Australian perspective, and Mattsson, Eilertsen and Rorrison (2011) editing a collection that analyses the 'practicum turn' largely from a Nordic perspective. It is important to stress that the 'practical turn' still very much includes a role for the school-based teacher mentor, but one that implies a pedagogical stance that emphasises copying effective practices for immediate impact rather than developing deeper understanding that might be applied in a range of different contexts. Not only does the practical turn have implications for what is expected of mentors, but it also reveals a particular view of the purpose of ITE itself. Zeichner (2012) illustrates a key motivation for the practical turn being 'a strong press for reducing the length of teacher education programs and for eliminating anything that is not seen as immediately useful to new teachers' (p.379).

Scottish ITE programmes have long been delivered 'in partnership' with schools, but the extent and formality of these partnerships has been questioned. Brisard et al. (2006) pointed to the 'goodwill' nature of teacher involvement in supporting students on placements, arguing that, at that point, teachers had resisted any formalisation of the role. A particular sticking point was around teacher mentors' roles in assessment, and while many more ITE programmes now adopt a shared approach to assessment, this is still generally very much led by HE colleagues. Brisard et al (ibid.) outline a long history of attempts to enhance university/school partnerships in ITE, but it was not until the publication of *Teaching Scotland's Future* (Donaldson, 2011) that formal partnership agreements were drawn up. Almost ten years after these partnership agreements were drawn up, practices remain variable, probably still reflecting, although maybe to a lesser extent, what Brisard et al. described as 'instrumental partnerships' (p.62), which are 'mostly geared towards the ITE needs for the HEI institution' (ibid.).

Underpinning these challenges is the debate on teacher education pedagogy more generally. While the university-led model of ITE in Scotland demonstrates a valuing of both theory and practice, the ways in which these two things come together is more contentious. Lillejord and Børte (2016) articulate this in terms of either the traditional model, 'where students are *first* presented [with] the theory they *later* are expected to "practice"' (p.557) vis-à-vis a model whereby 'students simultaneously investigate instructional practice through first hand experiences *and* consult the research knowledge' (ibid.). These two contrasting approaches reveal different conceptions of the process of learning to teach, which inevitably, but sometimes implicitly, point to different roles and expectations of teacher mentors. In the first model, the mentor's role is simply to ensure that the 'practice' is enacted in the school, whereas in the second model, the mentor's role is to actively support the student teacher's learning through enquiry, engaging in dialogic and collaborative meaning-making.

---

**Task 2.2    Reflecting on the purpose of initial teacher education**

- Given the above discussion, think about what you perceive to be the purpose of the school-based element of ITE.
- Now consider what that might mean in terms of the role you might play as an ITE student mentor – what activities/tasks will be important, and what tasks or activities might actually serve to limit the student's learning?

---

The important thing to take away from all of this is the underpinning philosophy that drives teacher education in Scotland, which, despite changes in structural and organisational approaches over time, has always valued the complimentary contributions of both schools and universities. Menter (2017), in his literature review on 'the role and contribution of higher education in contemporary teacher education', concludes by stating that the evidence he presents:

> is not a call for the maintenance of the status quo, but rather a recognition that through the involvement of the universities as a fundamental element of provision, we may continue to see innovation and improvement that will ensure that the teaching profession itself continues to be held in high esteem and that the continuing challenges of overcoming educational disadvantage are directly tackled by teachers and teacher educators who understand these challenges and are equipped with the skills to address them.
>
> (p.15)

So, while mentoring is part of an enduring philosophy in ITE, mentoring during induction, on the other hand, is shaped by a prescribed national policy: the Teacher Induction Scheme, established in 2002 and managed by the GTCS.

## The introduction of the Teacher Induction Scheme (2002)

Following years of a very loosely supported system of the GTCS requiring two years of 'probationary' service for new teachers, the early 2000s saw views galvanising around the need to introduce a more structured system of induction for new teachers in Scotland, with the McCrone review of teachers' conditions of service acknowledging that 'No amount of pre-service training can fully prepare newly qualified entrants for the challenges they will face when they become teachers' (SEED, 2000, p.7). The report went on to describe the situation of many new teachers at that time as being one with little support, in a series of short-term, temporary positions; conditions which meant it took many new teachers a long time to 'clock up' the days of service that entitled them to full GTCS registration. The final agreement that resulted from the McCrone report declared that 'All probationers should be guaranteed a one-year training contract with a maximum class commitment of 0.7 FTE, the remaining time available for professional development. Probation will be limited to one year and permanent employment restricted to fully registered teachers' (SEED, 2001, p.16), with new arrangements to be in place for the academic session starting August 2002. The process that resulted from this recommendation became known as the 'Teacher Induction Scheme' (TIS).

TIS became a process (rather than an experience), albeit one informed, certainly in the early stages, by research on mentoring. Conceptually, however, the resistance to using the term mentor – justified, in part, because of previous challenging experiences in the nineties with a 'Mentor Teacher Initiative' pilot, instigated by the then Scottish Office Education Department and run by Moray House (Smith et al., 2006) – is possibly a missed opportunity. Instead of adopting the term and wrestling properly with the conceptualisation of the 'mentor', TIS used the term 'supporter'. The choice of the word 'supporter' arguably implies a unidirectional process of support, rather than opening up possibilities of a mentoring relationship that can be two-way or, indeed, collaborative, serving as what Chambers et al. (2012) call a 'profession-building endeavor' (p.346). The positioning of the 'mentor' role within TIS is key to understanding its possibilities and limitations. We know that new teachers need some support in transitioning to the responsibilities of being the class teacher, but it is also posited that the new teachers contribute something to the school community (Helleve & Ulvik, 2011), and it is therefore argued that the mentoring role is not simply one of giving direction to the novice, but that a mentoring relationship can serve as a mutually generative source of professional learning both within teaching (Holland, 2018) and more widely (Eby et al., 2006; LaFleur & White, 2010).

The Organisation for Economic Co-operation and Development (OECD) (2019) acknowledges that mentoring can support quality induction, but goes on to warn that 'evidence on effective mentoring, and how to build the capacity of experienced teachers to become mentors is not yet robust enough' (p.12). There seems to be no argument in the literature, or indeed in practice, against the importance of 'effective' induction programmes, but what Moir and Gless (2001) encourage us to ask is, 'induction into what, and for what purpose?' (p.110), acknowledging that 'induction will happen, with or without a programme' (ibid.).

One aspect of induction programmes that seems to have become a *sine qua non* across the globe is the perceived need to frame the programme around a professional standard, and in this regard, Scotland is no different, with the establishment of the first 'Standard for Full Registration' in 2001, against which new teachers were assessed during their induction year. However, in their year-long ethnographic research with a sample of new teachers in Scotland, McNally et al. (2008) found 'a discourse for new teachers' experience that is largely at odds with the standard as written' (p.288), drawing a contrast between new teachers' experiences and the things that they deemed to be important, and the technical-rational nature of a professional standard that arose principally from a policy response to an increasingly neoliberal predilection with standardisation, homogeneity and public auditing.

The drive to shape induction programmes around professional standards is central to the messages emanating from the European Commission, who conclude: 'Professional competence frameworks can be used to raise quality standards, by defining the knowledge, skills and attitudes that teachers ... should possess or acquire. Similarly, the teacher educators who prepare teachers to undertake their tasks can benefit from frameworks of this kind' (EU, 2014, p.22). Indeed, teacher educators and mentors in some countries are required to meet specific professional standards related to this role. For example, with the expansion of school-based 'initial teacher training' in England, the Teaching Schools Council was invited to develop 'a set of non-statutory standards to ... help bring greater coherence and consistency to the school-based mentoring arrangements for trainee teachers' (2016, p.3). These standards reveal much more of a job description than a pedagogical orientation, and perhaps beg compliance rather than adaptation to context. Research internationally shows that there is often a tendency to use professional standards as a checklist, encouraging a compliance mentality, which, as McNally et al. (2008) argue, may well be counterintuitive to the professional learning experiences of new teachers. However, McNally et al. (ibid.) do suggest that there might be more productive ways to work with standards, something echoed by Bourke et al. (2018) in the US context, where 'counter discourses of resistance and reinterpretations of standards as deficit are also evident as some strive to maintain their professional autonomy' (p.90). Thus, we see that it is possible for teacher educators (including mentors) to use standards as both administrative tools for quality assurance and accountability, as well as for more creative developmental purposes. That said, the issue at point here is not so much about the possibilities regarding how standards *could* be used, but the discourses and practices that shape how they generally *are* used.

---

### Task 2.3   Standardising mentoring?

- What do you think might be the pros and cons of introducing a set of standards specifically for teacher mentors?
- How useful do you find the Standards for Provisional and Full Registration in supporting student and probationer teachers?

---

While it is perhaps fair to say that the main motivation for the development of the TIS in Scotland was one of quality, and there is plenty of evidence to support that as a sensible direction of travel (e.g., Moir & Gless, 2001; Stanulis & Floden, 2009), it was also expected to support teacher retention. There is clear, although not entirely uncontested (Glazerman et al., 2010), international evidence that structured induction support does indeed support teacher retention (Ingersoll & Strong, 2011). However, this evidence tends to look at the impact of induction systems as a whole rather than the impact of mentors within these programmes in particular, something that Haynes (2019) focused on in her EdD study. Perhaps unsurprisingly, Haynes concluded that in order to enhance retention, mentors required appropriate training, clear guidance about their role, time for the role and the space to foster trusting relationships with their mentee(s). The message here is that well-structured and smoothly administered induction programmes will only support retention if the mentoring is right. The mentoring role is absolutely fundamental to any induction programme.

### Mentoring in Scotland: contemporary perspectives

Mentoring is clearly a central and well-established part of early phase teacher education in Scotland, and has been for a long time. However, the above discussion suggests that the role is not particularly well conceptualised; recent findings from the 'Measuring Quality in Initial Teacher Education' (MQuITE) project (see www.mquite.scot" www.mquite.scot) help to unpack the various understandings of the role across key stakeholders.

In May/June 2018, the MQuITE project team issued surveys to three stakeholder groups, asking them about their perceptions of ITE quality: students graduating from ITE programmes; staff working on ITE programmes in universities; and teachers involved in supporting ITE students in schools. The surveys attracted the responses given in Table 2.1.

*Table 2.1* Numbers of survey responses for the MQuITE project, 2018

| Survey | Number of responses |
|---|---|
| Graduating students | 323 |
| University staff contributing to ITE programmes | 150 |
| Teachers involved in supporting student teachers on placement | 229 |

The survey asked the school-based mentors about their views on placement, and a common theme to emerge was a sense that the school mentor's job was principally about assessment (as opposed to supporting professional learning). The issue of assessing students on placements was seen to be a challenging one, but while 76.9% of mentor respondents reported feeling confident or very confident in assessing students against the Standard for Provisional Registration, only 67.3% reported actually being involved or very involved in this process – so nearly 10% of respondents felt confident about assessing students despite not actually being involved in doing it in practice, thereby raising questions about what their sense of confidence might be based on. The qualitative data revealed a perception that assessment decisions were ultimately the gift of the university tutor rather than the mentor, with respondents having strong views about what they perceived to be contradictory assessment decisions – '[universities have] a desire to pass students who are struggling' – and a perception that the teacher's/school's view is given less weight – 'the universities often overrule the schools'. These findings support the argument made earlier that the mentor's role is perhaps not sufficiently well defined, either in terms of what it entails in practice or in its relationship to the university tutor's role.

A clear theme emerging from the MQuITE data is that mentors lack consistent information about, and access to, appropriate education/training for the role, with one respondent naming the 'elephant in the room': 'there appears to be no quality control of the teachers with whom the students are placed'. When asked if they had undertaken any professional learning relating to mentoring students, 50% of respondents said they had. However, of this 50%, many had only engaged in very brief, instrumental 'training' type activities, such as a one-hour briefing session after school. This illustrates a lack of systemic attention to the role of the mentor, with the assumption made that if one is a good teacher, then one will also be a good mentor. Smith and Avetisian (2011) provide a challenge to this assumption, reporting that in their case study of a student teacher being mentored by two different 'cooperating teachers', the cooperating teachers' approaches to mentoring had a greater influence than his or her own teaching style on a teacher candidate's pedagogy, i.e., that the biggest influence on the student teacher is the mentor's capacity to mentor rather than the mentor's own teaching style. Smith and Avetisian (ibid.) go on to argue that a lack of attention on the purpose of student teaching is at the root of this, that is, when mentors do undertake professional learning for a mentoring role, it is more likely to focus on 'skills and responsibilities associated with the role' (p.349) than on exploring and sharing understandings of the purpose of the placement element of ITE or induction. They go on to argue that 'In the absence of shared understandings about the purpose of student teaching, [mentor teachers], understandably, develop approaches to mentoring that stem from their own experience and beliefs about student teaching' (Smith & Avetisian, p.350). This is of particular relevance in the Scottish context, where over 90% of the 229 school mentor responses in the MQuITE survey had completed their own ITE in Scotland, revealing a fairly homogenous experience of learning to teach upon which to draw as a mentor. This is important given the relative lack of systematic professional learning available to mentors of early phase teachers, despite the Donaldson Report (2011) recommending that 'All teachers should see themselves as teacher educators, and be trained in mentoring' (p.73).

## Task 2.4   What makes a good mentor?

- Thinking about the issues raised above, and your own experiences, list what you think are the key roles, skills and dispositions of a good mentor within the Scottish system.
- Again, thinking about the above discussion and your own experiences, what do you think are the key roles, skills and dispositions required of a good university-based tutor?
- Now think about the similarities and differences between these lists, and what this might mean for the mentor/tutor relationship.
- Where, when and how should/might teachers be educated in mentoring?

## Moving forward: challenges and suggestions

It seems, then, that while mentoring has had a secure place in early phase teacher education in Scotland for some time now, its role and purpose have not been particularly well conceptualised or articulated. In many cases it is positioned as an administrative role: jobs to do, forms to complete. In other places it is a quality assurance role, with assessments to be made against standards. However, in arguing for a more educative conceptualisation, Feiman-Nemser (2012) suggests that, 'in helping novices learn to teach, mentors take on an educational role, form a pedagogical relationship [and] engage in an educational activity' (p.241). This more educative role must surely therefore involve professional learning on the part of the mentor; this is not a skill learned, nor knowledge gained routinely, in ITE. Indeed, Langdon and Ward (2015) argue, from a New Zealand context, that despite growing recognition of the need for a more overtly educative conception of mentoring, practices remain largely focused on giving directive advice to new teachers on classroom management, sourcing and using appropriate resources, and passing on institutional knowledge about how things work in the particular school/department. This seems, then, to be a problem within and beyond the confines of Scotland, and limits possibilities for expansive learning on the part of both the mentee *and* the mentor.

The evidence, I suggest, is pretty compelling: we know that good mentoring, both in ITE and in the induction phase, has the capacity to support positive early phase learning for teachers, thereby also enhancing retention, and also that mentoring can be an exciting, fulfilling and expansive experience for mentors. However, we also know that we do not currently have a well-developed and shared understanding of the role, nor do we have clear and accessible national systems in place to prepare mentors systematically for this role. Stakeholders are considering proposals emanating from an 'independent panel on career pathways for teachers' (Scottish Government, 2019), which include a proposal to introduce a role of 'lead teacher'. If these proposals are approved, then there would appear to be a pretty persuasive case for introducing a 'lead mentor teacher', or perhaps a 'lead teacher in supporting professional learning'.

Not only does the Career Pathways report from the Scottish Government (2019) provide a potential route to making mentor education more systematic and valued, but the issue of mentor quality and capacity is beginning to be recognised more explicitly elsewhere too. The most recent Parliamentary Inquiry into 'initial teacher education and early phase teaching' is revisiting a recommendation made in the Scottish Parliament's Education and Skills Committee's 2017 report (Scottish Parliament, 2017), in which it is recommended that an 'emphasis on the importance of mentoring should feature in local working time agreements. This could include a specific allocation of non-contact time' (p.4), thereby promoting the idea that this role needs to be better supported and valued. The importance of quality mentoring has also been acknowledged by the Strategic Board for Teacher Education, and it has mandated Education Scotland to work on proposals for a coaching and mentoring strategy for Scottish education.

As well as a focus on developing experienced teachers' capacity to mentor, there is also merit in thinking about how we might include some of the skills of mentoring, or supporting colleagues' professional learning, as a pre-requisite in all ITE programmes: student teachers can learn about the role of observation, for example, and use this knowledge not only to help shape the observation processes involved in their own placement learning, but also use it to support peer observations within their own cohorts. We have the capacity, and potentially the policy provision, to upscale mentoring as a central element of the teacher role.

It would appear that we are at a cusp in Scotland, where there is clear recognition of the importance of quality mentoring and the possibility of resource being put into its further development. I sincerely hope this proves to be the case, but in developing a more systematic approach to mentoring, there are some important issues to be considered:

- Do we want to continue to entrench a 'mentor-matching' approach, where one early phase teacher is supported by one nominated mentor, or do we want to consider how we might establish more widespread collaborative mentoring through developing mentoring cultures?
- Is it time to revisit the idea of 'hub schools' that specialise in supporting teacher learning?
- Should we consider mentoring (and other skills relating to supporting professional learning) to be a core teacher skill, starting in ITE?

Finally, to return to Moir and Gless (2001), when we think about early phase teacher learning, into what are we inducting new teachers, 'and for what purpose?' From there, surely, will follow an appropriate conceptualisation of the mentor's role, around which we can build suitable systems for supporting and valuing mentors as school-based teacher educators.

## Summary and key points

Mentoring is a longstanding component of early phase teacher learning in Scotland, but its development and enactment are quite complex. Key points raised in this chapter include the following:

- mentoring in Scotland is set within a wider context in which learning to teach is seen as both an intellectual and a practical pursuit;

- mentoring in this context is more than a directive or administrative task, rather it might be seen as an opportunity for expansive collaborative learning on the part of both the mentor and the mentee;
- professional standards can serve as a helpful focus for professional learning conversations, but they should not be used as a mentoring checklist;
- to be a good mentor, it is not enough simply to be a good teacher – the role also requires specific knowledge, skills and dispositions; and
- there is arguably a need for greater resource to be invested in ensuring that all teachers are well-prepared to work as mentors, and that the system values this role overtly.

## Further reading

Mutton, T.A. (2015). 'Partnership in teacher education'. In G. Beauchamp et al. (Eds.), *Teacher education in times of change* (pp. 202–217). Bristol: Policy Press.
O'Brien, J. & Christie, F. (2008). A role for universities in the induction of teachers? A Scottish case study. *Journal of In-service Education, 34*(2), 147–163.
Rippon, J. & Martin, M. (2012). What makes a good induction supporter? *Teaching and Teacher Education, 22*(1), 84–99.
Shanks, R. (2020). *Teacher preparation in Scotland*. Bingley: Emerald Publishing.
Shanks, R., Robson, D. & Gray, D. (2015). New teachers' individual learning dispositions: a Scottish case study. *International Journal of Training and Development, 16*(3), 183–199.

## References

Bourke, T., Ryan, M. & Ould, P. (2018). How do teacher educators use professional standards in their practice? *Teaching and Teacher Education, 75*, 83–92.
Brisard, E., Menter, I. & Smith, I. (2006). Discourses of partnership in initial teacher education in Scotland: current configurations and tensions. *European Journal of Teacher Education, 29*(1), 49–66.
Chambers, F.C., Armour, K.A., Luttrell, S., Bleakley, W., Brennan, D. & Herold, F. (2012). Mentoring as a profession-building process in physical education teacher education. *Irish Educational Studies, 31*(3), 345–362.
Donaldson, G. (2011). *Teaching Scotland's future: report of a review of teacher education in Scotland*. Edinburgh: Scottish Government.
Eby, L., Durley, J., Evans, S., Ragins, B.R. (2006). The relationship between short-term mentoring benefits and long-term mentor outcomes. *Journal of Vocational Behaviour, 69*(3), 424–444.
European Commission (2015). *The teaching profession in Europe: practices, perceptions, and policies. Eurydice Report*. Luxembourg: Publications Office of the European Union.
European Union (2014). Council conclusions of 20 May 2014 on effective teacher education. *Official Journal of the European Union*. Retrieved from: https://eur-lex.europa.eu/legal-content/EN/TXT/PDF/?uri=CELEX:52014XG0614(05)&from=EN
Feiman-Nemser, S. (2012). *Teachers as learners*. Cambridge, MA: Harvard Education Press.
General Teaching Council for Scotland (GTCS) (2019). *Guidelines for accreditation of initial teacher education programmes in Scotland*. Edinburgh: GTCS.
Glazerman, S., Isenberg, E., Dolfin, S., Bleeker, M., Johnson, A., Grider, M. & Jacobus, M. (2010). *Impacts of comprehensive teacher induction: final results from a randomized controlled study* (NCEE 2010-4027). Washington, DC: U.S. Department of Education.
Haynes, S. (2019). *Mentors' impact on new teacher retention in K-12*. Unpublished EdD Thesis, University of Seattle.

Helleve, I. & Ulvik, M. (2011). Is individual mentoring the only answer? *Education Inquiry, 2*(1), 127-139.

Holland, E. (2018). Mentoring communities of practice: what's in it for the mentor? *International Journal of Mentoring and Coaching in Education, 7*(2), 110-126.

Hulme, M. & Kennedy, A. (2016). 'Teacher education in Scotland: consensus politics and the Scottish policy style'. In G. Beauchamp, L. Clarke, M. Hulme, M. Jephcote, A. Kennedy, G. Magennis, I. Menter, J. Murray, T. Mutton, T. O'Doherty & G. Peiser. (Eds.), *Teacher education in times of change: responding to challenges across the UK and Ireland* (pp. 92-109). Bristol: Policy Press.

Ingersoll, R.M. & Strong, M. (2011). The impact of induction and mentoring programs for beginning teachers: a critical review of the research. *Review of Educational Research, 81*(2), 201-233.

Lafleur, A.K. & White, B.J. (2010). Appreciating mentorship: the benefits of being a mentor. *Professional Case Management, 15*(6), 305.

Langdon, F. & Ward, L. (2015). Educative mentoring: a way forward. *International Journal of Mentoring and Coaching in Education, 4*(4), 240-254.

Lillejord, S. & Børte, K. (2016). Partnership in teacher education – a research mapping. *European Journal of Teacher Education, 39*(5), 550-563.

MacDonald, A. & Rae, A. (2018). 'Initial teacher education in Scotland'. In T.G.K. Bryce, W.M. Humes, D.G. Gillies & A. Kennedy (Eds.), *Scottish Education: fifth edition* (pp. 825-837). Edinburgh: Edinburgh University Press.

McNally, J., Blake, A., Corbin, B. & Gray, P. (2008). Finding an identity and meeting a standard: connecting the conflicting in teacher induction. *Journal of Education Policy, 23*(3), 287-298.

Mattsson, M., Eilertsen, V. & Rorrison, D. (Eds.). (2011). *A practicum turn in teacher education.* Rotterdam: Sense Publishers.

Menter, I. (2017). *The role and contribution of higher education in contemporary teacher education.* Edinburgh: Scottish Council of Deans of Education.

Moir, E. & Gless, J. (2001). Quality induction: an investment in teachers. *Teacher Education Quarterly, 28*(1), 109-114.

OECD (2019). *A flying start: improving initial teacher preparation systems.* Paris: OECD Publishing.

Reid, J. (2011). A practice turn for teacher education? *Asia-Pacific Journal of Teacher Education, 39*(4), 293-310.

Scottish Executive Education Department (2000). *A teaching profession for the 21st century: report of the Committee of Inquiry into professional conditions of service for teachers.* Edinburgh: The Stationery Office.

Scottish Executive Education Department (2001). *A teaching profession for the 21st century: agreement reached following recommendations made in the McCrone Report.* Edinburgh: The Stationery Office.

Scottish Government (2019). *Independent panel on career pathways for teachers: final report.* Edinburgh: Scottish Parliament.

Scottish Parliament (2017). *Teacher workforce planning for Scotland's schools.* Edinburgh: Scottish Parliament.

Smith, E.R. & Avetisian, V. (2011). Learning to teach with two mentors: revisiting the "two-worlds pitfall" in student teaching. *The Teacher Educator, 46*(4), 335-354.

Smith, I., Brisard, E. & Menter, I. (2006). Partnership in initial teacher education in Scotland 1990-2005: unresolved tensions. *Scottish Educational Review, 37*(Special Issues), 20-31.

Stanulis, R.N. & Floden, R.E. (2009). Intensive mentoring as a way to help beginning teachers develop balanced instruction. *Journal of Teacher Education, 60*(2), 112-122.

Teaching Schools Council (2016). *National Standards for school-based initial teacher training (ITT) mentors.* London: UK Government. Retrieved from: https://assets.publishing. service.gov.uk/government/uploads/system/uploads/attachment_data/file/536891/ Mentor_standards_report_Final.pdf

Zeichner, K. (2012). The turn once again toward practice-based teacher education. *Journal of Teacher Education, 63*(5), 376–382.

# 3 From student to employed teacher

*Jacqueline Morley, Elaine Napier, Charlaine Simpson and Pauline Stephen*

## Objectives

At the end of this chapter, you should be able to:

- understand the foundation values in the Professional Standards and critically reflect on how those values are embedded in mentoring;
- consider the key knowledge, skills and dispositions that mentors require to support student teachers effectively through the transition phase to become fully registered teachers in Scotland;
- identify the ways mentors can assist beginning teachers to evolve and develop their practice through self-assessment and target-setting; and
- critically reflect on the use of the Professional Standards as a framework for supporting the professional growth of teachers in the early career phase.

## The Scottish Context and Professional Standards for Teachers

Becoming, being and growing as a teacher in Scotland are underpinned by a strong foundation of Professional Standards. From student teacher to accomplished teacher, and opportunities to be a school leader, teacher professionalism in Scotland is exemplified through the benchmark Standards of Provisional and Full Registration and the aspirational Standards of Career-Long Professional Learning, Middle Leadership and Headship. Influenced by the context of Scottish education, which is built on a strong culture of negotiation and consensus, teacher collaboration and partnership is a central theme throughout our national Professional Standards (2021).

## Professional Values and Professional Commitment

Our increasingly interconnected and rapidly changing world faces many social, environmental and economic challenges, and an effective, responsive and inclusive education system is vital if we are to address these. The Professional Standards outline what it means to become, to be and to grow as a teacher in Scotland. A commitment to the professional values is at the

DOI: 10.4324/9780429356957-4

heart of the Professional Standards and underpins the relationships, thinking and professional practice of all teachers in Scotland.

The educational experiences of all our children and young people are shaped by the professional values and dispositions of all those who work to educate them. Values are complex; they are the ideals by which teachers shape their practice as professionals. Starting with teachers as individuals, values extend to the learners, colleagues and community, as well as to the world in which we live.

Professional Standards are premised on our professional values of social justice, trust and respect, and integrity. These values describe the actions, behaviours and dispositions that are expected of teachers in their daily practice. They underpin teachers' moral imperative and give the indefinable essence (Adoniou & Gallagher, 2017) of what it means to be a teacher. As a student teacher through the transition into probation (induction), new teachers navigate the complexity and importance of professional values as part of their teacher identity. This embodiment of being a teacher extends beyond the workplace, as personal and occupational values are intertwined.

A values-based approach to Professional Standards guides practice in a way that is focused enough to give confidence to the public about the role of teachers and the caring aspects of teaching, and broad enough to allow interpretation, innovation, creativity and contextualisation for all teachers, regardless of context, position and role. A values-based model for Professional Standards encompasses the realm of critical pedagogy (Giroux, 2011; Freire, 1992), where teaching is understood as a values-based practice that empowers teachers to support learners to "actively transform knowledge rather than simply consume it" (Giroux, 2001, p. 7).

Professional values help teachers to develop their professional identity and underpin a deep commitment to all learners' cognitive, social and emotional growth and wellbeing. They provide the foundation to support and encourage teachers to see the whole child or young person and their needs. They are integral to, and demonstrated through, professional relationships, thinking and actions, and all that we do to meet our professional commitment as teachers registered with the General Teaching Council for Scotland (GTC Scotland).

Professional values and professional commitment are interrelated and at the heart of our Professional Standards. As these elements are inherently linked to each other, one aspect does not exist independently of the others. It is this inter-relationship that develops the professionalism of teachers and leads to appropriate professional action and growth.

Upholding the professional values of social justice, trust and respect, and integrity requires a commitment to leadership that inspires confidence and encourages aspiration. This commitment underpins leadership of, and for, learning in all contexts and change for improvement. It values the contribution of others and applies critical thinking to make effective decisions, in the interests of maintaining and improving the quality of education and leading to improved outcomes for all children and young people in Scotland.

---

### Task 3.1   Reflecting on Your Professional Values

- How do you critically reflect on your assumptions, beliefs and values?
- How do your professional values influence your role as a mentor?

GTC Scotland has created a resource to explore how professional values underpin teacher professionalism. A professional lifeline tool to support reflection on your professional values is included within this resource, which can be found at https://www.gtcs.org.uk/professional-standards/key-cross-cutting-themes/professional-values

---

## Teacher Professionalism

Teachers have the potential to transform and have a profound impact on the learning experiences and life chances of our children and young people, playing a critical role in helping them achieve positive outcomes, to thrive and flourish in life. At the heart of this are professional values and teacher professionalism.

We are fortunate in Scotland that we already have a very strong foundation of teacher professionalism. This is underpinned by an "inspiring set of professional standards defined by the General Teaching Council for Scotland" (OECD, 2015, p. 17). The Professional Standards, with professional values at the centre, support and promote collaborative professionalism, leadership, enquiry and professional learning.

GTC Scotland has previously discussed teacher professionalism as 'our way of being'. It informs who we are as professionals, is about our professional identity, and is firmly rooted in our values, beliefs and dispositions. Teacher professionalism is encapsulated within the suite of Professional Standards and is built on professional values, the interconnectedness of teacher-as-learner and their learners, collaborative professionalism, professional judgement and enquiry, and leadership at all levels. It also requires teachers to be engaged in professional learning, collaboration, and adopting and developing an enquiring disposition to help the teachers of Scotland to ask critical questions of ourselves, our practices and the wider educational agenda, and respond to the needs of our learners.

---

### Task 3.2   Defining Teacher Professionalism

- What does teacher professionalism mean to you?
- How does the foundation of the Professional Standards influence you as a mentor?

---

## The Roles, Aims and Functions of GTC Scotland

GTC Scotland has a statutory role in Scottish education. This section provides an overview of the roles, aims and functions of GTC Scotland.

The legislation, The Public Service Reform (General Teaching Council for Scotland) Order 2011, conferred independence for GTC Scotland. The Act states two aims for GTC Scotland:

a)   To contribute to improving the quality of learning and teaching; and

b)   To maintain and improve teachers' professional standards.

(The Public Service Reform (General Teaching Council for
Scotland) Order 2011, Article 5)

GTC Scotland meets the aims of the Order (2011) through the following policies and functions:

- The suite of Professional Standards, which outline the expectations of teachers in Scotland, with the Standards for Registration as the benchmark for entry into the teaching profession and the aspirational Standard for Career-Long Professional Learning supporting professional growth of teachers. An aspirational or developmental leadership framework is also offered by the Standard for Middle Leadership and the Standard for Headship.
- Early career teachers are supported through the accreditation of Initial Teacher Education programmes, administration of the Student Placement System and through the Teacher Induction Scheme (TIS) and Flexible Route for probationer teachers.
- Professional Update, which is underpinned by high-quality, sustained and reflective professional learning, professional dialogue and high-quality professional review. Integral to this process of self-evaluation is the suite of Professional Standards and the embedded focus on professional values, an enquiring stance, leadership and collaborative practice.
- The national MyGTCS online resource supports professional learning and reflection, framed round the Professional Learning model, which provides guidance on what high-quality, effective professional learning looks like. This is supported with additional guidance and free access to educational journals and ebooks to help the development of the skills and dispositions of enquiry and research.
- Professional Recognition, which celebrates enhanced accomplished professional practice of individual teachers. Also, the Excellence in Professional Learning Award for schools and learning communities and Professional Learning Awards for organisations, which recognise excellence in the provision and promotion of professional learning and professional learning environments.
- Holding a searchable register of teachers in Scotland and a regulatory function that ensures the teaching profession remains fit to teach so that public trust and confidence in teachers is maintained and the learning of children and young people is protected.

Effective mentoring is at the heart of improving the quality of learning and teaching, and therefore central to the work of GTC Scotland. Supporting improved outcomes for children and young people starts with the effective development of teachers and teaching.

---

**Task 3.3    Reflecting on the Role of GTC Scotland**

Explore the GTC Scotland website. The 'about us' section provides information about the history of GTC Scotland and the arrangements for its independence as a body. Focus on the reason for the establishment of GTC Scotland and reflect on what this means for the value of the Professional Standards.

https://www.gtcs.org.uk/

---

## Student Teacher to Probationer

A key component of Initial Teacher Education (ITE), at the start of every teacher's journey, is professional placement. The national Student Placement System assigns student teacher placements in Scotland and, in itself, is an outcome of effective partnership between central government, local government, ITE providers and GTC Scotland. The student teacher's placement experience is largely shaped by collaboration with teachers in the individual school context and, in particular, through their relationship with their main mentor. As the student teacher moves into their first year of teaching, their probationary experience, a paid year of induction for those that choose it, they continue to benefit from a key mentor (supporter). This mentoring support is dependent on the needs and experiences of the probationer.

GTC Scotland now use the term supporter rather than mentor when working with probationer teachers, local authority colleagues and partners. A supporter needs professional self-awareness to draw upon this continuum, from mentor to coach, and a range of skills to support the probationer teacher. They need a depth of professional knowledge and judgement to appropriately facilitate the self-directed learning of the probationer teacher in an appropriate, challenging, encouraging and supportive manner. One of the inherent tensions in the Scottish education system is how to ensure the comprehensive provision of learning opportunities that develop skilled supporters who know how to provide the right kind of mentoring and/or coaching at the right time. The appointment of a supporter for probationer teachers provides opportunities for deep and meaningful conversations regarding both support and challenge. This necessitates a co-ordinated national strategy that prioritises and actively champions the development of these skills.

Whilst this support is invaluable in shaping probationers' understanding and practice in preparation for sole teaching responsibility, a number of tensions exist in this collaborative relationship. These include developing a shared understanding of the nature of each other's responsibilities, managing discrepancies between a probationer's aspirations of their role and the realities they face in a particular context, the dual role of the supporter in supporting and assessing the probationer teacher, and how skilled the supporter is in providing the right kind of mentoring support at the right time. This chapter aims to unpick aspects of these tensions and suggest how probationer–mentor relationships can be improved, including how best to support the supporter and how the education system can benefit from further enhancement of this approach.

## Mentoring Probationers

Scotland, like other education systems, such as Finland, Sweden, Canada and Australia, has invested in mentoring strategies to support student teachers as they move into the next phase of their professional learning journey as a probationer teacher. New Zealand has also heavily invested in mentoring, giving dedicated time for probationer teachers and mentors to undertake support activities. In Japan and Germany, after undergraduate qualification, probationer teachers undertake a 'clinical, real world' experience as they transition to being fully registered teachers. Germany has a two year 'internship', while Japan provides guidance on the number of days for teaching and support from a mentor. These education systems invest in mentoring as a means to provide support for new teachers as they develop and perfect their skills. This contrasts with 'sink or swim' approaches. In Northern America, for example, newly qualified teachers are given very challenging classes and have more direct teaching time, in addition to expectations around extracurricular duties (Andrews & Andrews, 1998; Darling-Hammond, 1997; Darling-Hammond & Sclan, 1996; Gold, 1996; Shanker, 1987; Weiss & Weiss, 1999).

Even within contested theories, mentoring is understood as a social practice that is based in human interaction and co-operation and that involves activities and a common discourse. The practice of mentoring is bound by the context and, as such, looks different in different settings. This means that the mentoring experienced by the probationer teacher is context bound and a product of the ethos of the learning community. The interactions and affordances in every context enable or constrain mentoring practices. According to Kemmis et al. (2004) these interactions and affordances are held within three spaces: the semantic space, where the language used can enable or constrain the way people work together in a school community; the physical space-time, which can promote or subdue mentoring activities by creating the mentoring ethos and environment; and the social space, where different relationships between mentors, mentees and other members of the learning community can support or suppress the development of the probationer teacher's professional identity. Given the variety of contexts and levels of mentoring support, any approach must be 'tailored to suit' – there is no one-size-fits-all approach.

As well as different conceptual models, there are also different intended outcomes from the mentoring process. Mertz (2004) offers three views of mentoring. The first is that mentoring may be employed to offer support, advice and guidance to probationer teachers as they develop their skills, knowledge and teacher identity. The second is a more instrumental approach, in which mentoring is viewed as a supervisory role as probationer teachers transition from being student teachers to fully registered teachers through their probation period. Thirdly, mentoring can be viewed as an orientation process during which student teachers are inducted into the teaching profession.

Regardless of the theoretical stance, arguably what is most important for probationer teachers is their experience of the mentoring process in providing the necessary navigation through the complexity of professional values and support in developing their teacher identity.

---

## Task 3.4   Reflecting on Your Role as a Mentor

- Reflecting on your experience as a mentor, how do you develop a shared under-standing of the responsibilities of the supporter and the probationer teacher?
- What strategies work best for you in developing a supportive relationship with your probationer teacher(s)?

---

The role of the mentor is a complex one that is difficult to define. Levinson et al. (1978) attribute multiple roles to the mentor, such as teacher, sponsor, exemplar, counsellor, host and guide, as well as developer of skills and intellect. These roles overlap and the skills of the mentor to move between these roles, responding to the needs of the individual mentee, is crucial. Howe's (2006) study of 'outstanding' teacher induction programmes from across the globe concluded that the skills and training of the mentor was a fundamental aspect of a successful induction process.

A mentoring culture enables teacher professionalism by supporting colleagues to con-tinue to develop knowledge, skills and abilities as part of their professional learning. Within a mentoring culture, teachers would support and be supported to have honest, authentic conversations that support professional growth. Within such a culture, it is important to recognise issues of ownership and learning agendas. Mentors need to acknowledge that they are working with peers rather than children and young people, and therefore be cog-nisant of adult learning and liberally use empathy and sensitivity (Lovett, 2002).

In the 'Teachers of Promise' study conducted by Cameron et al. (2014), probationer teachers themselves reported that working with a mentor and each other sustained their enthusiasm and developed their teacher identity and innovative practice. In Scotland, the commitment to mentoring probationer teachers is a fundamental aspect of the commitment to creating a high performing education system.

Since 2002, all probationer teachers in Scotland have been required to complete a one-year probation period. The Scottish Government have made a commitment to support pro-bationer teachers through the TIS. This commitment funds probationer teachers through a guaranteed one-year teaching post, including a reduced class commitment time of 0.82 full time equivalence and having access to a supporter. Many believe that a funded first year of teaching is a jewel in the crown of Scottish education.

The role of mentor is a critical one in supporting probationer teachers as they develop their teacher identity. This crucial role is also fundamental to probationer teacher retention, as one of the main reasons given by probationer teachers who leave teaching in the first few years is "poor induction into the profession" (Goddard & O'Brien, 2003; Kersaint et al., 2007).

In an ideal world, each school would ensure that the probationer teacher gets the best start into the profession by appointing them an experienced mentor who is actively engaged in professional learning and is enthusiastic about supporting new teachers. This can help to counteract the negative press teaching and teachers receive at the hands of those who either have become disenchanted with the profession or those who do not understand the complexities of teaching and being a teacher.

The desirable skills of a mentor are numerous and varied. Mentors must be skilled enough to enable the probationer teacher to develop and progress in their understanding and abilities to plan, deliver and assess high-quality learning experiences for the diverse range of children and young people they encounter. There is broad agreement that genuine empathy to support probationer teacher improvement and good interpersonal skills (Martin & Rippon, 2005) are required. O'Brien and Christie (2005) draw on the work of Clutterbuck (2001) in generating a list of generic mentor competencies, which include traits such as being self-aware and having behavioural awareness, having good communication skills, having a sense of humour, having professional clarity and know-how, and being committed to developing self and others through relationship building. Hudson (2013) would add enthusiasm, being committed to making a difference to the lives of children, being a life-long learner, and both engaging in and supporting reflective practice.

---

### Task 3.5   Reflecting on Your Support for Probationer Teachers

- How do you manage the expectations of probationer teachers as they transition from being a student teacher into the reality of the responsibility for the care and progress of learners?

---

## The Role of the Supporter (Mentor)

The supporter's role is to become the champion for the probationer teacher by offering support and guidance for continual progression. This sits in tension with the supporter's role of challenging the probationer teacher and assessing their progress towards the Standard for Full Registration, which is the benchmark standard to be achieved for entry to the teaching profession in Scotland. Parsloe and Leedham (2009) argue that the relationship between probationer teacher and supporter can be lost when the supporter also has to make decisions about the probationer's progress. In such situations, the professional dialogue can become directive rather than supportive. McIntyre et al. (2009) reached similar conclusions from their study of student physics teachers who were part of the Physics Enhancement Programme.

Acknowledging this tension, the supporter must establish a professional relationship with the probationer teacher, and "the construction of this relationship from the start is crucial before any actual mentoring can take place" (Doherty, 2020) (see also Chapter 1). This usually happens even before the probationer teacher is allocated to the school. Most schools invite probationer teachers to have a tour of the school and to meet their new colleagues and supporter on a more informal basis sometime in June to start the relationship-building process.

Developing trust is a fundamental aspect of being a supporter, and there is an assumption in literature about mentoring that the depth of trust in a relationship between supporter and probationer teacher can influence the success of the mentoring process. This trusting professional relationship is determined by the interpersonal skills of both supporter and probationer teacher (Martin & Rippon, 2005). In the most successful supporter–probationer relationships both the supporter and the probationer teacher have a high degree of emotional intelligence. This is described by Hargreaves (1998) as follows:

> Teaching is not simply about knowing your subject ... Good teachers are not just well-oiled machines. They are emotional, passionate beings who connect with their students and fill their work and their classes with pleasure, creativity, challenge and joy.
>
> (p. 835)

Supporters who have engaged in mentoring, either by being mentored themselves or undertaking professional learning in mentoring, tend to be more open to supporting probationer teachers (Jacobs et al., 2018). They understand the power of mentoring premised on a professional relationship and they have a desire to support others (Allen, 2003) – in this case, to support the new generation of teachers. Both supporters and probationer teachers understand that the probationer teacher's learning is their focus (Mackie, 2018), however, in this professional relationship, the supporter is also undertaking professional learning as they support the probationer teacher.

---

### Task 3.6    Reflecting on Your Mentoring Skills

- How do you maintain and enhance your mentoring skills?
- What networks of support do you have as a supporter?

---

Supporters also help probationer teachers to connect with their pupils, colleagues, curriculum and professional learning to help them reach the expectations of the Standard for Full Registration. Through modelling and guiding the probationer teacher, the supporter helps the probationer teacher to navigate the most difficult aspects to 'measure', such as professional values and professional commitment – the 'teacher being' elements of the Professional Standards as opposed to the teacher knowing and doing elements, which are more measurable.

Part of the role of a supporter is also to challenge the probationer teacher. Challenge is important to identify gaps for and with the probationer teacher and then support them to close such gaps through reflection, knowledge or skills development (Daloz, 2012) (see Chapter 1), thus invoking their agency to address their own learning needs. This can happen when the relationship has been established and the supporter judges that the probationer teacher either needs challenge to modify practice or is showing real promise and needs to be stretched. The supporter and probationer teacher can engage in "risky conversations" (Daly & Milton, 2017) that take a critical look at practice and enable them to co-create solutions. The judgement of the supporter in the timing of these conversations is crucial; if the probationer teacher is not ready for such conversations, they may lose confidence and trust in the supporter's judgement. The probationer teacher also needs to be able to engage in a critical conversation and be honest about their areas for development without feeling personally criticised. How this is handled by the supporter demonstrates their interpersonal skills in empathy and ambition for the probationer teacher.

Some Scottish local authorities, the employers of teachers, have managed the tension created by the supporter being both the probationer teacher champion and assessor by creating local-authority-wide supporter posts. Having a supporter in a 'third space' allows the probationer teacher to engage, perhaps more fully, in 'risky conversations'.

The professional relationship between supporter and probationer teacher is a symbiotic relationship where both parties benefit. The probationer teacher is guided and supported to create their own teacher identity and to engage with learning and learners within the systems and protocols of the learning context. At the same time, the supporter is deepening their own knowledge, self-awareness and critical reflection. This mutually beneficial relationship is described in 'Teaching Scotland's Future' (Donaldson, 2011): "The benefits and impact of taking on the role of being a mentor, particularly for mid-career teachers, are clear … Where mentors are trained and fully supported, they gain many valuable skills and refresh a range of their own competences" (2011, p. 52). Haggard et al. (2011) agree and suggest that this is "a reciprocal relationship, involving mutuality of social exchange as opposed to a one-way relationship" (2011, p. 292), with Eby et al. (2007) calling this a learning partnership.

## Supporting the Supporter

The literature on mentoring is vast but can be seen as working along a flexible continuum of professional support, as outlined in Figure 3.1. For more information, visit http://www.gtcs. org.uk/professional-update/coaching-and-mentoring.aspx.

GTC Scotland helps describe this flexible continuum through the experiences of a probationer teacher in their first year of teaching. At the start of the first term the probationer teacher may need to call upon the mentoring skills of their supporter, and the school team around them, to help gain knowledge and provide solutions to different issues as they occur. This support can be very directive, for example, direct instructions or offering advice and guidance as needed. However, later in the school year, the support could move towards a more collaborative mentoring approach, with the supporter helping the probationer teacher to draw upon their growing experience to develop solutions to their enquiry, and plan for actions and next steps (GTCS, n.d.). (See also Chapter 1.)

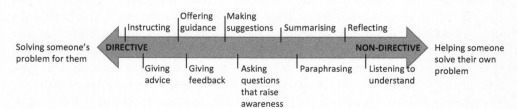

*Figure 3.1*

## Task 3.7   Reflecting on the Support You Provide

- How do you decide the approach to take with each probationer teacher?
- How do you navigate the tension between being a supporter and assessor of the probationer teacher? What are the main challenges for you in navigating this tension?

## Professional Learning for Supporters

The role of supporting the supporter is seen as part of a collaborative national approach to supporting the professional learning context of teachers in Scotland. In 2008, the Mentoring in Teacher Education report (HMIe, 2008) identified good practice that enabled mentoring in schools to support and develop the professional skills and knowledge of probationer teachers as they work towards the Standard for Full Registration. This necessitated a cohesive and co-ordinated approach from all education partners so that new teachers benefitted from mentoring that facilitated impactful continuous professional learning and development. This, according to the report, "can only take place with commitment from schools, education authorities and teacher education institutions to developing effective mentoring" (HMIe, 2008).

The 'Teaching Scotland's Future' report (Donaldson, 2011) builds on information contained in the 2008 HMIe report, which recognised mentoring as central to the professional learning and development of all teachers at all stages of their career, saying that teachers should "see themselves as mentors not just of students and newly qualified teachers but more generally" (2011, p. 98), thus identifying that mentoring skills should be developed through ongoing professional learning and development to support the professional learning of colleagues. Supporting the supporter involves developing professional confidence and self-awareness in mentoring, and addresses 'Teaching Scotland's Future's' recommendation number 39 that "all teachers should see themselves as teacher educators and be trained in mentoring" (2011, p. 73).

Supporters come from a range of backgrounds and are not required to undertake any formal qualification, as in other education systems. For example, in North Carolina, mentors are required to hold a mentor license (Andrews & Andrew, 1998). GTC Scotland supports the supporter through facilitating collaborative working with local authority officers and independent sector representatives. These officers and representatives play a lead role in the co-ordination, support and delivery of the probationary year for probationer teachers, their supporters, and schools in their local and regional settings. They are brought together throughout the school year as a supported professional learning community to share, develop and enable their skills and expertise to contribute to and build teacher professionalism. There is additional support through a dedicated team in GTC Scotland who offer support and guidance to local authority officers and independent school representatives on an ongoing basis. Likewise, GTC Scotland supports the local authority officers and independent sector representatives who play a lead role in the co-ordination, support and delivery of the Professional Update process, to enable and support teacher professionalism. These officers are also invited to learning community events to promote a shared culture of professional learning. Additionally, GTC Scotland Senior Education Officers are deployed to regional areas to support and collaborate with local authority colleagues and independent school representatives to meet local needs and developments.

Bringing together the key 'supporters of the supporters', at a national level, GTC Scotland assists with the induction and mentoring support for new local authority lead officers by creating the opportunities to work with, and learn from, more experienced colleagues. This helps build an informed community of practice and breaks down the potential isolation that the complexity and uniqueness of these roles can bring.

Local authorities, teacher education institutions and national bodies offer a wide range of enhanced professional learning programmes to support the role of supporter, particularly in relation to meeting the needs of probationer teachers. The GTC Scotland offering in this area is a facilitated four-day mentoring and coaching programme to support the understanding and development of mentoring skills of supporters, in supporting professional learning conversations and Professional Review and Development. This offering includes a range of online materials to support mentoring approaches (see https://www.gtcs.org.uk/professional-update/coaching-and-mentoring.aspx>).

Many local authorities have very comprehensive programmes for both mentoring and coaching, several of which have achieved GTC Scotland Professional Recognition, an award that recognises the enhanced, significant, sustained and reflective enquiry a teacher has undertaken, and the development of their professional learning in mentoring.

## Individual Benefit to System Benefit

There is no doubt that effective mentoring of probationer teachers supports their development as a teacher and provides a solid foundation for a fulfilling and successful teaching career. However, in general there is a lack of recognition of the importance of this work and a lack of recognition for the skills and time commitment of the supporters of probationer teachers, with it being seen as something that is expected to be done. In Scotland there are some exceptions to this, where those undertaking a coaching and mentoring diploma are awarded Professional Recognition by GTC Scotland, which is an award that recognises professional learning in a particular area, in this case coaching and mentoring.

Scotland's national model of professional learning for teachers recognises the need to "lead learning conversations underpinned by coaching approaches to stimulate, challenge and support thinking". The potential has also been identified for the establishment of a national coaching and mentoring strategy for Scotland's teachers. There is a view that this will build on national educational policy intentions of empowerment, agency, self-evaluation and improvement. As Scottish education develops an empowered system and considers new career pathways, mentoring approaches are being viewed as building capacity through supporting critical self-reflection to increase self-efficacy and a sense of agency.

It is necessary to consider the impact of effective mentoring on different groups within Scotland's teaching profession, with focused mentoring for specific role-related groups and minority ethnic teachers being explored and created. Often in an approach to develop system-wide, national-level approaches to issues in education, there are concerted efforts to ensure consistency of approach. Mentoring is not a linear approach (see 'Supporting the Supporter' section); success is built on relationships and dialogue, rooted in professional values, that take place with a full understanding of the impact of the individual context. What works as a process for one individual may not be what works for the next. Therefore, a national approach needs to embrace both the diversity of approaches and the tensions in-built within the role of supporter. It is through a deeper understanding of why mentoring works, and a shared view of what makes it effective, that the different approaches to how it is delivered can ensure teachers at all stages of their career, but particularly in the early phase, experience, model and benefit from effective relational approaches. This investment in teachers by teachers is a foundation for what it means to be a teacher in Scotland.

## Summary and Key Points

This chapter explored development from student to employed teacher with mentoring support. The key points discussed are as follows:

- the Professional Standards outline what it means to become, to be and to grow as a teacher in Scotland, and a commitment to professional values is at the heart of the Professional Standards and underpins the relationships, thinking and professional practice of all teachers in Scotland;
- the professional values are embedded in mentoring;
- mentors require key knowledge, skills and dispositions to support student teachers effectively through the transition phase to become fully registered teachers in Scotland;
- mentors can assist beginning teachers to evolve and develop their practice through self-assessment and target-setting; and
- the Professional Standards provide a framework for supporting the professional growth of teachers in the early career phase.

## Further Reading

Jyrhämä, R. & Syrjäläinen, E. (2009). "Good pal, wise dad and nagging wife" – and other views of teaching practice supervisors. In Papers from the ISATT 2009 conference. *Navigating in educational contexts: identities and cultures in dialogue*. 14th Biennal Conference of International Study Association on Teachers and Teaching. 1–4 July 2009. University of Lapland, Rovaniemi.

Kennedy, A. (2011). Collaborative continuing professional development (CPD) for teachers in Scotland: aspirations, opportunities and barriers. *European Journal of Teacher Education*, 34(February), 25–41.

## References

Adoniou, M. & Gallagher, M. (2017). Professional standards for teachers – what are they good for? *Oxford Review of Education*, 43(1), 109–126.

Allen, T.D. (2003). Mentoring others: a dispositional and motivational approach. *Journal of Vocational Behavior*, 62(1), 134–154.

Andrews, T.E. & Andrews, L. (eds) (1998). *The NASDTEC manual 1998–1999: manual on the preparation and certification of educational personnel.* Dubuque, IA: Kendall/Hunt.

Cameron, M., Baker, R. & Lovett, S. (2006). *Teachers of promise: getting started in teaching.* Wellington: New Zealand Council for Educational Research.

Clutterbuck, D. (2001). *Everyone needs a mentor: fostering talent at work* (3rd ed.). London: The Chartered Institute of Personnel and Development.

Daloz, L.A. (2012). *Mentor: guiding the journey of adult learners* (2nd ed.). San Francisco, CA: Jossey-Bass, Wiley Print.

Daly, C. & Milton, E. (2017). External mentoring for new teachers: mentor learning for a change agenda. *International Journal of Mentoring and Coaching in Education,* 6(3), 178–195.

Darling-Hammond, L. (1997). *Doing what matters most: investing in quality teaching.* National Commission on Teaching & America's Future.

Darling-Hammond, L. & Sclan, E.M. (1996). Who teaches and why: Dilemmas of building a profession for twenty-first century schools. In S.E.J. Sikula, T. Buttery & E. Guyton (eds), *Handbook of Research on Teacher Education.* New York: Association of Teacher Educators.

Doherty, E. (2020). *CollectivED working papers,* (10), 9–11. Carnegie School of Education, Leeds Beckett University. Retrieved from www.leedsbeckett.ac.uk/-/media/files/schools/school-of-education/collectived-issue-10.pdf?la=en

Donaldson, G. (2011). *Teaching Scotland's future: report of a review of teacher education in Scotland.* Edinburgh: Scottish Government. Retrieved from www.webarchive.org.uk/wayback/archive/20190701211038/https://www2.gov.scot/resource/doc/337626/0110852.pdf

Eby, L.T., Rhodes, J. & Allen, T.D. (2007). Definition and evolution of mentoring. In T.D. Allen & L.T. Eby (eds), *Blackwell handbook of mentoring: a multidisciplinary approach* (pp. 7–20). Oxford, UK: Blackwell.

Freire, P. (1992). *Pedagogy of hope: reliving pedagogy of the oppressed* (R.R. Barr, Trans. 2004 ed.). New York: Continuum Publishing Company.

General Teaching Council Scotland (GTCS) (n.d.). *Coaching and mentoring.* Retrieved from https://www.gtcs.org.uk/professional-update/coaching-and-mentoring/

Giroux, H. (2001). *Theory and resistance in education: towards a pedagogy for the opposition.* Westport, CT: Bergin & Garvey.

Giroux, H.A. (2011). *On critical pedagogy.* London: Continuum.

Goddard, R. and O'Brien, P. (2003). *Beginning teachers' perceptions of their work, well-being, and intention to leave* [Doctoral dissertation]. Routledge.

Gold, Y. (1996). Beginning teacher support. Attrition, mentoring, and induction. In C.B. Courtney (ed.), *Review of Research in Education,* 16, pp. 548–594. Washington, DC: American Educational Research Association.

Haggard, D.L., Dougherty, T.W., Turban D.B. & Wilbanks, J.E. (2011). Who is a mentor? A review of evolving definitions and implications for research. *Journal of Management,* 37, 280–304.

Hargreaves, A. (1998). The emotional practice of teaching. *Teaching and Teacher Education,* 14(8), 835–854.

HMIe (2008). *Mentoring in teacher education.* Retrieved from https://dera.ioe.ac.uk/998/7/mite_Redacted.pdf

Howe, E.R. (2006). Exemplary teacher induction: an international review. *Educational Philosophy and Theory,* 38(3), 287–297.

Hudson, P. (2013). Desirable attributes and practices for mentees: mentor teachers' expectations. *European Journal of Educational Research,* 2(3), 107–119. Retrieved from https://eprints.qut.edu.au/64234/1/Attributes_and_Practices_for_Mentees_-_mentors_expect.pdf>

Jacobs, J., Boardman, A., Potvin, A. & Wang, C. (2018). Understanding teacher resistance to instructional coaching. *Professional Development in Education,* 44(5), 690-703. DOI: 10.1080/19415257.2017.1388270

Kemmis, S., Heikkinen, H.L.T., Fransson, G., Aspfors, J. & Edwards-Groves, C. (2014). Mentoring of new teachers as a contested practice: supervision, support and collaborative self-development. *Teaching and Teacher Education,* 43, 154-164.

Kersaint, G., Lewis, J., Potter, R. & Meisels, G. (2007). Why teachers leave: factors that influence retention and resignation. *Teaching and Teacher Education,* 23(6), 775-794.

Levinson, D.J., Darrow, C.M., Klein, E.G., Levinson, M.H. & McKee, B. (1978). *Season's of a man's life.* New York: Ballantine.

Lovett, S. (2002). Teacher learning and development in primary schools: a view gained through the National Education Monitoring project. [Thesis] Retrieved from http://dx.doi.org/10.26021/9676

Mackie, L. (2018). Understandings of mentoring within initial teacher education school placement contexts: a Scottish perspective. *Professional Development in Education,* 44(5), 622-637.

Martin, M. & Rippon, J. (2005). Everything is fine: the experience of teacher induction. *Journal of In-service Education,* 31(3), 527-544.

McIntyre, J., Hobson, A.J. & Mitchell, N. (2009). Continuity, support, togetherness and trust: Findings from an evaluation of a university-administered early professional development programme for teachers in England. *Professional Development in Education,* 35(3), 357-379.

Mertz, N. (2004). What's a mentor, anyway? *Educational Administration Quarterly,* 40, 541.

O'Brien, J. & Christie, F. (2005). Characteristics of support for beginning teachers: evidence from the new Teacher Induction Scheme in Scotland. *Mentoring and Tutoring,* 13(2), 189-203.

OECD (2015). *Improving schools in Scotland: An OECD perspective.* Retrieved from http://www.oecd.org/education/school/Improving-Schools-in-Scotland-An-OECD-Perspective.pdf

Parsloe, E. & Leedham, M. (2009). *Coaching and mentoring: practical conversations to improve learning* (2nd ed.). London, UK: Kogan.

Shanker, A. (1987). Tomorrow's teachers. *Teachers College Record,* 88(3), 423-429.

The Public Service Reform (General Teaching Council for Scotland) Order 2011. Retrieved from https://www.legislation.gov.uk/sdsi/2011/9780111012246

Weiss, E.M. & Weiss, S.G. (1999). *Beginning teacher induction.* Eric Digest. (ERIC Document No. ED436487). Retrieved from  https://files.eric.ed.gov/fulltext/ED436487.pdf

# SECTION 2

# Mentoring at each stage of a teacher's career

# 4 'Meet my mentor' - the student teacher's view

*Jennifer Farrar and Maggie McColl*

## Objectives

At the end of this chapter, you should be able to:

- critically reflect on your own experiences of being mentored and the impact it had on your own development;
- use these reflections to inform your own practice and approach as a mentor;
- evaluate the impact that your approach to mentoring might have on the development of a beginning teacher's professional identity;
- consider the balance of the mentoring experience that you provide in terms of emotional and academic support; and
- develop ways of working with your mentee that enable you to realise their expectations – and your own – in manageable and productive ways.

## Introduction

This chapter focuses on the experience of 'being mentored' from the perspective of the beginning teacher. As the phrase in inverted commas implies, there is a sense that 'being mentored' can be something that is 'done to' a person rather than 'with' them. While we recognise that this is not and should not always be the case, a primary aim of this chapter is to draw attention to the complex dynamics that underpin the mentoring relationship with a view to making these power structures visible.

Drawing the findings from recent research literature alongside the views of some newly qualified teachers in Scotland, we build on emerging trends in mentoring scholarship to suggest strategies that may support mentors (and those being mentored) towards the creation of more equable and responsive mentoring relationships that are practically manageable and mutually beneficial. Towards the end of the chapter, we discuss how this can include an acknowledgement of the Funds of Knowledge (Moll et al 1992) that beginning teachers bring with them to the mentoring process and their potential contribution to existing communities of practice in school settings (Wenger-Trayner & Wenger-Trayner 2015).

DOI: 10.4324/9780429356957-6

## Task 4.1    What are your memories of being mentored?

Recall a time when you experienced mentoring within a professional context. This could be when you were mentored as a beginning teacher or, if that is not relevant, another time when you received advice from a more experienced colleague to support your professional development.

You might consider:

- What are your primary memories of being mentored?
- How did the experience make you feel?
- What aspects of the mentoring process led to those feelings?
- If you could meet your mentor now, what feedback would you give them?
- On reflection, to what extent is your current practice as a mentor influenced by your experiences as a mentee?

Completing the first reflective task has hopefully caused you to dwell on memories of mentoring that most probably took place in an earlier stage in your career. Were your memories positive or negative – perhaps a mix? As Lejonberg et al (2018) have noted, while mentoring has the potential to effect positive change in a mentee's development, outcomes can vary, meaning contrasting experiences are possible (2018: 524). Given the important role that mentoring can play in supporting the development of effective teachers (Spooner-Lane 2017) and in reducing attrition rates within those crucial first years of teaching (Caspersen & Raaen 2014), it seems vital to ensure that there is consistency and quality in the mentoring programmes provided (Hobson et al 2009; Mackie 2018) while also allowing for individual differentiation and personalised support.

So how might this be done? Research in this field is expanding. As other chapters in this book have explored, researchers in recent decades have unpacked the key features of successful mentoring relationships (eg, Beck & Kosnick 2000). Other scholars have examined mentee and mentor understandings of the mentoring process (Lejonberg et al 2018; Mackie 2018), highlighting the tensions that can occur and their possible effects (Zanting et al 2001). Of particular relevance to this chapter's focus on the beginning teacher's perspective are three growing sub-fields, which will be explored in more detail under the following, somewhat over-lapping, headings:

i.   Mentee and mentor expectations of mentoring
ii.  Power dynamics inherent in mentoring and mentoring models
iii. How to make the most of the mentoring experience: the mentee's view

## Mentee and mentor expectations of mentoring

Under this heading falls an emerging body of research that explores the ideas about mentoring that mentee and mentor bring to the relationship. Izadinia (2016) has drawn attention to the nuanced difference between *perspectives* of mentoring, in other words, how the mentoring relationship is understood through experience, and *perceptions* or *expectations* of mentoring, in other words, the values and ideals that participants ascribe to the concept of mentoring, possibly even before the process takes place. One of the ways Izadinia (2016) tried to explore this in her own small-scale study was to ask mentees and mentors to encapsulate their expectations of mentoring into the form of a metaphor.

According to Izadinia's analysis, the mentees in her project tended towards metaphors with connotations of support and guidance, including "parenting, gardening, advising and coaching" (2016: 395). As these words suggest, the mentees expected mentoring to be a process that involved cultivation, care and encouragement. Many of the metaphors selected by the mentors in the project mirrored those of the mentees, with images such as "bringing a new player onto some kind of sporting team" (2016: 396), indicating the importance of teamwork and supportive structures. Yet some of the mentor-chosen metaphors also reflected the hierarchical nature of the mentoring relationship, a feature we return to again in the next section. According to Izadinia, one mentor used an image of "the cup and the water" (2016: 396) to illustrate the steady hand the more experienced mentor requires to ensure the "correct" flow of their knowledge to the mentee as "cup", while another drew a "master and apprentice" parallel.

Interestingly, the metaphors chosen by the beginning teachers in Izadinia's (2016) study have much in common with the findings of earlier studies into student teachers' expectations of mentoring. For example, student teacher participants in Booth's 1993 study expected their mentors to offer "general support and encouragement, assistance in their professional development, and information and advice on subject-specific teaching, classroom management, and control" (Booth cited in Zanting et al 2001: 60). The student teachers in Zanting et al's own study (2001) wanted their mentors to be coaches and guides, not only in relation to aspects of pedagogy but also to aspects of classroom life and school routines (2001: 76). But as one of Izadinia's respondents noted, the beginning teachers did not want the support to be confused with "spoon feeding" (2016: 396).

Writing more recently, Lejonberg et al (2018) found that beginning teachers' perceptions of mentoring support were strongly influenced by their perceptions of how much "effort" their mentor put into the mentoring relationship (2018: 533). These authors also concluded that mentees' perception of their mentoring relationship as "safe" was "an important prerequisite" for their subsequent positive development through the mentoring process (2018: 536). The requirement for a safe mentee/mentor relationship is reminiscent of the need for trust discussed in Chapter 1, when reference was made to the traditionally defined role of the mentor as someone entrusted with the protection of another. As these findings indicate, the perceptions or expectations that mentees bring to the mentoring process – many of which are bound up with personal and emotional responses – can have a shaping effect on the experience and effectiveness of mentoring as a support mechanism where the mentee feels secure.

## Task 4.2   The view from probation

Read through the following quotations from recent probationer teachers in Scotland and consider them against your own experiences and the reflective prompts that follow.

*"My mentor started things off by setting out her expectations. She asked me, 'Have you ever been mentored before? What do you expect of me?' I told her I was looking for advice, guidance and a fresh pair of eyes. She laid out her expectations too and they were high but not too high. They were not out of the ordinary from the remit. I didn't expect her to ask me for my expectations but it really worked."*

*"If I become a mentor in the future, I will start things off with an open conversation and I will ask them what they want to gain from the year. I was asked this myself and it automatically gave me a doorway into a positive relationship because both of us started with a clear view of our priorities."*

*"It is important to have similar values as your mentor, but that is hard – how can you tell that is going to be the case? From my friends, I have heard of clashes between mentees and mentors. That must be so challenging because you are dealing with such mixed messages and trying to make the relationship work. I am quite a hesitant person and luckily the mentor I had was really understanding. He took time to get to know me and let me know that it was okay for me to ask questions."*

*"I felt lost at times in my mentoring relationship. Things that were promised in terms of support did not materialise, but I was still expected to hit the ground running. In fact, the feedback and support I was offered by the local authority was better than what I was offered by my mentor. It turned out that my mentor had never managed adults before, and it showed. I was left on the brink of 'Can I? Can't I?' for much of my probationary year."*

### Reflective questions

Consider the snippets from our real-life beginning teacher case studies above. What key themes or ideas emerge? How do these beginning teachers' experiences of mentoring map onto your own experiences and expectations? What advice would you offer these beginning teachers – and their mentors?

### *Practical tips for mentors*

- Use the initial meetings to discuss and establish your expectations.
- Don't promise things you cannot deliver due to time constraints.
- Seek training and support to help with the development of your mentoring skills, such as line management.

## Task 4.3    The mentor identity

- What impact did the mentoring you received have on your emerging sense ofprofessional identity?
- As a mentor, to what extent do you think your practice has a shaping effect on yourmentee's developing professional identity?

## Power dynamics inherent in mentoring and mentoring models

For Task 4.3, we aimed for you to consider the impact that your mentor, or mentoring experience, had on your developing sense of professional self. Similarly, we wanted you, as a mentor, to reflect on the impact you think you have on your mentees as they develop their professional identities. The idea that such reflection can be helpful for mentoring is supported by research that shows beginning teachers find the impact of mentoring to be "highly significant" on the formation of their professional identity (Izadinia 2016: 398). Yet, the same small-scale qualitative study in Australia also found that most mentors did not share their mentees' view; in other words, they were unaware that their mentoring could have such profound significance on beginning teachers' development (ibid).

As this example illustrates, mentors do not always fully recognise the power they wield over their mentees, both in terms of possible pedagogic influence and also in terms of authority. But given the power dynamics that are inherent in any relationship that positions a less experienced mentee or 'novice' under the guidance of a more experienced other, perhaps mentors should be more explicitly aware of the power structures at work within the mentoring relationship.

Such structures are visible in the definitions we use for mentoring, such as this neat summary by Hobson et al (2009):

> The one-to-one support of a novice or less experienced practitioner (mentee) by a more experienced practitioner (mentor), designed primarily to assist the development of the mentee's expertise and to facilitate their induction into the culture of the profession ... and into the specific local context.
>
> (Hobson et al 2009: 207)

As these authors suggest, the mentor's role is to help develop the mentee's professional and pedagogical expertise while also equipping them with sufficient *cultural capital* to induct them into their learning communities. By cultural capital, we mean the social assets (which might include specific 'insider' knowledge) that can enable mobility within social groups. In a school setting, this could equate to having access to specialised socio-cultural knowledge of 'how things are done around here', where 'here' can refer not only to the 'culture' of a specific school context but also to the 'culture' of the teaching profession as a whole. Once in possession of such knowledge or capital, it is assumed that mobility or acceptance is more likely.

While of course it is essential to provide beginning teachers with support during the initial stages of their careers, some researchers are critical of the way that such support is framed.

A look at the language used in dominant mentoring frameworks supports this concern. Maynard and Furlong (1995) described the early career stage as a period of "early idealism" that leads into "survival", with Katz and Raths (1985) also using "survival" as a label for the same period of career development. Berliner (1988) recommends the use of the term "novice". Given the negative connotations of these terms and the sense of struggle they convey, it is perhaps not surprising that some researchers feel that beginning teachers can be positioned as "helpless and in need of guidance into the tradition of the school" (Ulvik & Langørgen 2012: 43) by induction schemes (Ulvik & Langørgen 2012). Instead, Ulvik and Langørgen (2012) call on schools and researchers to re-position student and beginning teachers as *resources*, rather than risks or burdens. This can be done, they claim, through a change in focus, away from 'survival instincts' and towards an acceptance of the mentee as more of a 'community contributor'. Ulvik and Langørgen's own research found that beginning teachers "were not used [by schools] in a positive way, even though more experienced teachers could learn from them" (2012: 54).

Similarly, Correa et al (2015) have explored the issues caused by the positioning of new teachers as "deficient professionals" who are often seen to have little of value to offer schools (66). Like Ulvik and Langørgen, Correa et al problematise the terminology used in frameworks to describe the beginning stages of a teaching career. In particular, they highlight Veenman's (1984) explanation of the "reality shock" that new teachers experience, caused by "the collapse of the missionary ideals formed during teacher training as a result of the confrontation with the harsh and rude reality of everyday classroom life" (143, cited in Correa et al 2015: 67). According to Correa et al, phrases such as 'reality shock' are problematic in that they "reproduce and legitimise" existing power structures by "legitimising the division between the one who knows and the one who does not" (2015: 67). In turn, this reproduction of power makes change all the more challenging, as why would you trust someone in such a state of "shock", "collapse" and utter struggle to bring about innovation within the school setting?

Instead, Correa et al (2015) present an alternative perspective, through which the process of mentoring a beginning teacher is positioned and recognised as an ideal opportunity for a school and mentor to enact change, new ideas and to reflect on practices past, present and future (2015: 73). This does not mean that the level of challenge that new teachers face is forgotten or dismissed; the shift in practice comes via the change in discourse and its consequences. The perspective presented by Correa et al (2015) fits with the idea of the mentoring relationship being a dynamic one, as suggested in Chapter 1, where the roles of mentor and mentee are constantly evolving as contexts change.

## Task 4.4   The view from probation

Read through the following quotations from recent probationer teachers in Scotland and consider them against your own experiences and the reflective prompts that follow.

*"My mentor would bring his troubles to work and would take them out on me – or at least that is how I felt. As a mentee, you want to know that you can go and knock on*

that door, but I couldn't. I felt as if I was a child again. I worked with what I was told and did not ignore his suggestions, but it was awful. I often wondered why he had agreed to mentor me and really did start to believe I was the problem. I did not want to go to the Headteacher to ask for another mentor because I thought this would be held against me. So instead, I found another colleague who was more on my wavelength. I would go to this person instead for advice. I don't think I can ever repay them for what they did for me."

"It is really hard to get out of the student mindset into the probationary mind, but my mentor made it so much easier for me. She made me feel listened to and treated all of my opinions as valid. She also had a good relationship with the Headteacher and would pass on positive feedback about my work to the head. It made me feel so confident that my work was being recognised in this way."

"Before I retrained as a teacher and started on my probationary year, I had worked for many years and was used to doing a job well. I was also used to giving feedback to my colleagues within the business world. My mentor was in a senior management role in a small school. The feedback he gave me caused me to feel terrible. It was always picky and negative and not at all constructive. After an observation, he would not give anything away and would tell me he'd 'speak to me later'. Because my school was so small, I had no one else to share my experiences with. One person did tell me 'that's just the way he is', but I don't think that is an excuse. I felt rubbish and power-less and used to panic about whether I would ever be good enough."

### Reflective questions

Consider the power dynamics that are visible in these three brief accounts of mentoring relationships. How can Ulvik and Langørgen's (2012) idea of the beginning teacher as *resource* be applied to each example? For the first and third examples, consider in detail what steps would have to be taken to reposition the beginning teacher more positively in relation to the mentoring relationship. Again, what advice would you offer these beginning teachers – and their mentors?

## Practical suggestions for mentors

- Find out what skills your mentee brings with them to the mentoring relationship and how you might make the most of them.
- Review the models of mentoring used in your school and identify the power structures at work in the relationship: what can be done about them?
- Make sure your mentee has a clear idea of whom else they might speak to if, for any reason, they find it difficult to confide in you, as their official mentor.

---

### Task 4.5   Defining the responsibilities of the mentor

Think about the sort of support you currently provide for your mentee.

- To what extent do you think your role is to offer academic, professional support?
- To what extent do you think your role is to offer emotional support?
- How do these components balance out in the approach you plan to take as a mentor?
- Are there other components present?

---

## How to make the most of the mentoring experience: the mentee's view

Drawing together some of the ideas and issues covered above, this section considers how the mentoring experience might be improved for both parties. As we have seen from the research discussed already in this chapter, beginning teachers place a high value on the mentoring experience, but, as the studies by Correa et al (2015) and Ulvik and Langørgen (2012) have shown, new teachers can feel undervalued and underused within their school settings, leading to feelings of inadequacy, invisibility and powerlessness. Caspersen and Raaen's (2014) study into the coping strategies employed by beginning teachers in Norway found that many newly qualified educators found it difficult to encapsulate and express their training needs, meaning they were not able to fully benefit from the experience of engaging with the professional support offered to them via induction programmes (2014: 205).

For mentors, the challenge then becomes how best to help mentees *articulate* these training needs and goals, and this can be a complex task. As discussed above, the power dynamics of the mentoring relationship might make such conversations seem more of a challenge or risk, with beginning teachers reluctant to admit to something they fear might be interpreted as a weakness.

Having explored beginning teachers' perspectives on mentoring, Izadinia's (2016) findings suggested that a successful mentoring arrangement would offer both academic and emotional support. Writing about the experiences of mentors and student teachers in Scottish schools, Mackie (2018: 628) organised her findings under two main headings that are similar to Izadinia's: the personal and professional. As Mackie notes, this dual view of mentoring goes beyond the traditional idea of an "instructional-based supervisory notion" under which "mentors advise, dominate talk, view themselves as the expert and are product rather than process focused" (2018: 632) towards a view of mentoring as a "multidimensional process" (ibid: 634).

As some of the research already cited in this chapter has indicated, one of these 'multidimensions' is the mentee and their potential role as a resource for innovation and change in the classroom (Ulvik & Langørgen 2012). To help mentors and mentees recognise and understand the resources that beginning teachers bring with them on probation, and how to make the most of them to support and enrich the school community, we outline two theoretical concepts: Funds of Knowledge and Communities of Practice.

## Funds of Knowledge (Moll et al 1992)

While the date of this original paper by Moll et al (1992) might now seem quite old, the concept continues to gain traction in education through application and further diversification (for example, see Esteban-Guitart & Moll 2014). Back in the 1990s, Moll et al (1992) used the term 'Funds of Knowledge' to refer to the rich and abundant historical and cultural knowledge that exists within families, but which is not always recognised within schools. One of the original aims of this approach was to develop "participatory pedagogies" (Moll et al 1992: 139) that could encourage a greater and more culturally responsive exchange of knowledge between home and school. The 'Funds of Knowledge' concept has since been used to explain how teachers' professional knowledge is inherently connected to the knowledge that comes from their home life with families and cultural communities (Hedges 2012). According to Hedges, the concept can help make visible the ways that "experiences like being a parent, being a teacher, sharing ethnic and religious backgrounds and being a part of the local community can influence the teacher knowledge drawn on in daily practice and ... pedagogical decision making" (2012: 11).

With this application in mind, we suggest that the Funds of Teacher Knowledge approach (Hedges 2012) can be used as a tool to help mentors unlock aspects of their mentees' personal and professional knowledge linked to learning and teaching. Doing so would help to deepen mentors' understanding of their mentees as resources in the classroom by understanding more about their mentees' background and opening up spaces for dialogue about the 'hows' and 'whys' of teaching. It could also help to create more culturally responsive ways of mentoring by acknowledging and encouraging reflective conversations linked to diversity of practice. It is true that this approach may lead to some challenging conversations, but it could be argued that all mentoring conversations carry some form of risk or challenge. As with any mentoring conversation, it is important to ensure that the mentee feels secure enough to share such personal details.

Some prompts linked to Funds of Knowledge may include the following:

* What aspects of your family life have influenced the approach you take as a teacher?
* What aspects of your community life have informed your teaching practice?
* Tell me about a teacher who profoundly influenced your own teaching style and why.

## Communities of Practice (Wenger-Trayner & Wenger-Trayner 2015)

Wenger-Trayner and Wenger-Trayner (2015: 1) defined a Community of Practice (COP) as "groups of people who share a concern or a passion for something they do and learn how to do it better as they interact regularly." Woodgate-Jones suggests that a school can be considered as a COP, given that the key components are a *shared domain of interest* (teaching and learning); a *community* (all the staff working in and towards the shared domain); and a shared repertoire of *practice* (the sum of all activity enacted by members of the community) (2012: 149). As 'newcomers' to the school community, beginning teachers can sometimes experience tensions with the 'old timers' – that is, the longer-established community members (2012). According to the original COP theory (Lave and Wenger 1991), such "uneasy relationships" between community members old and new can lead to transformation and renewal, with benefits for all COP members, including the very newest (Woodgate-Jones 2012: 149), although such developmental journeys are not always easy for the beginning teacher. Woodgate-Jones's research showed the benefits of working with beginning teachers within a COP given that it could support the professional development of the 'old timers' (2012). Staff also gained from the new skills offered by the beginning teacher and appreciated the opportunity to revisit and reflect upon aspects of their teaching practice and underpinning philosophies after years without explicitly doing so (2012: 154).

Related to this, research by Correa et al (2015) also explored how beginning teachers experienced being a newcomer in a COP. The newly qualified teachers in this study reported feeling as if they lacked a sense of agency within the COP and were concerned about the ideological clashes they perceived between their own beliefs and the established practices of the COP (2015: 73).

For the aims and purposes of this chapter, the COP can be understood as a tool for making visible some of the taken-for-granted assumptions about teaching practice that might otherwise remain invisible within a school setting. To return to a quotation used earlier in the chapter, one of the mentor's roles is to facilitate the mentee's induction into the "culture of the profession ... and into the specific local context" (Hobson et al 2009: 207); in other words, to the Community of Practice. By doing so, both mentors and mentees may benefit from conversations that may begin with "how are things done around here?" but can progress into an explanation of the COP's underpinnings via questions such as "why are things done that way around here?" and "what might happen if we did it a little differently?"

## Task 4.6   The view from probation

Read through the following quotations from recent probationer teachers in Scotland and consider them against your own experiences and the reflective prompts that follow.

*"You can make the most of mentoring by making your mentee feel comfortable. My mentor made the effort to take me out for a coffee in June, way before I started at the school in August, and suddenly I had one less thing to worry about on my first day. Try to make your mentee feel as confident as possible because this will help them to take the initiative, and if that happens, it will have a positive impact on your own role."*

*"To make the most of your mentoring practice for your mentee, give them a voice. Let them tell you what is going well or is not going so well and use this alongside your own feedback. And on the subject of feedback, use it to build confidence via constructive criticism rather than endless negatives."*

*"Don't forget to smile. I know it sounds obvious, but it can sometimes be forgotten. Of course, you are not to be your mentee's best pal but do smile and make yourself*

*available. If you have agreed to be a mentor, you have to show that you are willing to adapt your approach to the student's needs. It cannot be a case of one size fits all."*

### Reflective questions

- What advice would you offer these beginning teachers – and their mentors?
- How might you use the concepts of the COP or Funds of Knowledge to help explain what is going on in the probationer's quotations?
- How will you ensure your mentee has a voice?

## Practical tips for mentors

- Think of creative ways to help your mentees articulate their training needs. This could be done via a focus on the Community of Practice or Funds of Knowledge.
- Use the mentoring experience as an opportunity to boost your own professional development and skills as a reflective practitioner.
- Think carefully about how you will handle any tensions that emerge between the beginning teacher's knowledge and that of the wider school community. What will you do to ensure the mentee has agency while also learning 'what they need to know'?

## Summary and key points

In this chapter, we have focused on the experience of 'being mentored' from the perspective of the beginning teacher. In close contact with the research literature, we have considered the mentee's experience from varied vantage points, including mentees' expectations of mentoring; the power dynamics inherent in mentoring and models of mentoring; and how to make the most of the mentoring experience. We have highlighted two theoretical tools, Funds of Knowledge and Communities of Practice, and have set out the ways they could be used to initiate and support conversations between mentors and mentees that reposition beginning teachers as competent colleagues. Ensuring that taken-for-granted school practices are unpacked and made visible is a helpful way to support induction but also makes transformational change a possibility.

## References

Beck, C. and Kosnik, C. (2000). Associate teachers in pre-service education: Clarifying and enhancing their role. *Journal of Education for Teaching*, 26(3), 207-224.

Berliner, D.C. (1988). *The Development of Expertise in Pedagogy*. Washington, D.C.: American Association of Colleges for Teacher Education.

Caspersen, J. and Raaen, F.D. (2014). Novice teachers and how they cope. *Teachers and Teaching: Theory and Practice*, 20(2), 189-211.

Correa, J.M., Martínez-Arbelaiz, A. and Aberasturi-Apraiz, E. (2015). Post-modern reality shock: Beginning teachers as sojourners in communities of practice. *Teaching and Teacher Education*, 48, 66-74.

Esteban-Guitart, M. and Moll, L.C. (2014). Funds of identity: A new concept based on the Funds of Knowledge approach. *Culture and Psychology*, 20(1), 31–48.

Hedges, H. (2012). Teachers' funds of knowledge: A challenge to evidence-based practice. *Teachers and Teaching: Theory and Practice*, 18(1), 7–24.

Hobson, A., Ashby, P., Malderez, A. and Tomlinson, P.D. (2009). Mentoring beginning teachers: What we know and what we don't. *Teaching and Teacher Education*, 25, 207–216.

Izadinia, M. (2016). Student teachers' and mentor teachers' perceptions and expectations of a mentoring relationship: Do they match or clash? *Professional Development in Education*, 42(3), 387–402.

Katz, L.G. and Raths, J.D. (1985). Dispositions as goals for teacher education. *Teaching and Teacher Education*, 1(4), 301–307.

Lave, J. and Wenger, E. (1991). *Situated learning: Legitimate peripheral participation*. Cambridge: Cambridge University Press.

Lejonberg, E., Elstada, E., Sandvik, L.V., Solhaugb, T.A. and Christophersen, K-A. (2018). Developmental relationships in schools: Pre-service teachers' perceptions of mentors' effort, self-development orientation, and use of theory. *Mentoring and Tutoring: Partnership in Learning*, 26(5), 524–541.

Mackie, L. (2018). Understandings of mentoring within initial teacher education school placement contexts: A Scottish perspective. *Professional Development in Education*, 44(5), 622–637.

Maynard, T. and Furlong, J. (1995). Learning to teach and models of mentoring. In T. Kerry and A. Shelton-Mayes (eds.) *Issues in Mentoring*. London: Routledge, pp 10–14.

Moll, L.C., Amanti, C., Neff, C. and González, N. (1992). Funds of knowledge for teaching: Using a qualitative approach to connect homes and classrooms. *Theory Into Practice*, 31(2), 132–141.

Spooner-Lane, R. (2017). Mentoring beginning teachers in primary schools: Research review. *Professional Development in Education*, 43(2), 253–273.

Ulvik, M. and Langørgen, K. (2012). What can experienced teachers learn from newcomers? Newly qualified teachers as a resource in schools. *Teachers and Teaching*, 18(1), 43–57.

Veenman, S. (1984). Perceived problems of beginning teachers. *Review of Educational Research*, 54(2), 143–178.

Wenger-Trayner, E. and Wenger-Trayner, B. (2015). Communities of practice a brief introduction. Retrieved from 20/01/2022 from: https://wenger-trayner.com/wp-content/uploads/2015/04/07-Brief-introduction-to-communities-of-practice.pdf

Woodgate-Jones, A. (2012). The student teacher and the school community of practice: An exploration of the contribution of the legitimate peripheral participant. *Educational Review*, 64(2), 145–160.

Zanting, A., Verloop, N. and Vermunt, J.D. (2001). Student teachers' beliefs about mentoring and learning to teach during teaching practice. *British Journal of Educational Psychology*, 71, 57–80.

# 5 Mentoring new teachers in Scotland

*Margery McMahon*

## Objectives

At the end of this chapter, you should be able to:

- understand the dimensions of the mentoring relationship to reflect on your experience of being a mentor;
- know the elements involved in preparation for mentoring through formal programmes and informal approaches; and
- build on the knowledge and experiences gained through mentoring relationships to develop your own professional and pedagogical practice as an accomplished practitioner.

## Introduction

The relationship between a mentor and a newly qualified or probationary teacher is one of the most critical and formative professional relationships that early career practitioners will have. Their experiences from this, whether positive or negative, can have a significant impact on their own professionalism and pedagogical practice that can endure for many years. While the impact for the beginning teacher can be significant, it is also clear that mentoring brings considerable professional gains for mentors as well, developing and advancing their practice – both pedagogical and reflexive. The mentoring relationship is one way in which the teaching profession renews itself, sharing with and modelling for beginning teachers the values, standards and professional practices that assure quality and commitment in the service of children and young people.

The focus of this chapter is on the role of the mentor and how mentors are supported to fulfil the different dimensions of this role. The chapter begins by considering who mentors are and how they come to that role. It will explore the knowledge, understanding and skills that are required to support probationary/early career teachers. In particular, the extent to which mentoring is now embedded in regulatory professional standards is discussed. While the chapter has a key focus on the Scottish context, effective mentoring practices from beyond the United Kingdom are also explored, so that global perspectives on mentor knowledge, skills and development can illustrate international approaches to developing and supporting early career teachers.

DOI: 10.4324/9780429356957-7

## Mentoring new teachers in Scotland

Mentoring of new teachers, and indeed mentoring at any career stage, can be formal and informal, collective and individual. This chapter is primarily concerned with those with formal responsibilities for mentoring, assigned as part of their job remit, but it recognises that much of the mentoring of new teachers often occurs informally alongside the formal requirements of a mentoring scheme, such as Scotland's Teacher Induction Scheme. The sense of collective professional responsibility for supporting new entrants to teaching reflects the strengthened professional culture that has evolved in Scotland as a result of the 2011 *Teaching Scotland's Future* report (Donaldson, 2011). The emphasis in that report that 'all teachers should see themselves as teacher educators and be trained in mentoring' (Recommendation 39, p.99) has gone some way to embedding support for new teachers as an innate professional respon-sibility of all teachers. While mentoring was seen as essential for the early career phase, the *Teaching Scotland's Future* report also foresaw that mentoring should be available beyond this phase, and linked to teachers' career-long professional learning and annual performance and development review (Donaldson, 2011: p.95).

Formal mentoring for newly qualified teachers in Scotland occurs through the Teacher Induction Scheme (TIS). This scheme, introduced in 2002, was one of the first to formalise an induction programme for new teachers that included the guarantee of a one-year, salaried, teaching position. The scheme emerged as part of a workforce remodelling package entitled 'A Teaching Profession for the 21st century' (SEED, 2001). A key purpose of the scheme was to address concerns about the fragmented and inconsistent experience of newly quali-fied teachers across Scotland. Through it, a programme of induction and mentoring would support newly qualified teachers' introduction into the teaching profession. This included a guaranteed teaching post for one year following initial qualification; a reduced teaching time-table to enable participation in induction events organised by the local education authority; and an assigned mentor/induction supporter. Successful completion results in full admission to the teaching profession, confirmed by achieving the *Standard for Full Registration* with the General Teaching Council for Scotland (GTCS). The assignment of a mentor, who has respon-sibility for a newly qualified teacher, or group of teachers, as part of their formal remit, is a critical lynchpin in the TIS, and how this occurs is explored below.

## Who are the mentors?

In Scotland, the assignment of mentors for newly qualified teachers occurs at school level, though who undertakes this role can vary depending on the sector and size of the school. There is further coordination at the level of the local education authority, which is the direct employer for all teachers and headteachers coming under its governance. At this level, and depending on its size, a local authority officer is usually assigned responsibility for proba-tionary teachers, and while not having a direct mentoring role, their oversight of the locally administered TIS connects them closely to mentors and probationary teachers. In a small primary school, mentoring for a new teacher might be undertaken by the headteacher; in a larger, post primary school it is often the remit of a subject or faculty head, or a member of the school's senior leadership team. In either case, there is an expectation that the mentor will be an experienced and accomplished practitioner. The GTCS *Standard for Career-long Professional Learning* (GTCS, 2021a: p.11 sees this as integral to developing and advancing career-long professional learning and expertise, and leading and contributing to the professional learning of colleagues, including student and probationer teachers (ibid). While there have been efforts to involve other staff in mentoring, through schemes such as the Chartered Teacher scheme in Scotland or the Advanced Skills Teacher initiative in England and Wales, responsibility for mentoring often continues to be assigned to those with leadership and line management duties.

In the refreshed GTCS *Professional Standards Scotland* (GTCS, 2021b), mentoring is firmly located within the leadership standards, with Middle Leaders (Department or Faculty Heads) expected to 'develop coaching and mentoring skills and promote the use of coaching and mentoring principles and approaches which support professional learning and foster a culture of peer support, commitment and collegiality' [*Standard for Middle Leadership and Management*] (GTCS, 2021c: p.13). Headteachers are expected to create the conditions for this and to 'establish, enable and sustain coaching and mentoring principles and approaches which support professional learning including the PRD process' [*Standard for Headship*] (GTCS, 2021d: p.13. The association of mentoring with leadership roles can sometimes present challenges for the mentoring relationship, particularly when the mentor is already 'overwhelmed with other duties' (King *et al*, 2019: p.15). Shanks *et al* (2020: p.1) also found that persistent challenges to effective mentoring endure, including 'having time for observation and feedback but also in terms of how to mentor'.

The focus and emphasis on school empowerment, shared leadership and collaborative practice, which has been a key feature of education policy in Scotland in recent years, is an opportunity to engage more teachers in the mentoring and support of new entrants to the profession. For this to be successful, professional learning opportunities for mentors are essential, although, in the absence of a national scheme, provision for this varies across local education authorities and providers, as Livingston noted in Chapter 1.

---

**Task 5.1   Reflecting on mentoring in your context**

- Review how mentors are assigned in your own professional context. Is there scope to involve more staff who, while not holding a formal leadership role, have the expertise and experience for mentoring new teachers?
- If you are already a mentor, reflect on how this came about. How well prepared were you for your first mentee(s)? What would have assisted you?
- Is there a case for a national scheme for all mentors?

---

## Developing as a mentor

Experience and expertise are critical to being an effective mentor. There is recognition that this need not necessarily equate with longevity or position, though it often does. Regardless, professional learning and training for new mentors is essential, and even the most experienced mentors should have access to ongoing development opportunities to ensure they are up to date with recent policy and regulatory guidance, and changes to curricula in initial teacher education. Such opportunities are usually provided through the local education authority, although can include other agencies involved with the teacher induction scheme, such as the General Teaching Council or professional associations. Formal programmes are also available for mentors through higher education providers as part of their postgraduate Master's programmes. There is, however, no mandatory requirement for mentors to have a formal qualification in mentoring. Given this, what can be expected of mentors and how are they supported to continue to develop their own professional knowledge and skills to ensure meaningful and successful mentoring relationships? In discussing the multi-faceted nature of mentoring, Livingston, in Chapter 1, drew from Orland-Barak (2010), who argued that learning to mentor should focus on the actions of a mentor. There are a number of elements that are critical to this, including understanding teacher learning; familiarity with teacher education programmes and requirements of regulatory standards; appreciation of wider policy contexts; the interpersonal skills required for effective mentoring; and credibility and legitimacy as an accomplished practitioner. Each of these elements is now considered.

### Understanding teacher learning

In the last 20 years there has been a significant shift in how teacher learning is viewed and understood, and organised and resourced. While there are varied approaches to this across education systems (a mandatory, minimum specification of hours for engaging in professional learning, for example), the need for teachers to continue to engage in and take forward their development is central. The responsibility and resourcing for this can be a source of tension among teachers, their professional associations, employers and governments. Consequently, teacher learning can become polarised across the agency, empowerment and accountability agenda. Programmes and initiatives to support teacher learning have expanded considerably during this time period, with a growing focus on career-long professional learning and an ambition for this to be at an advanced level. In some systems there is a formal requirement to have a Master's qualification (for example, Finland), while in others the requirement is for this learning to be at Master's level but without the need to have a Master's degree, such as in Scotland.

This greater focus on teachers' ongoing learning has generated more research on how teachers learn. Drawing from theories of adult learning, or andragogy (Knowles, 1980; Gray, 2018), and research from other professions, there is a growing body of literature on teachers' professional learning (Cordingley *et al*, 2015; Campbell, 2017; Harris and Jones, 2017). Timperley's (2007) research synthesis on teacher professional learning and development identified essential features for effective professional development that included the folllowing:

- demonstrable links between professional learning experiences and student learning outcomes, with what students need to know and do driving what teachers need to know and do; and
- the promotion of deep teacher learning, which leads to effective changes in practice.

(Timperley, 2007: pp.8–12)

For Timperley, 'collegial interaction' focused on student outcomes helps integrate new learning into practice, and so there should be multiple opportunities for this in environments that offer both 'trust and challenge' (2007: pp.15 and 19). Timperley work has influenced subsequent approaches to professional learning, where emphasis is placed on the need for teacher learning to encompass opportunities for learning from experience, reflecting critically on professional and pedagogic practice (individually and collectively), learning collaboratively, and gaining further cognitive development through advanced reading, enquiry and research (Forde and McMahon, 2019). The evolution of formal and informal programmes for teachers' learning has shown that professional learning is a complex and ongoing process in which the agency of the individual teacher is central; that successful professional development needs to be seen as a process and not an event; and that professional learning that improves teacher quality requires rethinking and potentially radically changing traditional approaches to teacher learning (Forde and McMahon, 2019).

An understanding of how teachers, and particularly newly qualified teachers, learn is therefore imperative for effective mentoring. In modelling, mediating and scaffolding professional experiences for mentees, insight into how teachers learn, and the stages of teacher growth and accomplishment, is central to enriching the mentoring relationship (Bullough and Baughman, 1995). Hence, it is important for mentor training programmes to include teacher learning as part of course content. Linked to this is the need to know what and how early career teachers have learned in their programmes of initial teacher preparation so that mentors can work with their mentee to build on and grow from these foundations.

## Teacher education: programmes and standards

To be able to support probationary teachers fully, it is important that mentors are familiar with programmes of initial teacher preparation, with a broad understanding of curriculum content and the professional skills and competences that a new teacher will bring to their first teaching post. While each provider of initial teacher education may have features distinctive to their programme, the accreditation by a regulatory body, such as a teaching council (for example, in Scotland, the General Teaching Council), ensures a set of common expectations about what is required for a beginning teacher to be awarded (in the Scottish context) the *Standard for Provisional Registration* (post qualifying) and the *Standard for Full Registration* (post induction period).

Understanding the purposes of professional standards and how to balance development with performance and accountability is a highly skilled task and can sometimes be problematic for mentors, particularly where they have a dual role of supporter and assessor of professional competence (Shanks *et al*, 2020: p.10). Support, training and professional development for mentors is therefore essential. The changing nature of initial teacher education partnerships has enabled more integrated models for induction support and mentoring to emerge, which may take the form of specialised postgraduate programmes for induction mentors, offered through partnership providers or embedded as part of school-based partnerships. A recent study of mentoring programmes for new teachers in Demark, Malta and Scotland found that, in the latter, 'the participating NQTs, mentors and university tutors valued the opportunity to learn in a partnership community and the mentors highlighted the benefits and challenges of supporting NQTs to undertake enquiry in the classroom' (Shanks *et al*, 2020: p.10).

Knowing how teachers learn, and what new teachers are expected to know and be able to do, are critical elements of effective mentoring. While these are focused on the individual in the classroom and school context, knowledge and appreciation of the wider policy contexts for education is an important third dimension.

### Wider contexts for mentoring

Understanding the wider policy contexts that shape and influence the educational decisions and actions taken in schools and classrooms is essential for mentors and mentees, and mentors have a key role in mediating classroom, school and system-level experiences for beginning teachers. Such sensemaking (Weick *et al*, 2005; Weick, 2009) is part of the social-isation dimension of the mentoring role, where the mentor can assist a newly qualified teacher to make sense of external drivers for education, such as policy and research. The need for political awareness and acumen is increasingly acknowledged in teacher profes-sional standards and, given the micro and macro politics that beginning teachers will experi-ence, mentors have a key role in helping to navigate what, for many new teachers, may be unfamiliar territory. This can take many forms, for example, helping a beginning teacher to understand the role of national-level professional associations for teachers or the influence on national education systems of transnational organisations, such as the Organisation for Economic Cooperation and Development (OECD).

The rapid expansion of social media and its development and use for teachers to share practice, debate policy and contribute to global conversations about teaching and learning has underlined the need for digital literacy for mentors and mentees. This articulation of the 'public self' requires careful guidance as beginning teachers begin to assert their own professional identity as a teacher. Here, through their own engagement in online spaces, mentors can share useful sources, links, threads and connections. Such modelling of practice in the online environment is arguably as important as modelling good practice in the class-room. Guiding new teachers through an unfamiliar policy landscape and introducing them to wider connections through new networks (often online) requires mentors to induct without imposing, to introduce without compelling. This again underlines the highly complex nature of the role of mentor and of the mentoring relationship. It requires mentors to have highly developed interpersonal skills to be able to support beginning teachers to grow as confident educators.

### Mentors – essential attributes

Effective mentoring requires the enactment of a wide repertoire of interpersonal and profes-sional skills, which are essential for a successful mentoring relationship. This repertoire of skills and competences includes 'brokering relationships, building and maintaining relationships, coaching, communicating, encouraging, facilitating, goal setting, guiding, listening, man-aging conflict, problem-solving, providing feedback, reflecting, and valuing difference' (Wyre *et al*, 2016: p.76). For Wyre, Gaudet and McNeese (2016), effective mentoring goes beyond simply possessing these skills – mentors should feel comfortable using them (ibid). Strong communication skills are at the heart of a successful mentoring relationship, as are empathy and trust. Given the responsibility associated with mentoring, particularly where the mentor may have a role in a final assessment, mentors need to be secure in their own professional and pedagogic practice as well, and confident in their own professional identity. Emotional intelligence and self-awareness are therefore essential to a mentoring relationship. Beyond this, however, mentors should have credibility and legitimacy as expert practitioners, and it is to this we now turn in the final section.

---

### Task 5.2    Developing as a mentor

The section above has explored four key dimensions of developing as a mentor.

- Reflect on which aspects you feel most secure about? Which do you feel you require further knowledge about and where could you source this?
- What would you add to these dimensions?

---

## Mentor expertise – recognising and developing

There is an expectation that mentors should be accomplished practitioners, having established themselves within the profession and amongst their peers as expert teachers. As mentioned previously, within some formal schemes that aimed to develop and recognise accomplished practice, such as the Chartered Teacher Scheme in Scotland or the Advanced Skills Teacher initiative in England and Wales, mentoring for early career teachers was seen to be part of the role and contribution for those recognised for and awarded enhanced professional status through these schemes. However, Wexler (2020, p.211) cautions that it should not be assumed that being a good teacher equates to being an effective mentor, and that 'merely having a mentor is not sufficient; the practices mentors enact and the ways in which they enact the practices matter for novice teacher learning'. It is important, he argues, to provide mentors with opportunities to learn how to be educative (ibid). There is recognition that, through mentoring, the learning is reciprocal for the mentor and mentee, with emphasis placed on educative mentoring where mentors are 'able to engage in co-constructive enquiry-based mentoring activities, termed as "educative"' (Langdon *et al*, 2019: p.250). Langdon *et al*'s research, and the twelve principles subsequently derived from it, evolved the mentoring role from the model of the 'buddy mentor' (Stanulis and Brondyk, 2013 in Langdon, 2019: p.250) to one where

> mentors undertake a role as teacher-educator, going beyond passing on advice about practical teaching as a more experienced 'expert'. The mentor is positioned as a co-learner who is able to co-construct knowledge and understanding about teaching that

can lead to the development of altered beliefs and practices for both mentor and mentee about pupils' learning and about the role of the teacher.

(Langdon *et al*, 2019: p.251)

Langdon *et al*'s study, looking at induction and mentoring in New Zealand and Wales, found that although there had been significant developments structurally and systemically to support beginning teachers, induction and mentoring remained 'privatised practices' between mentor and mentee in many of the participating schools, and that 'the collective learning resource that is constituted by all members of a school community appears to be underutilised' (Langdon *et al*, 2019: pp.261–262). This aligns with the findings of Shanks *et al* (2020), who found that in all three systems in their study (Denmark, Malta and Scotland) 'any induction programme needs to be endorsed by the school leadership team and be part of a policy of developing collaborative school cultures' (Shanks *et al*, 2020: p.11).

Research is increasingly showing the need for understandings and practices of mentoring to continue to evolve, beyond socialisation and enculturation and away from, what Stanulis *et al* (2018: p.567) describe as, "cheerleading" or simply "cooperation" between mentors and student teachers. They argue instead for a conceptualisation that focuses on growth, continuity and inquiry (p.567), and call for 'a movement of educative experiences through a mentoring process that is itself educative' (ibid). For them, this is a sustained collaborative learning endeavour where 'teachers should not be alone in learning to mentor, nor should they just be provided with a handbook or a 1-day workshop (Stanulis *et al*, 2018: p.578). Such a model is integral, therefore, to how teacher learning is promoted across a school learning community. This can exist without formal preparation at the national level, as Shanks *et al* (2020) argue:

> Whether there is a national teacher induction scheme or not, does not appear to be as important as the infrastructure of support, training and education involved and how support is shared and communicated. Whatever model is in place, an authentic partnership between schools, NQTs and mentors that anchors new teachers into the teaching profession is needed.

(Shanks, 2020: p.11)

## Mentoring during and after the Covid pandemic

Wexler's (2020: p.225) advice to look at the experiences of new teachers through their own eyes, to understand their learning as a student and what they bring to their first teaching role, takes on added significance when the impact for new teachers of the global pandemic is considered. Whereas prior to the pandemic the learning and experiences that new teachers brought to their first teaching post evolved from an academic programme of study with planned practicum experiences embedded in a systematic way, full, partial and localised lockdowns of schools and teacher education providers curtailed and limited school-based placements. Where it was possible for them to continue, the adjustments to the student practicum/placement have meant a very different experience for student teachers. Given the anxieties and uncertainties that the pandemic has given rise to for schools, the school-based mentor has a critical role for student and new teachers as they adjust to different ways of teaching and working collaboratively in schools. In instances where university tutor visits could not take place, and were replaced with online professional dialogues and virtual observations, the school-based mentor's role is critical in not only supporting the new teacher but in sustaining the link with the wider school and teacher education provider.

A key theme throughout this book has been the importance of the mentoring relationship and the shift towards mentoring as both an individual and collective endeavour and responsibility. As schools adjust to the post pandemic challenges, support for new teachers needs to remain a priority for all, to continue to build professional capability and personal confidence and resilience for those entering teaching in an unprecedented time in the history of the teaching profession.

The following quotation from the headteacher of a secondary school that welcomed 12 probationary teachers during the pandemic reinforces the commitment to supporting newly qualified teachers while recognising the skills and expertise that they bring to their first teaching post:

> While schools are operating in unchartered territory, we have not paused in our improvement journey and high aspirations for our community. We are continuing to move forward as our current young people won't get this time back. This is their school experience and it shouldn't be defined by COVID-19 and what we can't do as a result of the pandemic. The more uncertain the future looks, the more visible our values of Aspiration, Compassion, Creativity, Integrity, Perseverance and Respect need to be through our decisions, actions and interactions.
>
> The same applies to our support and mentoring of NQTs who also missed out significantly last session and did not have the support of a school community to cope with the anxiety and uncertainty of lockdown. Education will never be the same again. The pre-COVID 'normal' no longer exists and won't return. We now have an opportunity to shape a future of education – curriculum, exams, technology – so what better time to be entering the profession as we navigate the future together?
>
> Our probationers all come with much needed skills in technology, given the rollout of the iPads and the preparation for home learning, blended learning and other alternatives to full-time learning in school. They are comfortable with video, online teaching platforms and other aspects of technology that we are all learning together.
>
> Whether on a student placement or a probationary year, the next generation of teachers need to know their worth and importance to our community and to the profession. This is a year that defines their professional future and educational values, and we have the responsibility to care for them, learn from them, nurture their skills and talents, support their development, confidence, contribution and sense of belonging to our school community.
>
> (Headteacher, Scotland, October 2020)

---

### Task 5.3   Becoming a new teacher in challenging times

Read again the previous quotation from the headteacher.

- Does it resonate with your experience as a mentor?

Think about your own context and consider any adjustments that have been made during the pandemic to the mentoring programmes for new teachers.

- Do new teachers require more support/different support as a result of their learning and experiences during the pandemic? How do you know?
- What are the implications for mentors if more support/different support is needed?

---

## Summary and key points

This chapter has explored the development of mentors. The key points discussed in this chapter are:

- the mentoring relationship as one means by which the teaching profession renews (but does not replicate) itself;
- positive relationships, grounded in trust and empathy, are essential to effective mentoring, which enables support and challenge;
- core foundations for 'educative mentoring' include having a deep understanding of teacher learning, teacher education programmes and standards, wider contexts for mentoring and the essential attributes for mentors;
- the emphasis in recent research on the collective and collaborative cultures that support positive mentoring experiences; and
- the importance of mentoring as schools and teachers at all stages adapt to different ways of working as a result of the global pandemic and its aftermath.

## References

Bullough, R. V., and Baughman, K. (1995) 'Changing contexts and expertise in teaching: First-year teacher after seven years.' *Teaching and Teacher Education*, 11(5), 461–477.

Campbell, C. (2017) 'Developing teachers' professional learning: Canadian evidence and experiences in a world of educational improvement.' *Canadian Journal of Education*, 40(2), 1–33.

Cordingley, P., Higgins, S., Greany, T., Buckler, N., Coles-Jordan, D., Crisp, B., Saunders, L., and Coe, R. (2015) *Developing great teaching – A review of the evidence about Continuing Professional Development and Learning*. Available online at http://www.curee.co.uk/publication/developing-great-teaching-review-evidence-about-continuing-professional-development-and- [Accessed August 23, 2020].

Donaldson, G. (2011) *Teaching Scotland's future: Report of a review of teacher education in Scotland*. Edinburgh: The Scottish Government.

Forde, C., and McMahon, M. (2019) *Teacher Quality, Professional Learning and Policy: Recognising, Rewarding and Developing Teacher Expertise*. London: Palgrave Macmillan.

General Teaching Council of Scotland (GTCS) (2021a) Standard for Career-long Professional Learning. Available online at https://www.gtcs.org.uk/wp-content/uploads/2021/09/standard-for-career-long-professional-learning.pdf [Accessed February 1, 2022].

General Teaching Council of Scotland (GTCS) (2021b) Professional Standards for Teachers Learning. Available online at https://www.gtcs.org.uk/professional-standards/professional-standards-for-teachers/ [Accessed February 1, 2022].

General Teaching Council of Scotland (GTCS) (2021c) Standard for Middle Leadership. Available online at https://www.gtcs.org.uk/wp-content/uploads/2021/09/standard-for-middle-leadership.pdf [Accessed February 1, 2022].

General Teaching Council of Scotland (GTCS) (2021d) Standard for Headship. Available online at https://www.gtcs.org.uk/wp-content/uploads/2021/09/standard-for-headship.pdf> [Accessed February 1, 2022].

Gray, J. (2018) 'Leadership coaching and mentoring: A research-based model for school partnerships.' *International Journal of Education Policy and Leadership*, 13(12), 1–17.

Harris, A., and Jones, M. (2017) 'Leading professional learning: Putting teachers at the centre.' *School Leadership & Management*, 37(4), 331–333.

King, F., McMahon, M., Nguyen, D., and Roulston, S. (2019) 'Leadership learning for pre-service and early career teachers: Insights from Ireland and Scotland.' *International Studies in Educational Administration*, 47(2), 6–22.

Knowles, M. S. (1980) *The modern practice of adult education*. Chicago, IL: Association Press.

Langdon, F., Daly, C., Milton, E., Jones, K., and Palmer, M. (2019) 'Challenges for principled induction and mentoring of new teachers: Lessons from New Zealand and Wales.' *London Review of Education*, 17(2), 249–265.

Orland-Barak L. (2010) Introduction: Learning to Mentor-as-Praxis Foundations for a Curriculum in Teacher Education. In: *Learning to Mentor-as-Praxis. Professional Learning and Development in Schools and Higher Education*, vol 4. Boston, MA: Springer. https://doi.org/10.1007/978-1-4419-0582-6_1

Scottish Executive Education Department (SEED) (2001) *A Teaching Profession for the 21st Century* (the Agreement based on the McCrone Report) (online). Available online at www.scotland.gov.uk/library3/education/ tp21a–03.asp [Accessed August 23, 2020].

Shanks, R., Attard Tonna, M., Krøjgaard, F., Paaske, K. A., Robson, D., and Bjerkholt, E. (2020) 'A comparative study of mentoring for new teachers.' *Professional Development in Education*, DOI: 10.1080/19415257.2020.1744684 [Accessed August 23, 2020].

Stanulis, R. and Brondyk, S. (2013) 'Complexities involved in mentoring towards a high-leverage practice in the induction years.' *Teachers College Record*, 115(10), 1–34.

Stanulis, R. N., Wexler, L. J., Pylman, S., Guenther, A., Farver, S., Ward, A., Croel-Perrien, A., and Whit, K. (2018) 'Mentoring as more than "cheerleading": Looking at educative mentoring practices through mentors' eyes.' *Journal of Teacher Education*, 70(5), 567–580.

Timperley, H. (2007) *Teacher professional learning and development*. Belgium: The International Academy of Education.

Weick, K. E. (2009) *Making sense of the organization, vol. 2: The impermanent organization*. Chichester, UK: Wiley.

Weick, K. E., Sutcliffe, K. M., and Obstfeld, D. (2005) 'Organizing and the process of sensemaking.' *Organization Science*, 16(4), 409–421.

Wexler, L. J. (2020) '"I would be a completely different teacher if I had been with a different mentor": Ways in which educative mentoring matters as novices learn to teach.' *Professional Development in Education*, 46(2), 211–228.

Wyre, D. C., Gaudet, C. H., and McNeese, M. N. (2016) 'So you want to be a mentor? An analysis of mentor competencies.' *Mentoring & Tutoring: Partnership in Learning*, 24(1), 73–88.

# 6 Mentoring in the career-long professional learning phase of teacher education

*Kay Livingston, Lynne Shiach, Fiona Allen and Niccy Smith*

## Objectives

At the end of this chapter, you should be able to:

*   reflect on mentor roles and mentoring processes when working with mentees in the career-long professional learning phase;
*   recognise the learning needs and benefits for mentors' own professional learning when engaging in mentoring;
*   recognise the conditions necessary in school to support effective mentoring for teachers beyond the induction phase; and
*   reflect on the balance of mentoring for individual teacher's professional learning and school improvement.

## Introduction

The focus of this chapter is mentors and mentees in the career-long professional learning phase of teacher education. Benefits of mentoring for experienced teachers are shared, as well as benefits for mentees who are experienced teachers. As discussed in Chapter 1, the report of the review of teacher education in Scotland (Donaldson, 2011) suggested that 'Mentoring is central to professional development at all stages in a teacher's career and all teachers should see themselves as mentors not just of students and newly qualified teachers but more generally' (Donaldson, 2011, p.98).

Professional dialogue between peers at all career stages was also recognised in the report as important for the professional learning of all teachers: 'Whether or not a teacher has direct responsibility for mentoring of student teachers and probationers at any particular time, every teacher will be engaged in professional dialogue with peers' (Donaldson, 2011, p.73).

According to Bressman and colleagues, 'Mentoring teachers during the induction years has long been recognized as a powerful means to support and acclimate new teachers to the profession' (Bressman et al., 2018, p.162). However, post-induction there has tended to be limited opportunities for teachers to engage with a colleague in peer mentoring to develop their professional learning. Falconio and Carlough (2016) argue that providing meaningful mentoring for experienced teachers can help them feel empowered and can have a positive impact on their pupils' learning.

DOI: 10.4324/9780429356957-8

It is acknowledged that experienced teachers have different professional development needs from newly qualified teachers (NQTs). Chapter 1 outlined various models for implementing mentoring. To select an appropriate mentoring approach with experienced teachers it is necessary to understand their interests for professional development and the challenges they face in order to support their career-long professional learning while respecting their experience and knowledge. Bressman et al. (2018) suggest that by looking at mentoring through a new lens – one that meets the needs of experienced teachers and benefits both the mentee and the mentor – a unique, value-added model for school improvement can emerge.

This chapter presents and discusses a series of case studies written by mentors who were in the career-long professional learning phase and were working with both beginning teachers and experienced teachers. These case studies aim to help you to reflect on the roles of mentors working with teachers with different professional learning needs at different stages of their careers and on the benefits of mentoring for mentors. They also provide an opportunity for you to reflect on the conditions needed in school to encourage, support and develop mentoring for all teachers. The final case study is designed to help you reflect on the balance of mentoring for individual teacher development and school development in the career-long professional learning phase. All names used in the case studies are pseudonyms.

## Mentor roles and mentoring processes when working with mentees in the career-long professional learning phase

Case Study 6.1 in this section outlines how the roles of a mentor, who had previously worked with beginning teachers, changed when mentoring a teacher in the career-long professional learning phase. Helen is a teacher in a primary school and has experience of mentoring beginning teachers. She valued her role as a mentor of beginning teachers and recognised the impact mentoring had on their professional development, as well as on her own professional learning. Mentoring gave her opportunities to reflect on her own practice and think about what she might do differently in her own classroom. Helen had recently been appointed as a Principal Teacher, and while she was excited by her new role, she was also aware there would be challenges in leading tasks across the school with colleagues she knew well and had worked alongside for many years. Her headteacher suggested the possibility of Rachel, the other Principal Teacher in the school, acting as Helen's mentor. Rachel had been in post as a Principal Teacher for several years and was a trained mentor of beginning teachers. She was keen to engage in peer mentoring with Helen because mentoring a colleague in the career-long professional learning phase (CLPL) would be a new experience for her and she thought it would be useful in her ambition to progress her career. The case study is told from the perspectives of both Helen and Rachel.

### *Case Study 6.1: Mentoring an experienced teacher*

*Rachel and Helen both recognised that the principle of trust that is central to mentoring new teachers is also central to mentoring a more experienced colleague. Even though they had worked together in the same school and knew one another, they had to work at establishing a trusting relationship with one another. Rachel was aware that, as a mentor to a colleague in the CLPL phase, she had to respect the experience that Helen brought to her new role as Principal Teacher. She did not want to come across as a judge or as an assessor of Helen's practice. To help develop trust, Rachel and Helen began by discussing what each expected from the mentoring process. Helen said she wanted to understand how to approach colleagues in her new role, and how to ask them to engage in a new initiative she was to lead on literacy and numeracy across the school. She said she was friends with some of the teachers and met with them socially after school and she had shared her challenges as a teacher with some of them in the past. Helen wanted to know how Rachel managed to motivate and lead colleagues who were friends. This honesty and openness at the start was important in making clear to each other what they expected from the mentoring relationship. Helen was nervous at the start to express the challenges she felt she faced in her Principal Teacher role. Rachel reassured her by talking about the expectations and challenges she had faced when she took up her role. This helped Helen to feel more at ease and she felt that Rachel had credibility as a mentor because she was already a Principal Teacher and knew what the role entailed. Helen felt that Rachel could provide the specific professional development support she needed. She knew the school context and understood the challenges that Helen would face in her new role.*

---

### Task 6.1   Reflecting on mentor and mentee expectations of mentoring processes in the context of the career-long professional learning phase of a teachers' career

If you were offered a mentor (no matter what stage you were at in your career), what would be your expectations of the mentoring process? List your expectations.

---

*There were so many things that Rachel wished she could have asked a mentor when she first took up her role as a Principal Teacher, and she was very tempted to tell Helen what to watch out for and what to do. However, Rachel knew from her experience of mentoring probationary teachers that mentors need to listen to their mentee. While Rachel found it hard to stop herself from telling Helen about how she had overcome the challenges she faced as a Principal Teacher, she knew she had to focus on her role as a listener so she could personalise the questions she would pose to support and challenge Helen. She recognised that to support Helen in developing her own approach to the Principal Teacher role, it was necessary to encourage and facilitate her to talk about her challenges and the ways of working she was considering.*

*Rachel began the mentoring conversation by asking Helen what had interested her in becoming a Principal Teacher and what she would like to achieve in the role. This enabled Helen to share her ideas for her new role and start the professional conversation on a positive note. It helped Rachel to understand more about what Helen was aiming to do. Rachel asked Helen to tell her more about some of her ideas so she could better understand the specifics. She needed to understand more precisely what Helen had in mind so she could be more focused in the questions she asked. Helen immediately felt reassured that Rachel was listening to her and that the mentoring process was about helping her to shape her ideas and develop her professional learning. Rachel then asked Helen what she thought the main challenges were in putting her ideas into action. The challenges expressed by Helen were not challenges that Rachel was used to hearing about from the probationary teachers she usually mentored. The challenges Helen talked about concerned taking up a leadership role, how to set aims for teachers related to the initiative, and how to support and challenge them when implementing it. Some of the challenges identified by Helen were also challenges that Rachel still faced herself. Rachel realised in her role as mentor to Helen that she could use the approach of asking for clarification to assist Helen in uncovering and breaking down the specifics of the challenges and she could ask probing questions to help her reflect on possible ways of overcoming these challenges and prioritising where to start. Listening to Helen's responses, Rachel quickly understood that Helen had lots of ideas. Her challenge was how to focus on her next steps and identify her starting point in working with her colleagues in a different role. Rachel asked Helen which of her ideas she would prioritise and then which challenges particularly related to the priority area. This enabled Helen to stay focused and reflect more deeply on specific next steps. Together they talked through different possibilities. Helen felt the focused collaboration with Rachel had enabled her to see more clearly the detail of what she needed to do, and she felt relieved that she had a sounding board to try out thoughts and ideas with someone who understood the role and who asked her questions that were specific to her professional learning needs and helped her to decide on a concrete plan of action.*

*Rachel quickly realised there was much that she could learn from engaging in the mentoring conversation. She found that by asking clarifying and probing questions to facilitate Helen's professional learning, she was also reflecting on and learning more about strategies needed in her Principal Teacher role. In other words, she recognised that mentoring with Helen would not be one-way professional learning. Rachel could see there were benefits for both of them and realised they had, towards the end of the mentoring conversation, been engaged in problem-solving in a collaborative way. Both Rachel and Helen agreed that they could adopt a co-mentoring approach with each other, where they could interchange the roles of mentor and mentee to assist them both in their career-long professional learning and in working through ongoing challenges that emerged in their teaching and in their leadership roles.*

---

**Task 6.2   Reflecting on the similarities and differences of the roles of the mentor when mentoring at different stages of their mentees' professional careers**

Reflecting on Case Study 6.1, what similarities and differences were there in the mentoring process for Rachel when mentoring an experienced teacher rather than a beginning teacher?

What qualities, characteristics and dispositions does a mentor and mentee need to ensure the roles of mentor and mentee can function successfully in a mentoring relationship between experienced teachers?

---

## Learning needs and benefits for a mentor's own professional learning

When asked to mentor a newly qualified teacher or another colleague, some teachers may see it as an additional challenge to take on and may ask themselves, why should I become a mentor? There is a growing body of research suggesting that mentors often feel re-energised as a teacher when they engage in mentoring and that there are benefits for their own professional learning (e.g., Bressman et al., 2018). This section aims to enable you to reflect on the benefits of mentoring and on how becoming a mentor can support and challenge your own professional learning.

The case study in this section is told from the perspective of Anna. She has worked as a mentor for over ten years, in a school-based mentor role alongside her classroom teacher role and as a mentor working across different schools full-time. The role as a full-time mentor involved supporting a group of probationer teachers across a variety of school settings, from small, two-teacher rural primary schools to large primary schools in towns. Anna is often asked by teachers why she is so interested in mentoring and what the benefits of mentoring are for a mentor's own career-long professional learning (CLPL). In Case Study 6.2, Anna explains how her own professional learning has benefitted from her role as a mentor.

### Case Study 6.2: Benefits of mentoring for mentors' own career-long professional learning

*Each year I mentored brought a new cohort of probationers, with each having their own unique learning needs, which created a range of learning and development needs for me. It was ever-changing and each year presented new learning challenges as well as opportunities, and throughout all my years as a mentor my own CLPL developed. In supporting probationers' development and helping them to make a positive impact on pupil learning and attainment, I was also continually reflecting on my own practice. An area of professional learning for me was around the language of mentoring and understanding how critical the use of positive language is as a mentor and as a teacher. I share three scenarios to demonstrate how my professional learning about the use of language developed with probationers and with teachers in the CLPL phase.*

### Scenario A

*The first scenario involves a probationer who recognised, at a very early stage in her practice, that there was a high level of disruptive behaviour that was impacting on learning in the classroom. This became a focus in our weekly meetings and it was agreed that a classroom observation would be helpful. It was also agreed that the focus of the observation would be the use of language in behaviour management. To help focus in on the language used, the probationer agreed, in the pre-observation meeting, to the sound being recorded for a short part of the lesson. This gave us both an accurate record of the language used, which we could then discuss together. In the post-observation meeting, a ten-minute section of the recording was analysed collaboratively. It transpired that the probationer was using language as a tool to manage behaviour, but the language used was predominantly negative. In the ten-minute segment, on nine occasions, the probationer told a pupil what not to do then* apologised, saying 'sorry'. It was a real light-bulb moment when the probationer heard herself say 'sorry' so many times. She had not been aware she was saying this or aware of how it was impacting on her behaviour management. We agreed that positive language in behaviour management strategies would be beneficial. The probationer agreed to speak to more experienced colleagues in school to find out about the behaviour management approaches already used in the school, and I offered to take a supporting role by researching positive behaviour management programmes and tools. In this way, we both embarked on looking for examples of behaviour management strategies that focussed on the use of language and positive re-affirmation. Next time we met I shared my research with her. She saw the value of my research, together with her own research, and over time she changed her practice in a positive way. I benefitted too by working on my research skills. I was able to extend my repertoire of behaviour management strategies through the research I did and the strategies the probationer shared from other teachers in the school. We talked together about selecting and using strategies appropriate to the context, and how to adapt them and develop them in order to feel ownership of managing behaviour in your own classroom. The new strategies were helpful for me not only as a mentor to discuss with other probationary teachers but also for me when I returned to my role as a classroom teacher.

---

### Task 6.3 Learning together to benefit the mentor and mentee

List all the benefits for your own career-long professional learning that you have experienced as a mentor.

---

### Scenario B

The second scenario involves a probationer who was continually negative when talking to other teachers in the staff room about how his teaching was going. The constant use of negative language gave the impression to the Senior Management Team that all was not well in the classroom and concerns were raised with me as his mentor about his progress. The probationer in question was actually managing the class well but was concerned that if he talked positively in the staff room he would come across as a show-off. This led me to take my CLPL in a new direction, exploring the relationship between perception and reality. I had to think how to handle this situation. I reflected on different examples I had experienced over the years – some with pupils, some with parents and some with teachers. Once I felt confident in sharing anonymised examples of where perception can become reality, we considered the different examples together and thought about what messages we would have 'read into' the examples. I encouraged the probationer to talk about how he would have perceived the behaviour and then I was able to talk about what the person in each example was actually doing. This enabled the probationer to realise for himself that he was creating a negative impression of his practice that was open to misinterpretation. He realised that he needed to address the situation by sharing his practice in the classroom in a more positive way. It led me to think more about the unintended messages that a mentor can send, based on what is said *in mentoring discussions, and how careful mentors have to be in choosing their words and how they convey them. It also reminded me about the importance of checking what mentees are hearing in a mentoring conversation by asking them to summarise the main points of what they have heard.*

---

### Task 6.4   What people say, what people hear and how interpretations can be different from reality

What can be learned from Scenario B about how what you say or do as a mentor, as a teacher or as a leader can be misinterpreted by others?

What unintended message might you be communicating as a mentor to your mentee? (Unintended messages can be communicated by what you say, how you say it, how you start a conversation, by your body language, or even by how you handle the arrangements for meeting up with your mentee.)

What benefits can be gained for you as a mentor and as a teacher in developing your understanding of the difference between what people say and what others hear, or how they interpret what is said? Make a list of the benefits for you.

---

### Scenario C

*The third scenario illustrates another area that involved language use and how this bene-fitted my own CLPL. In this particular scenario, a colleague in the CLPL phase had identified a focus for a professional conversation we planned. When we met, as time is always short, I started immediately with the focus we previously agreed and asked how the particular area of development was going? However, I mis-read the signs of emotional stress that my colleague was feeling and she was not able to focus on responding to my question, appearing close to tears. To avoid further emotional distress, I turned the focus away from what we had agreed and suggested we go for a cup of tea. After the move to a different and more private space, and a complete change of conversation, my colleague shared some of the pressures she was currently experiencing. These pressures left her feeling overwhelmed with every-thing she had to do. This made me realise that even though we know colleagues well, tuning in is always important. It reminded me that a mentor should always pay attention to non-verbal cues. If I had tuned in more quickly and read the situation I could have suggested postponing our planned conversation to another day and focused our conversation imme-diately on what the mentee wanted to talk about. Also, I reflected on the importance of flexibility. Any discussion about the planned focus was unlikely to be helpful at that time. It is challenging in busy schools to find time to meet for mentoring conversations, but pro-fessional learning does not always coincide with specific timetables. I am always struck by the highly dynamic nature and the complexity of the learning needs of probationer teachers and teachers at the CLPL stage, and how this impacts my own practice as a mentor. On this occasion, I realised the importance of readiness, as a mentor, to always ask oneself when is the appropriate time to support and challenge your mentee? As a mentor as well as a teacher, it is important to listen, but it is also important to look and reflect on all the cues and messages (verbal and non-verbal) that a person is sending out. This scenario reminded me that my professional learning as a mentor and as a teacher needs constant renewal to develop my skills to meet the emerging and developing learning needs of the teachers with whom I work.*

---

### Task 6.5 Tuning in to verbal and non-verbal messages

As a mentor, how might you handle a scenario where someone is feeling overwhelmed? What are the benefits for you as a mentor in dealing with unexpected situations?

---

## Conditions necessary in school to support effective mentoring beyond the induction phase

Encouraging and enabling all teachers in the career-long professional learning phase to engage in peer mentoring is challenging. Not all teachers in this phase may see the need or the benefits of mentoring. Some may even be suspicious of a hidden agenda in mentoring or may worry that it suggests a deficit in their teaching. Yet for other teachers, mentoring may be welcomed as an opportunity to share practice, to think more deeply with colleagues about how to improve practice, and explore new approaches to learning, teaching and assessment. The conditions in school to support and enable mentoring can have a significant influence on how teachers feel about mentoring and can impact on their willingness to participate. The case study in this section is designed to encourage you to reflect on the conditions needed in school to support peer mentoring for all teachers. The case study is about a new headteacher and explores how he went about implementing mentoring in his school.

### *Case Study 6.3: Conditions needed in school to support mentoring for all teachers*

*Daniel is a former experienced mentor of newly qualified teachers. He recently took up a new post as Headteacher in a small suburban secondary school, working with two Deputy Headteachers as a management team. Daniel's leadership priority is to lead change and improvement, following a school inspection prior to his arrival that rated Learning, Teaching and Assessment, and Raising Attainment and Achievement as Satisfactory. It was commented in the Inspection Report that many of the pupils were underachieving. This rating was below the school's own self-evaluation of professional practice and pupil achievement. In discussion, Daniel felt that despite low morale the teaching team were committed to making overall improvements, but in his view, there was a lack of cohesive teamwork between teachers at varying stages of their professional development. The management team aimed to establish a professional learning community with a shared focus on improving the interdependent aspects of learning, teaching, pupil attainment and achievement in school. Daniel aimed to achieve this through mentoring.*

## Task 6.6   Reflection on supports and barriers when introducing mentoring in a school

What opportunities and barriers may be present when trying to introduce a mentoring approach to professional learning within a school?

   What strategies could be used to overcome these barriers?

*Daniel's in-service plan is to support teachers in making regular use of short, focused mentoring conversations to facilitate small-action steps towards improvement in practice and pupil learning outcomes. He identified pairs of teachers, who he asked to meet fortnightly, to engage in peer-conversations, with a whole-school focus on enhancing pupils' understanding and using self and peer assessment. When asked by an experienced teacher what criteria he used when selecting teacher pairs, Daniel explained that the Management Team had decided that contrasting length of experience and different curriculum area responsibility in the teachers selected would extend the opportunity for developing new relationships and sharing different perspectives. The question about the criteria for selecting the mentor pairs led Daniel to reflect on the wisdom of the Management Team identifying the pairs. His reflection led to a deeper exploration of the selection process and a change of strategy. He recognised that one of the conditions for successful teacher mentoring in the CLPL phase is the cred-ibility of the mentor in the eyes of the mentee, and that all teachers need to feel ownership of the mentoring process. On reflection, he realised that without trust in their mentor it is unlikely that the teachers would fully engage in open and honest conversations, which would make it difficult to support and challenge each other in developing their practice. Daniel decided to create an in-service activity at the next whole-staff meeting where groups of teachers with mixed levels of experience and curriculum areas would discuss and decide on the criteria to guide self-selection of mentoring pairs.*

*At the staff meeting the teachers voiced their significant concern about when they would find time to mentor one another and asked if everyone would be trained to mentor their peers in the career-long professional learning phase. They also asked for clarification of why Daniel wanted to implement mentoring for all teachers and if the outcomes of the mentoring conversations had to be recorded in some way. Daniel and the Management Team recognised that the teachers' concerns were legitimate and needed further consideration. Daniel agreed that time for mentoring conversations would be challenging and agreed they needed to con-sider meeting arrangements through further discussion with the staff. The need for some flexibility was recognised and a minimum number of times for mentors and mentees to meet across two terms was agreed. This allowed the teachers more flexibility in deciding when to meet.*

*Following the staff meeting one of the teachers asked Daniel if she could have a quiet word. She said, 'I am glad the school has implemented peer mentoring and I am looking forward to it, but not everyone is so enthusiastic about it. Some of the more experienced teachers think it is not appropriate for them. They feel it's condescending to suggest that after their years of experience they should have a mentor. They really do like working together so perhaps it would be better to avoid using the term mentoring.' Daniel welcomed the feedback and acknowledged that teachers have different expectations and concerns about mentoring. He recognised that whole-school mentor training would be necessary for everyone in school to develop the skills and dispositions needed to understand how to go about a professional conversation with peers at different stages in their career.*

---

**Task 6.7    Reflection on first steps in introducing mentoring for all teachers**

Reflecting on the way that Daniel introduced mentoring to the teachers, what did you learn about the first steps in introducing mentoring for all teachers in a school?

What might Daniel have done differently to engage all teachers in mentoring, particularly those that are more reluctant to mentoring in the career long professional learning phase of their career?

---

## Balancing mentoring for individual teacher's professional learning with school improvement

Every teacher has unique areas of strength and areas for development, and every school has unique strengths and areas for improvement. Sometimes these areas match, but often they do not or the link is not immediately apparent. However, there is a need to find a balance between individual teacher professional learning and the school improvement agenda to raise pupil attainment and achievement, and for mentoring to be recognised as a legitimate form of professional development for all teachers. As stated in Chapters 1 and 5, mentors need to understand the contexts that shape and influence educational decisions and actions taken in schools and classrooms because they have a key role in mediating classroom and school experiences for their mentees.

The final case study in this chapter presents a narrative from a mentor who was mentoring a probationary teacher. However, through an encounter in the school staff room with a teacher in the CLPL phase, the value of mentoring for all teachers' individual professional learning and for the headteacher in linking individual teacher development and school improvement was demonstrated. The case study is also designed to support your reflection on how, as a mentor, you manage your role of supporting an individual teacher and your role as a mentor in whole-school development.

### Case Study 6.4: Balancing individual professional development of a teacher in the CLPL phase and school improvement

*I was chatting in the staff room with a probationer teacher about a twilight workshop about the teaching of numeracy that is provided as part of the induction scheme in the local authority. The conversation was overheard by another teacher (Emma) who was in her fourth year as a teacher. Emma commented that she wished she could attend the workshop too.*

*She said, 'sometimes I bore myself in my numeracy lessons! I think I'm a bit stale.' I asked her if she would like to chat to me about it later and she agreed.*

*Before I met Emma, I enquired whether the twilight workshop would be open to all teachers as well as probationers. The answer was that it would be alright if the headteacher was happy for the cost to come out of the school CLPL budget. This commitment would only happen if numeracy was part of the school improvement plan.*

*When I met up with Emma, at first, she just wanted to talk about all the difficulties of the job and how a workshop would maybe help to give her a boost and 'tick a CLPL' box. Using my skills as a mentor, I asked Emma to clarify what was concerning her. There seemed to be a bit more going on than just wanting to attend a workshop. We agreed to meet again and Emma said she would bring the targets she had set on her GTCS profile for her professional development as well as a copy of the school improvement plan, so that we could see if there was any overlap.*

*At the next meeting, we looked at Emma's targets. She had not mentioned numeracy specifically, but she had set a target to find ways to improve pupil engagement in learning. Looking at the school improvement plan the emphasis was on improving attainment in literacy. In-service days were planned and time was set aside to work collegiately with stage partners, specifically looking at good practice and teaching strategies. When we looked at Emma's targets and the improvement plan side by side, we could see that her target matched the school improvement plan, as improving engagement in learning would focus on improving pupil attainment. Through our mentoring conversation, Emma realised that her focus on ways to improve pupil engagement in learning was linked to the school improvement plan and could be explored through a numeracy lesson to support her professional learning, and then, potentially, the engagement strategy could be adapted to support attainment in literacy. We also talked about alternatives to attending the twilight workshop. We agreed that she would ask the probationer to talk her through the strategies discussed at the workshop. We also agreed to set up a meeting with the headteacher to share our discussion.*

*When we met with the headteacher, Emma was candid in saying that she had spent the first few years of her teaching concentrating on the pupils in front of her and hadn't completely appreciated how her professional development targets and school improvement aligned. The headteacher was also candid. She said that she lived and breathed the School Improvement Plan and should have done more to check that teachers had the same level of understanding. She undertook to make sure the School Improvement Plan and teachers' individual professional learning were discussed in more detail at a staff meeting. She did not agree to Emma attending the numeracy twilight for probationary teachers but agreed that meeting with the probationer afterwards was a good idea. She also suggested she could arrange for Emma to have a series of mentoring conversations with another teacher in the school who had recently focused on developing her practice in numeracy. Emma agreed that she would find this helpful in meeting her own professional learning target.*

*I found the conversations with Emma, as a teacher in the CLPL phase of her career, refreshing. An ideal mentoring conversation involves both the mentor and mentee working in a collaborative partnership; the mentee, with mentor facilitation, often working out for themselves what their next step should be. Probationer teachers frequently need more prompting and structure to achieve this, sometimes even straightforward direction, especially at the*

*beginning of their probation year. Emma approached me voluntarily, and through collab-*
*oration and looking at her own professional learning and the school improvement plan,*
*together we were able to identify concrete steps that supported Emma and the school. The*
*process also gave me experience of mentoring a teacher in the CLPL phase and an oppor-*
*tunity to reflect on the importance of a mentor understanding teachers as individuals and*
*also in terms of the school context in which they work.*

---

### Task 6.8   Reflection on mentoring for individual teacher development and school improvement

As a mentor, what challenges are there in building and maintaining trust with the teacher you are mentoring and in keeping the headteacher informed?

How would you follow up on a series of discussions with a teacher in the CLPL phase and with the headteacher to sustain mentoring and identify the benefits for the individual teacher and the school?

---

## Summary and key points

In each of these authentic case studies the mentors received ongoing mentor training, and they were aware that mentoring all teachers entailed building trusting relationships; actively listening to their mentee; choosing language in mentoring conversations and mentoring strategies appropriate to the individual learning needs of their mentee; and tuning in to the context of their mentee and the school as a whole. In all the case studies the mentors were mindful and respectful of the knowledge and experiences that the teachers in the CLPL phase brought to the mentoring process. At the same time, they aimed to support and challenge their mentee to develop their professional learning. The importance of the headteacher and management teams in creating the necessary conditions in school for successful implementation of mentoring was demonstrated, particularly in Case Study 6.3, including recognition of the importance of clarity in aims for mentoring; teacher ownership of the mentoring process; mentor training for all teachers; and flexibility and provision of time when implementing peer mentoring. Across the case studies the mentors and school leaders reflected on the benefits of mentoring for the development of their own professional learning.

This chapter has explored the mentoring of teachers in the career-long professional learning phase of their career. The key points raised through the 'voices of mentors' in the case studies are:

- some mentor roles and mentoring processes are similar whether working with mentees in the induction phase or the career-long professional learning phase, such as building a trusting relationship, tuning in to their professional learning needs, and providing support and challenge at appropriate times;
- there are differences in the experiences of beginning teachers and teachers in the career-long professional learning phase of their career and in your role as mentor. It

is necessary to respect the different experiences of each teacher you mentor in your selection of mentoring strategies;

- mentors learn from engaging in mentoring with colleagues and the experience provides benefits for their own career-long professional learning;
- the introduction of mentoring approaches for all teachers in school needs to be carefully thought through to provide the conditions necessary to support effective mentoring; and
- mentors should have an understanding of the context in which they mentor and take account of individual teacher and school needs, as they can have a key role in supporting an individual teacher's professional learning and school improvement.

## Further reading

Achinstein, B. & Athanases, S.Z. (2006). *Mentors in the making*. New York: Teachers College Press.

## References

Bressman, S., Winter, J.S. & Efron, S.E. (2018). Next generation mentoring: Supporting teachers beyond induction. *Teaching and Teacher Education*, 73, 162–170.
Donaldson, G. (2011). *Teaching Scotland's future: Report of a review of teacher education in Scotland*. Edinburgh: The Scottish Government.
Falconio, J. & Carlough, S. (2016). Field notes: Solving root problems with teacher voice and support. *Disrupting Inequity*, 12(6). Retrieved from https://www.ascd.org/el/articles/field-notes-solving-root-problems-with-teacher-voice-and-support

# 7 Mentoring for leadership

*Morag Redford and Sandra Clarke*

## Objectives

At the end of this chapter, you should be able to:

- reflect on the distinctive role that mentoring has in leadership development for promoted posts in schools;
- consider the ways in which formal and informal mentoring is used to support professional learning in leadership programmes;
- reflect on a series of practice examples of mentoring for teacher, middle, school and systems leadership, with feedback from practitioners and learning activities for mentors; and
- reflect on the use of mentoring for leadership development in other countries and consider future developments of mentoring for leadership in Scottish education.

## Introduction

In this chapter we explore the role of mentoring as a supporting structure for leadership development in Scotland. We begin by reflecting on the distinctive role that mentoring has in leadership development for promoted posts in schools. We then analyse the use of mentoring in leadership programmes as part of a progression of mentoring practices, considering the ways in which formal and informal mentoring is used to support professional learning across leadership roles in education. We support this through a series of examples and feedback on mentoring practice for teacher, middle, school and systems leadership, through the National Framework for Educational Leadership (Education Scotland, 2020a). In each strand we consider different mentoring roles and relationships, as explored by Livingston in Chapter 1, and link practice examples with feedback from practitioners and learning activities for mentors. To conclude, we reflect on the use of mentoring for leadership development in other countries and consider the future development of mentoring for leadership in Scottish education.

## Mentoring for leadership development

Mentoring is a key part of the structures and systems that support professional learning for leadership in schools in Scotland. It is used both in formal structures, in leadership programmes,

DOI: 10.4324/9780429356957-9

and in informal structures, in school and local education authorities, to support individual professional development for leadership roles. The development of mentoring for leadership began in the late 1990s as part of a new postgraduate award, the Scottish Qualification for Headship (SQH) (Cowie, 2005). This national programme was delivered through a work-based learning model, where each participant was 'supported' by their current Head Teacher in a mentoring role. An evaluation of the programme in 2005 (Menter *et al*.) identified positive outcomes for the participants, their Head Teacher 'supporters' and the school community. In particular, the evaluation found that the mentoring role of the 'supporter' had an impact on the programme participants, their mentors and activated distributed leadership in the school community (Menter *et al*., 2005). This finding, of the wider impact of the SQH programme on the affective dimensions of school leadership, has directly influenced the development of mentoring for school leadership in Scotland since 2003.

The current Into Headship and In Headship programmes (Education Scotland, 2020b) utilise a similar mentoring structure to SQH, while more recent developments in teacher and middle leadership follow the structure and ideas of mentoring as used in initial teacher education and induction year, as explored by Kennedy in Chapter 2. The developments in mentoring for leadership, and in leadership, have grown as the profession has embraced mentoring as a tool to support career-long development (Donaldson, 2011) and link directly to the Standards Framework of the General Teaching Council for Scotland (GTCS, 2012). The professional learning opportunities for leadership in school, local education authorities and taught postgraduate programmes in universities are framed through the Standards for Career Long Learning (GTCS, 2012) and the Standards for Leadership and Management (GTCS, 2012). There is an expectation across the standards that all teachers will become expert practitioners who take responsibility for their own learning (Torrance and Forde, 2017) and, from that, raise the attainment of children and young people through improved prac-tice (OECD, 2015). This focus on improved practice sits at the heart of mentoring structures across the Scottish leadership continuum (Education Scotland, 2020a).

## A progression of practices

The role of mentor and mentee in leadership development changes according to the stage of development being supported. Teacher leadership, linked to the Standard for Career Long Professional Learning (GTCS, 2012), as discussed in Chapter 3, is individually focused professional learning that is often supported by mentoring through network activities or by a colleague as a critical friend or sounding board (Connor and Pokora, 2017). Indeed, mentoring for teacher leadership is often carried out as part of network-based learning, sometimes with a critical colleague in school, and often enabled and demonstrated through practitioner enquiry (GTCS, n.d.). In schools, mentoring relationships to support teacher leadership are established informally by the individuals concerned, often through an existing relationship (Starr, 2014). In contrast, mentoring for middle leadership development or to support those in middle leadership roles is formally agreed by school management, as an existing middle leader will mentor an aspiring middle leader. Teachers often require nomin-ation by their Head Teacher to participate in middle leadership programmes, and that nom-ination is reflected in the mentor support provided to lead an area of practice in their school.

The mentee here is less likely to have a choice of mentors, but they will agree the structure and focus of the mentoring sessions with their mentor. Participants in the national Into Headship programme must be nominated by their local authority employers and are mentored by their current Head Teacher. The learning dialogues (Conner and Pokora, 2017) in this relationship are set to support leadership of change in their work setting. This programme supports and develops the role of Head Teachers in mentoring teachers across the leadership continuum. Here, mentoring is closely linked to personal review structures in school and leadership opportunities linked to school development. Mentoring continues to be used as a tool to support educators in systems leadership roles, particularly in specific areas of their development. The role of mentoring for leadership works with the understanding that professional learning for teachers is most effective when it is based on self-development, work-based learning and critical reflection (Stoll *et al.*, 2006). Recent research found that mentoring throughout teaching careers can impact directly on practice and prevent teachers leaving the profession stressed and disillusioned (Ernst and Erikson, 2018; Spooner-Lane, 2017), and that undertaking a mentoring role with colleagues (Davey and Ham, 2010) supports individual professional learning.

---

**Task 7.1    Reflecting on mentoring for leadership**

Reflect on the use of formal and informal mentoring and the option of individual choice in matching a mentor to mentee in leadership development in your own setting.

---

## Mentoring for teacher leadership

The role of teacher leadership in schools and professional learning communities is a developing area of teaching practice in Scotland, and nationally it sits with a focus on the empowerment of teachers (Scottish Government, 2019a) and the Standard for Career Long Professional Learning (GTCS, 2012). There is a growing expectation that class and subject teachers will take leadership roles in their school communities, where, as leaders of teaching and learning in their classrooms, they are in a position to innovate and lead change in practice and curriculum. Mentoring for teacher leadership is an informal arrangement, often with a colleague or school leader supporting the teacher through a series of mentoring conversations. These conversations reflect the mentoring culture in Scottish schools and a range of existing mentoring relationships (Starr, 2014). Development for teacher leadership is provided through professional learning programmes, where a school-based leadership project is part of the work of the programme and is supported by the participant's school and employer. These programmes provide a structure and timeline for leadership projects and a focus for the mentoring conversations. An example of this is a Developing Leadership programme offered in two rural local authorities, which explores what teacher leadership means and feels like through the values of leadership and practitioner enquiry. In this programme the teachers work together in a group, in person or virtually, supported by an experienced school leader. They are mentored individually in their workplace to identify and agree on an enquiry to lead. The mentoring approach is informal, decided by the teachers. As you read the following quotations from programme participants, reflect on your informal experience as a mentor.

> *A more informal approach can be hugely beneficial – knowing there is someone you can turn to for advice and who knows the pitfalls, and emotionally and professionally how it can feel.*
> *The benefit for me of having my informal mentor was that it felt very relaxed because it was very natural. As a result, I was probably more open during the whole process, which I think was really useful in helping me to improve my practice.*

The use of informal conversation as a mentoring tool is a key part of the development of teacher leadership where the mentor does not hold management responsibility for their mentee (Starr, 2014). The mentor role is defined by existing relationships and the focus of the leadership project, where the mentor will have relevant experience and knowledge that they can share with their mentee. Mentoring for teacher leadership supports teachers with no leadership experience to explore their own knowledge and develop leadership skills in their workplace. It provides the teachers with an opportunity to develop new skills and consider leadership within their own career, and offers teachers a starting point for leading change and making a difference in practice (Lieberman and Miller, 2004). This experience gives those who go on to hold leadership posts in schools a depth of understanding about leading change.

---

### Task 7.2    Further reflection on mentoring for leadership

- Consider how you can be an effective mentor for teachers or how you would like to be mentored as a teacher in your setting.
- Read Chapter 2 on the roles of a mentor, as listed by Connor and Pokora (2017:34), and reflect on the roles of a mentor as supporter, challenger, sounding board, networker, role model, critical friend, strategist and catalyst. Which of these are appropriate to teacher leadership in your setting?

---

## Mentoring for middle leadership

The term middle leadership refers to teachers who hold a leadership post, as a Principal Teacher or Depute Head Teacher, and to those who have a leadership role in their school community through experience or a specific skill set. Mentoring in and for middle leadership is formally arranged in schools, with those in middle leadership posts mentoring those who are considering applying for a middle leadership post. Schools and local authorities often have a formal nomination process and professional learning programmes to support aspiring middle leaders. For example, in Argyll and Bute, the Middle Leadership programme requires teachers to be endorsed by their Head Teachers and provided with a school-based mentor for the duration of the programme. In secondary and larger primary schools, the mentor is usually a teacher who is in a middle leadership post; in smaller schools, it is often the Head Teacher who acts as mentor. There is an expectation that the participant and mentor meet on a regular basis, with discussions focused around the middle leadership part of the Standards for Leadership and Management (GTCS, 2012). This formal mentoring arrangement, with discussion structured around the Standards, builds on the mentoring model used in induction and reflects research identifying such practice as being effective (Forde, 2016). Those mentoring middle leaders in this programme work from the combined perspective of holding a middle leadership post and their own experience of mentoring to support their mentee. The mentor is expected to establish a mentoring relationship of 'benevolence and respect' (Starr, 2014:34), and the mentee to work with the mentor in establishing that relationship. The knowledge that mentors hold of school systems is particularly key here. As you read the following quotations from programme participants, consider the ways in which you share systems knowledge within your mentoring relationships.

> *My mentor has supported me by the regular focussed discussions on my role in school and also how the project I identified as part of the programme meets the school improvement priorities and is developing to benefit the young people.*
>
> *She was providing me with the opportunity to lead on an area of school improvement to gain first-hand experience of this, including feeding back to staff, pupils, parents and partner agencies.*

---

### Task 7.3    Reflecting on effective mentoring for leadership

- Reflect on the leadership opportunities in your workplace and the ways in which mentoring is part of that process.
- Read Chapter 2 of Starr (2014) to develop your understanding of different mentoring relationships.

---

## Mentoring for school leadership

In Scotland, from August 2020, all teachers taking up their first permanent post as a Head Teacher in a local authority or grant-aided school must hold the national Into Headship qualification (Scottish Government, 2019b). This is a part-time postgraduate programme supported by Education Scotland, and delivered by universities in partnership with local authority employers. All teachers participating in the programme are nominated by their employer and mentored by their current Head Teacher. The structure of the programme expects teachers and their mentors to meet on a regular basis as the teachers lead change in their setting. These mentoring conversations connect the professional reading the participant is undertaking to the change project they are leading, and actively support the development of the skills and knowledge required for school leadership. In this programme, the role of the mentor is key in supporting the individual's transition from Depute or Principal

Teacher to Head Teacher in their local authority area. As you read the following quotations from participants, reflect on your role in mentoring for leadership.

> *A mentor needs to know what their mentee is expected to achieve and the timescales. They also need experience of working at that level. She is very experienced in the role and showed me how to think as a Head Teacher rather than a Principal Teacher.*
>
> *I received a lot of support from my mentor when I was going through the Into Headship programme and this helped build my confidence in going forward.*

---

### Task 7.4   Reflection on relationships in mentoring for leadership

- Reflect on the structure of professional relationships required to support mentoring for leadership in your workplace.
- Read Chapter 3 of Connor and Pokora (2017) and explore the skills and knowledge required to be an effective mentee.

---

## Mentoring for newly appointed Head Teachers

Mentoring is used as a structure to support newly appointed Head Teachers in many local authorities, usually as part of an induction programme. Newly appointed Head Teachers often cite the isolation of headship as being particularly challenging. Some Head Teachers will comment that it is only other Head Teachers who will understand how they feel, and therefore Head Teachers mentoring others can offer empathy and help newly appointed Head Teachers through a challenging time in school. Another benefit to the mentee in this arrangement is the knowledge the mentor can share of legislation, education policy, and working with parents and staff successfully under both positive and challenging circumstances. As you read the following quotation from a newly appointed Head Teacher, consider the range of components (see Livingston, Chapter 1) contained in this mentoring role.

> *The role of Head Teacher can feel overwhelming at times. It's easy to feel isolated, especially given our rural setting. Having a professional mentor that I can call on has helped me cope with the practical and emotional demands of the role. If I didn't have that relationship, I couldn't do the job.*

In Argyll and Bute new appointees are mentored by an experienced Head Teacher leading a similar school. This is particularly important in rural primary schools, where teachers often move directly from a teaching role into headship (Forde, 2016). In this rural authority, newly appointed Head Teachers participate in an induction programme dedicated to providing support and challenge, with mentors working closely with them in planned sessions. They are partnered with an experienced Head Teacher who has experience in a similar context and a structure of meetings is arranged to support mentor/mentee meetings. The induction programme includes a residential professional learning programme that supports the development of a strong mentoring partnership. In this authority, as the newly appointed Head

Teachers move through the planned programme, they are encouraged to continue to work with their mentor as they need support, with further opportunities for meetings throughout the year. In this structure, the mentor supports the newly appointed Head Teacher as they develop the knowledge, skills and behaviours linked to the role of Head Teacher in that local authority. This organisational socialisation (Hallinger and Heck, 2010) supports the development of a leadership network, as is done nationally through the In Headship programme (Education Scotland, 2020b). This one-year, part-time programme follows Into Headship and is available to Head Teachers who are within the first 18 months of appointment as Head Teacher. This programme is delivered by universities in partnership with Education Scotland, and supports newly appointed Head Teachers to develop a national network and, locally, to identify a critical colleague to support them with their professional learning. As you read the following comments from newly appointed Head Teachers, reflect on the impact of being mentored or mentoring a newly appointed Head Teacher.

For newly appointed Head Teachers being mentored into a post:

1. *creates a sense of what is possible in the post you are moving into;*
2. *provides clarity of purpose;*
3. *prevents time being wasted on searching for information or re-inventing the wheel; and*
4. *supports the establishment of strong teams and shared purpose.*

For those mentoring newly appointed Head Teachers:

*It has been a positive experience for me as I have felt that I am able to support someone else and I do have the knowledge and experience to help solve problems or advise on issues.*

---

**Task 7.5   Reflecting on mentoring for school leadership**

- Read Chapter 5 of Starr (2014) to develop your understanding of the process to support your development as a mentor or mentee for school leadership.
- Reflect on the impact of mentoring on your own or others' professional development.

---

## Mentoring in headship with members of teaching staff

As school leaders and managers, Head Teachers often adopt a non-structured mentoring approach with staff to support school improvement. This non-structured approach is also found in the informal mentoring support for teacher and middle leaders, where a Head Teacher mentors teachers to enable them to develop and lead aspects of school improvement. In these situations, the Head Teacher uses mentoring structures to enable colleagues to identify the actions that will support the development they are leading. The Head Teachers will have frequent, often weekly, dialogue with teachers to support particular actions, but it is the teachers who are designing, implementing and evaluating. The use of mentoring to support teachers builds capacity and skills within the school itself and can give a sense of empowerment. It is important in this approach that there is a common understanding of the vision and values of the school, and that the Head Teacher enables the teacher or middle leader to develop policy and practice, thus becoming more empowered. As you read the following quotations from a mentor and mentee, reflect on your experiences in mentoring or being mentored.

For Head Teachers mentoring teachers:

> *Being a mentor involves being responsive and available, a listening ear, able to be solution focused and also to have practical, workable suggestions that will minimise workload and maximise impact. You need to have the ability to signpost to others who can help ... Building a shared working knowledge of the setting and challenges that the mentee faces.*

For teachers being mentored:

> *Relationships are key – you have to be able to be honest with your mentor, particularly if things aren't going to plan. You also have to be capable of accepting criticism/feedback and action this in a positive way.*

---

### Task 7.6   Reflecting on your experience as a mentor or mentee

- Read Chapter 6 of Starr (2014) and explore the challenges involved in mentoring and being mentored.
- Reflect on your experience as a mentor or mentee.

---

## Mentoring for systems leaders

Education staff appointed to local authority officer roles and those working in national teams are recognised as systems leaders in Scottish education. This wide-ranging group are usually formally mentored as they begin a new role in education, and may also look to establish an informal mentoring arrangement with a colleague. For many, becoming a systems leader is a move from a school-based post to a strategic role that requires an expanded knowledge base of areas that support the schools system, such as reporting to and working with local councillors, interpretation of national legislation into policy and practice, and dealing with formal complaints. The following quotations reflect experiences of formal and informal mentoring for systems leaders. As you read, consider the importance of both approaches.

Formal mentoring for systems leaders:

> *There is a strength in having the space to talk through a wide range of issues with someone you trust to allow you to develop into the practitioner you become, which should not necessarily be a version of the person who is providing the mentoring.*

Informal mentoring for systems leaders:

> *I miss not being given the time for rich debate, dialogue and reflection – this is done entirely at my own discretion. I miss the engagement of a supportive, caring mentor who gives you confidence when things aren't going so well, who raises my aspirations, who makes me be the very best person I can be.*

---

### Task 7.7    Final reflection on mentoring for leadership

- Read Chapter 7 of Starr (2014) in which the author summarises the key points about being mentored and being a mentee.
- Consolidate your learning and reflect on the ways in which you wish to develop as a mentor or mentee.

---

## Mentoring for leadership

The development of leadership programmes in Scotland over the last twenty years mirrors international developments in educational leadership, where the requirement to produce more school leaders has supported the growth of leadership programmes across the world (Brundrett and Crawford, 2008). The structure and content of these programmes varies but all include mentoring, with networking and coaching, as a key development tool (Bush, 2008). Many of these programmes, such as the National Professional Qualification for Headship in England (United Kingdom Government, 2014), use mentoring to support individual leadership development in a national leadership programme. The success of such programmes is limited by the challenges of sustaining and further developing leadership beyond the timeline of the programmes (Brundrett, 2006). The use of mentoring for leadership development provides the local structure to support the development of mentoring relationships and shared understanding of individual development needs beyond the leadership awards.

The illustrations of mentoring for leadership in this chapter, from a range of different programmes, identify the importance of relationships, the need for flexibility of structure and the availability of time to support leadership development in education. As one programme participant reflected, to be an effective mentor for leadership:

> *You need to have allocated time, a positive relationship, develop trust and have a good understanding of the life of a school to be a good mentor.*

Mentoring for leadership in Scotland follows from the experience of teachers as they are mentored in their induction year and when they, as experienced teachers, mentor inductees. These practices establish mentoring as a key tool in professional learning, and provide knowledge and understanding of being a mentor and mentee that is utilised in leadership development programmes and enables the move between formal and informal mentoring for leadership. A range of local and national programmes reflect the international use of mentoring as a key tool to support leadership development for teachers, middle leaders and school leaders. These programmes would support the further development of mentoring for experienced Head Teachers and systems leaders.

With thanks to the educational leaders in Argyll and Bute who shared their experiences of mentoring.

## Summary and key points

Mentoring for leadership requires a range of approaches and relationships. The key points discussed in this chapter are:

* the use of formal and informal mentoring in leadership development;
* the varied roles of a mentor, as supporter, challenger, networker, role model and critical friend, in mentoring for leadership;
* the ways in which mentoring supports leadership development in your workplace;
* the professional relationships required to support mentoring for leadership; and
* the impact of mentoring for leadership on your own and others' professional development.

## Further reading

Brent, M. and Dent, F. (2015) *The Leaders Guide to Coaching and Mentoring*, London, Financial Times.
Kay, D. and Hinds, R. (5th ed.) (2012) *Using Coaching and Mentoring Skills to Help Others Achieve Their Goals*, How to Books.

## References

Brundrett, M. (2006) The impact of leadership training: Stories from a small school. *School Leadership and Management*, 34 (2), 173-183.
Brundrett, M. and Crawford, M. (2008) *Developing School Leaders: An international perspective*, London, Routledge.
Bush, T. (2008) *Leadership and Management Development in Education*, London, Sage Publications.
Connor, M. and Pokora, J. (3rd ed.) (2017) *Coaching and Mentoring at Work*, London, Open University Press.
Cowie, B. (2005) Pupil commentary on assessment for learning. *The Curriculum Journal*, 16 (2), 137-151.
Davey, R. and Ham, V. (2010) 'It's all about paying attention!' ... but to what? The '6 Ms' of mentoring the professional learning of teacher educators. *Professional Development in Education*, 36 (1-2), 229-244.
Donaldson, G. (2011) Teaching Scotland's Future: Report of a Review of Teacher Education in Scotland. Available online at: https://www.webarchive.org.uk/wayback/archive/2019070 1211038/https://www2.gov.scot/resource/doc/337626/0110852.pdf [Accessed 15.04.20]
Education Scotland (2020a) The SCEL Framework for Educational Leadership. Available online at: https://professionallearning.education.gov.scot/media/1088/scel-framework-information-leaflet.pdf [Accessed 12.08.19]

Education Scotland (2020b) Leadership Programmes. Available online at: https://professio nallearning.education.gov.scot/learn/programmes/ [Accessed 15.04.20]

Ernst, J. and Erickson, D. M. (2018) Environmental education professional development for teachers: A study of the impact and influence of mentoring. *The Journal of Environmental Education*, 49 (5), 357–374.

Forde, C. (2016) Leadership development. In Jim O'Brien (ed.) *School Leadership*, Edinburgh, Dunedin, pp. 107–131.

GTCS (n.d.) Practitioner Enquiry. Available online at: https://www.gtcs.org.uk/professional-update/ [Accessed 15.04.20]

GTCS (2012) Professional Standards. Available online at: https://www.gtcs.org.uk/professional-standards/professional-standards-for-teachers/ [Accessed 15.05.20]

Hallinger, P. and Heck, R. (2010) Collaborative leadership and school improvement: Understanding the impact on school capacity and student learning. *School Leadership and Management*, 30 (2), 95–110.

Lieberman, A. and Miller, L. (2004) *Teacher Leadership*, San Francisco, Jossey-Bass.

Menter, I., Holligan, C. and Mthenjwa, V. (2005) Reaching the parts that need to be reached? The impact of the Scottish Qualification for Headship. *School Leadership and Management*, 25 (1), 7–23.

OECD (2015) Improving Schools in Scotland: An OCED perspective. Available online at: http://www.oecd.org/education/school/improving-schools-in-scotland.htm [Accessed 15.04.20]

Scottish Government (2019a) Empowering Schools: Education reform progress update. Available online at: https://www.gov.scot/publications/empowering-schools-education-reform-progress-update/pages/2/ [Accessed 15.04.20]

Scottish Government (2019b) Standards for Headteachers: Business and regulatory impact assessment. Available online at https://www.gov.scot/publications/head-teachers-education-training-standards-scotland-regulations-2019-business-regulatory-impact-assessment-bria/ [Accessed 12.01.22]

Spooner-Lane, R. (2017) Mentoring beginning teachers in primary schools: Research review. *Professional Development in Education*, 43 (2), 253–273.

Starr, J. (2014) *The Mentoring Manual*, Harlow, Pearson.

Stoll, L., Bolam, R., McMahon, A., Wallace, M. and Thomas, S. (2006) Professional learning communities: A review of the literature. *Journal of Educational Change*, 7, 221–258.

Torrance, D. and Forde, C. (2017) Redefining what it means to be a teacher through professional standards: Implications for continuing teacher education. *European Journal of Teacher Education*, 40 (1), 110–126.

United Kingdom Government (2014) National Professional Qualification for Headship. Available online at: https://www.gov.uk/guidance/national-professional-qualification-for-headship-npqh [Accessed 15.05.20]

# SECTION 3
# Different facets of impactful mentoring

# 8 Supporting sustained teacher development through reflection

*Willie McGuire and Jane Essex*

## Objectives

By the end of this chapter, you should be able to:

- identify the role and importance of reflection in the mentoring process;
- suggest practical approaches that mentors can use to engender deeper reflection; and
- understand some common barriers to the effective use of reflection by school mentors and how these may be overcome.

## Introduction

The specific focus of this chapter is on reflection and how mentors can harness its potential to develop teachers' proficiency and self-efficacy. This chapter will consider critically how mentors can support teachers to develop their reflective skills and enhance the professional success of both parties. This is important, regardless of the career phase of the mentee, so that they can best respond to the challenges and opportunities of their role. Promoting reflection and reflective practice aligns closely with the aspects of mentoring that are set out in Chapter 1, most especially the counselling role, and it is an important element of the diverse functions of a mentor.

The notion of reflection in this chapter is encapsulated at a practical level throughout the chapter and is defined very succinctly by Hatton and Smith (1995:40), as follows:

> *Deliberate thinking about action with a view to its improvement.*

This will be complemented by a second definition (Zwozdiak-Myers, 2012:5), which encompasses both reflection and the associated actions, termed 'reflective practice'. It provides a lengthier but more complete definition and alludes to the importance of the 'mind set' of the people undertaking reflection, the changes that are wrought by reflection and makes explicit reference to the intended changes:

> *A disposition to enquiry, incorporating the process through which student, early career and experienced teachers structure or restructure actions, beliefs, knowledge and theories that inform teaching for the purpose of professional development.*

This chapter will focus on how to promote a sustained approach to actively and analytically thinking about the real-life situations encountered by a mentee. As the definition

DOI: 10.4324/9780429356957-11

of reflective practice implies, reflection is inextricably linked to action, and so the chapter considers how mentors can use action as the focus of reflection and how reflection can inform future actions. Although reflection does not automatically enhance pupil performance, it is nevertheless a powerful mechanism to improve teaching and teacher understanding. By so doing, it supports the development of flexibility and responsiveness, which are needed in the rapidly changing educational landscape. Crucially, it is a process and associated outlook that can readily be embedded into all mentoring interactions, making it a powerful and accessible strategy.

## Reflection: A multi-faceted process

Reflection is treated in the following chapter as both a 'lens' through which events are seen and analysed, and as a tool for enhancing practice through its contribution to contextual analysis and action planning. Although the chapter focuses on the practicalities of reflection, it is important that mentors and mentees understand that different writers have had different views of reflection. Three of these are described briefly to illustrate some of the many ways in which refection has been considered. It should be noted that the models focus largely on teaching, but for those working with experienced mentees, it is possible to substitute other processes, such as decision making, leading and managing, as appropriate to the context.

John Dewey (1933) described reflection as a rational and sequential process, which may remind you of the scientific process. He sees reflection as an intellectual process that happens recurrently, punctuated and fuelled by experience that, in turn, forms the basis of the next round of reflection. However, he does believe that reflection can ultimately provide a solution to the problem and, as such, can have an endpoint.

Figure 8.1 represents the relationship between the different stages of the reflective cycle, and signals the importance of analysis at all stages.

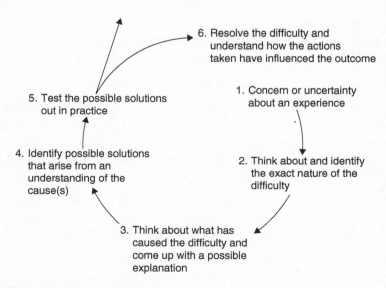

*Figure 8.1* The stages in Dewey's reflective cycle

In line with the definition given previously, Dewey understood the focus of the process to be problem-solving, and he notes that those undertaking reflection need to bring doubt (brought about by a 'disturbance' to their deliberations). This questioning approach is what distinguishes reflective actions from the habitual 'intuitive' actions, which are actions teachers do without consciously thinking about them.

A conversation that illustrates how Dewey's ideas of reflection might look in practice is set out here, alongside the corresponding stage:

1.  Concern/uncertainty: *What challenges or difficulties did you experience during the lesson? Did anything happen that you weren't expecting? Were there any decisions that you made during the lesson of which you weren't very confident?*
2.  Identify the nature of the difficulty: *Was the main problem that she was disturbing other pupils or that you felt she undermined your authority in the classroom? How has she behaved in other lessons that you have observed her in? Has she behaved similarly when other tasks were set in your lessons?*
3.  Thinks about what has caused the difficulty and a possible explanation for this: *Why were you hesitant about moving the pupil from where she chose to sit when she was disruptive? Do you still feel that it's not 'your' class? Did you worry that you wouldn't have any options if she point blank refused to do what she was asked? Why do you think she was disruptive?*
4.  Identify possible solutions: *Your major issue is that she undermined your standing in front of the other pupils. A way to solve this would be to establish that you **are** the teacher and that the lesson runs according to your plan. This could be re-established by you starting the lesson with the regular class teacher nearby, but not in the room, and signalling that **you** are leading the lesson. You noted that the task that triggered the outburst was an extended writing task. You understand that writing is important, not least for assessment purposes, but that there are alternatives in the short term. You will look at ways to promote learning that do not require a lot of writing and consider, in the medium term, how to develop confidence in writing for the pupils who find it challenging.*
5.  Test the possible solutions: The two hypotheses (loss of standing and writing being the trigger for the outburst) will be tested by planning and executing a lesson that enables the exploration of the chosen options: *You will reinforce your role by ensuring a swift and purposeful start to the lesson, making it clear that this is happening because **you** have chosen this approach. You will choose an activity that is intended to be engaging for all the pupils but that does not involve lots of writing, since this was what triggered the last confrontation.*

David Kolb's (1984) model differs in a few subtle ways. Firstly, he explicitly states that personal experience is the 'engine' of reflection, with which it starts and upon which any intellectualisation rests. Secondly, he assigns a different role to the participant at each stage of the cycle. Thirdly, Kolb recognises the importance of experience that is not intellectual, and so allows for the emotions and physical experiences that are important aspects of experience. A fourth distinction is that the learner moves through a four-part cycle again and again, with an end-point never being reached because further experience inevitably presents new problems and questions. Like Dewey, Kolb understood reflection to be an intellectual

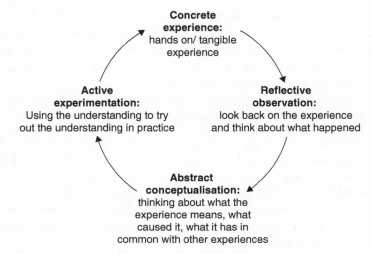

*Figure 8.2* Diagram showing the key stages in Kolb's cycle of reflection

process but he saw it as being influenced by other aspects of the experience. More recent academics suggest that emotional responses are a more important part of any experience than Kolb suggested, and have a strong influence on subsequent thinking and actions.

1. The *concrete experience* stage puts the reflector in the role of actor in the situation. Their experiences at this stage incorporate sensory and emotional experiences, as well as observations. These experiences are captured as a description by the mentor (or video or audio recording, if permitted) of events. It must be noted that the actor's written account will inevitably be a retrospective observation and so may be prone to errors of recall. For this reason, it is important to conduct the de-brief as promptly as possible. Suitable questions for this stage would be simple prompt questions, such as:

   *How well did you feel the pupils met your learning intentions?*
   *Which aspects of the lesson do you think went best?*
   *How closely did you manage to stick to your lesson plan?*

2. *Reflective observation* is the stage at which the descriptions of events and feelings are subjected to an in-depth analysis. The analysis seeks to link what happened to how the teacher understands it. Inconsistences in understanding, areas of unfamiliarity and unexpected events should all be probed through questioning and seeking elaboration of descriptions. Questions that convey a suitably analytical tone might include:

   *Did (named aspect of the lesson) go as you had anticipated? If so, what aspects of your planning do you think underpinned that success? If not, what hadn't you predicted when you planned the lesson?*
   *Has the experience of teaching the lesson identified any areas about which you now feel the need to find out more?*
   *What was in your mind at the point when you moved away from the planned lesson and did something different instead?*

The stage of reflective observation is very significant, as it marks one of the points at which experience is transformed to give it deeper meaning.

3.  *Abstract conceptualisation* follows on and is the stage during which the understanding generated by reflective observation is extrapolated to identify possible future actions and responses. It is the point at which multiple possible explanations and actions can be explored and is crucial for the introduction of the 'doubt' that Dewey felt was important for reflection. Some would argue that identifying multiple possibilities is the key role of reflection, and is certainly the way in which reflection is raised from being formu-laic to being authentically challenging of accepted and routine practices or beliefs. So, during abstract conceptualisation, the mentee's observation that he omitted part of his planned lesson because he realised that he didn't have time to complete everything he had planned for might be met with questions such as:

*Are you generally finding it difficult to estimate how long activities will take?*
*What strategies have you used to monitor timings of lessons?*
*Were there any aspect of the earlier activities today that made them especially hard to plan for in terms of timings or that meant they took longer than originally anticipated?*
*Were all the pupils slower in completing tasks than you had anticipated or was it a sub-group who worked more slowly?*
*If it was a sub-group, are they pupils who you might have expected to take longer?*
*Were there any 'down times' in the lesson, when time wasn't being used for learning that could have been? If so, what caused these periods of down time and could they be avoided to give more learning time?*
*In what different ways could you modify future plans in light of this experience?*

Note that the questions are open and intended to stimulate thinking about the multiple possible causes, here of a mis-timed lesson, without privileging any one answer. At the conclusion of this stage, the action to be taken in Stage 4 should be agreed on, to avoid the mentee leaving the meeting still unclear as to what to do next.

4.  *Active experimentation.* This phase is characterised by the enactment of one, or more, of the solutions identified during the abstract conceptualisation phase. Since the iden-tified solutions are only provisional solutions to the 'problem', their impact will then need to be reflected on further. Thus, the actions that arise provide further concrete experiences, which may well have a new focus, and so the cycle starts over again.

## Task 8.1

To what extent do your own experiences lead you to support the idea that professional learning is primarily an intellectual activity? Have you had any experiences, either dir-ectly or indirectly through someone else's experiences, where the emotional response of the adult learner has shaped the learning? Where do you feel the balance between intellectual and emotional responses lies?

Donald Schön (1987) used earlier work to think about how professionals learn and how they can be helped to develop reflective skills to improve their practice. Like Kolb, he viewed experience as a key stimulus for reflection. A key difference with their beliefs, however, is that Schön sees reflection as a tool for making unrecognised knowledge, which informs Dewey's 'routine actions', explicit, and so open to questioning, change and improvement. The greater their understanding of why they do what they do, the greater their capacity to adapt and change rapidly. This is a characteristic of an expert teacher (see Chapter 12 for a description of expert teachers). Schön distinguishes, in a way very similar to Dewey, between *'knowledge-in-action'*, which is tacit knowledge that informs daily routines, and *'reflection on action'*, which is purposeful retrospective thinking about previous actions. This distinction augers the need for carefully structured questioning by the mentor in order to reveal the tacit knowledge (see the section headed 'How to promote reflection'). He believes that repeated reflection on action will make teachers more able to respond to unexpected situations because they have a wider range of rehearsed interventions to call upon. With repeat rehearsal, such reflection will enlarge the stock of intuitive responses that will only be evident in actions. This means that the accumulation of knowledge-in-action over time is not just a way to improve the technical aspects of teaching, or even to achieve a greater understanding of the role, but gives rise to highly accomplished teaching. This long-term, holistic endpoint distinguishes the model from Dewey's or Kolb's.

## Task 8.2

Think about an excellent teacher with whom you have worked. Do you agree with Schön that much of what they did they did not have to consciously plan for? Or, were they able to talk about the basis of the decisions they made, if asked? As a mentor, how would you go about enabling your mentee to reflect on action to improve their teaching?

A more recent author (Zwozdiak-Myers, 2012) has provided a framework for reflection that synthesises the ideas of many key writers, including those considered above, to provide a nine-part framework of reflective practice. This is shown, in summary, in Figure 8.3. Although drawing upon a vast body of literature, it is constructed to provide a clear summary of the key processes that underpin reflective practice of both mentors and mentees. Note that the dimensions are shown as intersecting at the description of reflective practice, but it is as much a cycle as the previous models, since the final dimension ('continue to improve teaching') takes you back to dimension 1 ('study their own teaching'). The model provides a useful reminder of the different areas of focus during sustained reflection, and it can be shared and used to guide mentor and mentee practice. Although the last process (9) is a medium- and long-term process, and processes (7) and (8) are the strategic intentions of mentoring, the earlier ones ((1) to (6)) can be executed as soon as the mentee is teaching (or executing other skills, such as leading or managing).

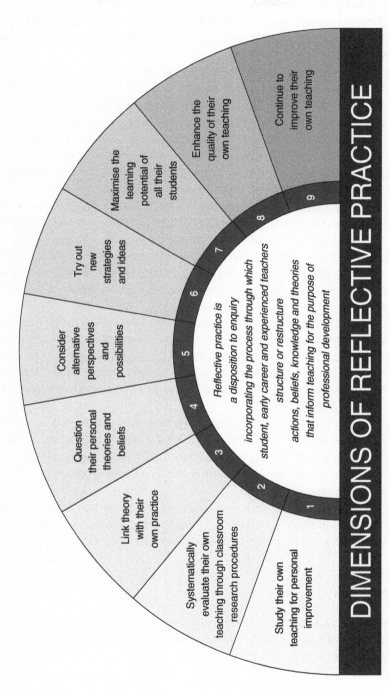

Figure 8.3  Dimensions of reflective practice

Dimension 1. Study their own teaching for personal improvement: This attitude of analysing how the teacher impacts upon learning is a crucial aspect of reflection and a pre-cursor to development. Teachers need to understand that pupils' and teachers' behaviours are hugely inter-related, and teachers need to be aware of how they can alter events in the classroom.

Dimension 2. Systematically evaluate their own teaching through classroom research procedures: This means that teachers need to consider evidence on the relationship between what they do and how pupils learn. For this to be studied over time, it is essential that teachers evaluate their work regularly and record their evaluations for future consideration. Their evaluations need to focus not simply on what they did but on evidence of outcomes, specifically the extent to which intended outcomes were met.

Dimension 3. Link theory with their own practice: This may be published theory but is also likely to be personal 'theories' and assumptions.

Dimension 4. Question their personal theories and beliefs: Theories are only as good as the practice they support and must never be viewed as 'beyond suspicion'. Evaluation requires explicit recognition of their personal theories and beliefs, either formal or informal, and then robust evaluation of these, preferably supported by a mentor or critical friend.

Dimension 5. Consider alternative perspectives and possibilities: As with Dimension 3, these may be identified by individual research, but are also frequently offered by a mentor or colleagues.

Dimension 6. Try out new strategies and ideas: Knowing alternatives is not enough – they have to be considered seriously and implemented as appropriate to the situation.

Dimension 7. Maximise the learning potential of all their students: The deepened understanding of their own role in shaping learning, and the concurrent recognition of the pupils as the environment to which teaching must be matched, will enable a teacher to become ever more effective.

Dimension 8. Enhance the quality of their own teaching: This is achieved by carrying out the processes described in the earlier dimensions. It should be noted that the quality of teaching does not always bring about demonstrable rise in assessment performance but may also manifest itself in shifts in other ways, such as engagement in lessons or attendance at lessons.

Dimension 9. Continue to improve their own teaching: This dimension requires a sustained effort to critique practice, to understand changing educational situations in which their practice is located, and to respond to unexpected events and opportunities.

## Task 8.3

Looking at Zwozdiak-Myers' (2012) definition of reflective practice, and the nine dimensions, consider how you might use the nine dimensions to assist your mentee in developing reflective and self-evaluation skills.

## Task 8.4

How do you think that you might apply each of the four models described (Dewey's, Kolb's, Schön's and Zwozdiak-Myers') to your own work as a mentor? Are there any modifications you would want to make to them in order to capture more accurately the process that you believe will best develop reflection in a mentee?

## Personal and professional attributes for reflection

As with all aspects of mentoring, the process of reflection should be mutualistic, with both mentor and mentee showing a 'disposition to enquiry'. While this sounds slightly abstract, the following account, based on Dewey's writing, shows the qualities needed in order to foster deep reflection and undergo what Kemmis et al. (2014) call 'collaborative self-development'.

1.  *Open-mindedness*: As the previous exemplar questions illustrate, the willingness to consider multiple factors when analysing a situation is essential. This can include aspects that one of the pair consider implausible. For example, inexperienced teachers frequently see disruptive behaviour as simply a failure by a pupil to exercise self-restraint, whilst the mentor may need to advance the possibility that it was a symptom of the work being unsuitable in some way, such as being too demanding or irrelevant, or simply that the instructions were not understood in the first place. Similarly, open-mindedness requires mentors to consider alternatives to their preferred routines and guards against the limitations of an 'imitative apprenticeship' style of mentoring. Being open-minded requires both parties to accept challenge to their practices and beliefs, and to consider the validity of alternative views. For this reason, it can be an uncomfortable process that needs handling sensitively.

2.  *Responsibility*: The acceptance that decisions about actions will have consequences for all involved. As well as recognising this, a responsible teacher accepts the consequences of their decisions, whether they affect an individual pupil, a colleague, a whole class or the entire school's ethos. Exercising responsibility should not, however, make the mentor or mentee averse to risk, as risk-taking can lead to breakthroughs in understanding. What should be thought about is how to mitigate the risk, for example, by having a backup plan or arranging for additional help to be at hand if needed.

3.  *Wholeheartedness*: This is a term that captures the interest in, and enthusiasm for, the subject being reflected upon. It can be equated to the motivation of the mentoring team to solve the problem at hand as effectively as possible. Wholeheartedness will be demonstrated by both parties being willing to engage in open-minded consideration of issues, and by their taking their respective responsibilities seriously.

## Task 8.5

Think about a mentee or colleague with whom you have worked and thought was making (or had already made) good progress as a teacher. Consider the extent to which they demonstrated the three qualities listed earlier. Focus on what they said and what they did; what were the 'markers' of their 'disposition'? Now, consider how *you* could demonstrate those same qualities in the way that you work with a mentee.

## Task 8.6

Think about how you might introduce the idea of the importance of the previously listed qualities to a mentee with whom you are working.

## How to promote reflection

This chapter has considered what reflection is, the processes associated with it and what the potential benefits are. The following section looks at possible actions that a mentor can take to promote reflection in their mentee, as well as themselves.

1.   *Model reflection yourself.* As part of this process, a mentor may need to model reflection as well as eliciting it in their mentee. Attitudes and beliefs need to be articulated and shared openly, and your mentee should also be able to observe the teaching that you do based on these. Admitting when you are having difficulties or having a teaching problem to solve does not make you a poor role model; it gives you a valuable opportunity to share how you undergo reflection to make progress with the issue. Work at demonstrating the three personal qualities of open-mindedness, responsibility and wholeheartedness as you describe your reflections. Being open does not mean that you are competing with your mentee for attention; rather, it reassures them that everyone has challenges and that these can be addressed by approaching them reflectively and then acting upon those reflections. By being open, you give your mentee a plausible role model and, in turn, will encourage them to share openly.

2.   *Demonstrate mutualism in reflection.* This is closely related to point 1. but should remind you that mentoring offers mentors valuable professional development if approached in this light. You should invite thoughts and ideas from your mentee about your own as well as their practice. Exchanging perspectives is likely to give a more rounded analysis and a wider set of possible options to evaluate and draw upon.

3.   *Ensure access to a range of other models of reflection.* Observing other teachers is eye opening, regardless of how experienced a teacher you are. However, observations are likely to result in much better learning experiences for the observer if they focus on a particular skill. Having access arranged to a variety of lessons and then listening afterwards

to the teacher's reflections will give a mentee insight into different approaches to reflection.

4.  *Have reflective conversations that encourage a shift in thinking.* The importance of matching questions to a reflective focus has been exemplified previously in this chapter and is part of the broader mentor role. For example, in Chapter 1 you met Anderson and Shannon's (1988) expectation that a mentor will clarify and probe. Likewise, Dewey's and Kolb's models both state the expectation that questioning will occur, even though they associate different types of questions at different stages in a reflective cycle. It is, therefore, useful to consider possible questions according to the depth of reflection that they will engender. The framework that follows (Zwozdiak-Myers, 2012) rests on the work of a range of writers, but there is general concordance about the qualities of three distinct categories of discourse. They may well remind you of the conversations and questions associated with the first three stages of Kolb's (1984) cycle. The shift in the focus of the conversation is demonstrated by the differential use of a How? What? Why? When? Next? framework.

   A.  *Descriptive conversations*: These are discussions about what, in the perceptions of those involved in the conversation, happened. These are almost a verbal reconstruction of events and are the most common type of comments made during lesson observations. Despite the unfiltered quality of them, it should be remembered that what is noted is what the observer judges as important enough to record, and this is why a mentee might helpfully suggest a focus for the observation. This stage of the conversation is characterised by 'What?' and 'Who?' questions. So, in a typically descriptive observer's account we find answers to the questions of 'What happened?' and 'Who were the pupils whose learning was not as expected?'

   > *09.00 Pupils come in, X. greets them at the door and tells them to get their jotters and pencils out.*
   > *09.08 J. shouts that she has no pencil, N. joins in, saying that he has lost his jotter.*

   Although these descriptions provide a hugely believable account of a lesson, they convey little meaning that can be used, in this form, to improve practice.

   B.  *Comparative conversations*: These involve evaluative consideration of what happened. They may involve comparing different aspects of one lesson, or comparing the lesson taught to the plan that was prepared, or comparing the lesson to previous ones. At this stage, early teachers are commonly thinking in a positivistic way, believing that there is one right answer. (More on the different stages of teacher development is given in Chapter 12.) Such comparisons naturally give rise to questions about the reasons for the differences observed. These are typically 'What (was different or the same)?' and 'Why?' questions. For example:

   > *What was different about J. and N.'s behaviour today?*
   > *Why do you think that they behaved differently to the way they have behaved in your other lessons?*

C.   *Critical conversations*: These are the conversations in which contextual factors are considered, and through which a relativistic understanding of the teacher's role is explored. It corresponds to Orland-Barak's (2010) action of 'connecting experiences, beliefs and knowledge'. Such conversations look at the role of context and background factors in shaping events in the classroom. Over time, such conversations will help an early teacher to understand that there not 'right answers' but that the best action depends on the situation. Nevertheless, there are important principles, such as upholding pupil well-being and treating all pupils equally, which set the boundaries for the range of acceptable solutions. These wider, contextual considerations should be brought to bear at this stage. Such exploration will be supported by further 'How?' and 'Why?' questions, this time with a more analytical focus. 'Next?' questions, which may have been considered at the comparative conversation stage, will yield a wider range of alternatives at this stage, as the multiple contributory factors are brought into focus. For example, a mentor might wish to raise the question of how disadvantage or learning difficulties may have had a bearing upon events:

> *How might J. have felt as you emphasised the need for a pencil at the start, knowing that she didn't have one?*

> *How could you ensure that all pupils have the necessary equipment without causing distress to those who don't, or can't, bring it?*

> *Next lesson, what strategy will you try out to avoid disruptions regarding equipment? What alternative strategies can you envisage and why do you think that the one you have chosen is the best option in this situation?*

> *Which school systems could you use to find out whether J. or N. have support needs that might explain their apparent lack of preparedness?*

5.   *Balance the challenge and support provided by your intervention*: In Chapter 1, Daloz's (2012) model was mentioned, which shows the importance of offering high levels of both challenge and support for optimal development. Posing searching questions about practice, assumptions and beliefs can be productively challenging, especially if support is available to help the mentee act. However, a mentee who is feeling anxious may hear questions intended to elicit description as veiled criticism. This is a judgement that a mentor must make each time they work with their mentee.

---

## Task 8.7

Consider these five strategies to engender deeper reflection and evaluate the relative importance of each of them in your own professional development and that of the mentees with whom you have worked.

---

## Reflecting on the impact of reflection

You should, by now, understand that reflection is an important way to enhance a mentee's practice, as well as your own. You may also appreciate that reflection requires commitment and time of both mentor and mentee. It is, therefore, important that you evaluate the impact that reflection and follow up action is having, in order to ensure that you are working as productively as possible. You have now encountered various frameworks with which to describe and self-audit practice, but assessing what you do is not the same thing as knowing that it is working! A word of caution, however, as studies have noted that reflection commonly does not produce a quantifiable difference in 'performance' (Lee and Sabatino, 1998) but is, nevertheless, rated as very helpful by the vast majority of participants. The inference of this is that the affective benefits may be more discernible in the short term than the practical ones. The very slight increments in practice over the short time of an evaluative study are illustrated by the typical time scales given for professional development, as shown in Chapter 12.

Previously documented outcomes, which may serve as a marker of positive impact for which you can look, include:

- Participants feel that they have a safe space in which to explore issues and ideas without judgement (Foster-Fishman et al., 2005).
- Learners who are guided in reflection show a greater ability to understand what they have been taught and how to apply this understanding in practice. Participants reported that this benefit endures after the intervention, which provides further evidence of long-term benefits that would require longer-term tracking to demonstrate (Lee and Sabatino, 1998).
- Reflection offers an enhanced learning experience, with learners reporting that they learn more easily and faster. This may be associated with the meta-cognitive (thinking about learning) quality of reflective conversations (Lee and Sabatino, 1998).
- Possibly associated with the existence of a safe space in which to undertake exploratory conversations, coupled with the improved experience of learning, participants feel that they are more empowered in their learning (Foster-Fishman et al., 2005).

## Task 8.8

Consider your own experiences of being reflective, along with those of any mentees with whom you have worked. To what extent does the absence of discernible short-term impacts make you feel that reflection may be an over-rated tool for understanding or development? Can you identify other impacts of reflection, not listed here, that you have experienced or observed?

## Summary and key points

The key points discussed in this chapter are:

- there are different theories of reflection, which differ in the extent to which reflection is seen as an intellectual and rational process, or as a more holistic one;
- different models share the idea that reflection is deep and sustained thinking, intended to solve problems and enhance practice;

- a cycle of reflection is central to all the different models of reflection that have been considered;
- effective questioning can stimulate wide and deep thinking about the circumstances that cause a problem, and likely solutions;
- personal attributes and dispositions of both mentor and mentee can help to foster reflection; and
- reflection provides essential support in the short-term and enhances professional learning over the long-term.

## Further reading

Crichton, H. and Valdera Gil, F. (2015). Student teachers' perceptions of feedback as an aid to reflection for developing effective practice in the classroom. *European Journal of Teacher Education*, 38 (4), 512–524.

Kuswandono, P. (2014). University mentors' views on reflective practice in microteaching: Building trust and genuine feedback. *Reflective Practice: International and Multi-disciplinary Perspectives*, 15 (6), 701–717.

Thomassen, W. and Munthe, E. (2021). Educating Norwegian preservice teachers for the multicultural classroom – what knowledge do student teachers and mentor teachers express? *European Journal of Teacher Education*, 44:2, 234–248.

## References

Anderson, E.M. and Shannon, A. (1988). Toward a conceptualization of mentoring. *Journal of Teacher Education*, January–February, 38–42.

Daloz, L.A. (2012). *Mentor: Guiding the Journey of Adult Learners*. New York: Wiley.

Dewey, J. (1933). *How We Think: A Re-statement of the Relation of Reflective Thinking to the Educative Process*. Boston: D.C. Heath and Company.

Foster-Fishman, P., Nowell, B., Deacon, Z., Nievar, M.A. and McCann, P. (2005). Using methods that matter: The impact of reflection, dialogue and voice. *American Journal of Community Psychology*, 36 (3/4), 275–291.

Hatton, N. and Smith, D. (1995). Reflection in teacher education towards definition and implementation. *Teaching and Teacher Education*, 11 (1), 33–49.

Kemmis, S., Heikkinen, H.L.T., Fransson, G., Aspfors, J. and Edwards-Groves, C. (2014). Contested architectures of mentoring: Support, supervision or collective self-development. *Teaching and Teacher Education*, 43, 154–164.

Kolb, D.A. (1984). *Experiential Learning: Experience as the Source of Learning and Development (Vol. 1)*. Englewood Cliffs, NJ: Prentice-Hall.

Lee, D. and Birdsong Sabatino, K. (1998). Evaluating guided reflection: A US case study. *International Journal of Training and Development*, 2 (3), 162–170.

Schön, D.A. (1987). *Educating the Reflective Practitioner: Toward a New Design for Teaching and Learning in the Professions*. San Francisco, CA: Jossey-Bass.

Zwozdiak-Myers, P. (2012). *The Teacher's Reflective Practice Handbook*. Abingdon, UK: Routledge.

# 9 Mentoring through dialogue

*Lorele Mackie*

## Objectives

At the end of this chapter, you should be able to:

- understand the importance of establishing an appropriate mentoring relationship to foster effective mentor/mentee dialogue;
- identify the key components of effective dialogue on pre-and post-lesson mentoring discussions;
- analyse the ways in which dialogue can support the professional learning of teachers; and
- recognise a range of practical strategies that can be used to enhance the quality of mentor/mentee dialogue.

## Introduction

In the context of a knowledge society and its inherent lifelong learning agenda, teaching and learning are multifaceted processes requiring broader, more complex knowledge, skill and competence bases (Forde, McMahon, McPhee and Patrick 2006). This has implications for the mentoring practices required to promote such bases in beginner teachers. Beginner teachers learn to teach through relationships with others (Harrison, Lawson and Wortley, 2005). Therefore, collaborating with a mentor, who is part of the teaching community, is necessary (Hargreaves and Fullan, 2000) in respect of developing requisite aspects, such as subject and pedagogical knowledge, self-evaluation, depth of comprehension of learning, metacognitive awareness, critically reflective thinking and communicative capacity, interpersonal skills, and transference of knowledge, understanding and skills to other contexts (Certo, 2005; Carnell, MacDonald and Askew 2006; Hargreaves, 2007). Dialogue is central to this professional learning relationship. In this respect, collaboration is an essential component of mentoring, as it addresses improvement in teaching and issues of social justice and equality through practices such as critical reflection, active trust, self-regulation, respect and reciprocity (Hargreaves, 2000). A situated learning model is relevant here, which equates with the social constructivist view of learning where meaning is constructed both individually and through social interaction (Vygotsky, 1978), and depth of comprehension is key as opposed to acquiring de-contextualised knowledge and skills (Fosnot, 1996; Selley, 1999).

DOI: 10.4324/9780429356957-12

---

**Task 9.1    Reflections about collaboration**

- Consider your experiences of being collaborative as a beginner teacher – which experiences stand out most and why?
- Identify key collaborative practices you use as a mentor teacher. Why do you use these in particular?

---

## Dialogic mentoring

The following sections make use of case studies of primary school student teachers on placement in Scottish school contexts to describe and explore salient elements of collaborative, dialogic mentoring, namely communication, constructive dialogue, quality questioning, listening to respond and self-evaluation (Mackie, 2016, 2018, 2020a, 2020b). To maintain participant confidentiality pseudonyms are employed, for example, class teacher mentor A – CTA, student teacher A – STA (*ibid.*).

### *Personal and professional dimensions of mentoring relationships*

Dialogic mentoring requires a relationship comprised of different dimensions. As noted in Chapter 1, the literature suggests that mentoring relationships are comprised of several components, for example, structural, supportive and professional dimensions (Yeomans and Sampson, 1994); pragmatic, managerial and interpersonal elements (Kwan and Lopez-Real, 2005); and relational, developmental and contextual aspects (Ambrosetti, Knight and Dekker, 2014). Such models commonly emphasise both personal and professional dimensions (relational and developmental components). The existence of, and connection between, these two dimensions is essential within a dialogic mentoring process to foster professional learning (Mackie, 2018), for example, to develop mentee confidence by way of support to experiment and take risks (Rajuan, Beijaard and Verloop 2007; Ambrosetti, 2010). Mentees are also reported to attribute more value to mentor feedback within mentoring relationships that include a personal dimension (Laker, Laker and Lea, 2008), particularly in situations where there are difficulties with their teaching practice (Yeomans and Sampson, 1994).

---

### Case Study 9.1 Friendship

Friendship was viewed as facilitating dialogue between mentor and mentee.

> *I think you have to develop ... a sort of friendship, trust. And especially ... with (participant name) ... who was extremely nervous when she came to me at first ... I think that it's important to try to make her feel ... at ease. So there has to be a wee bit of a personal rapport between you.* **CTB**

> *I think there has to be an element of friendship. You're in somebody's classroom ... you're working alongside them daily ... at the end of the first day, she was ... 'so how was it?' ... I said, 'I'm absolutely shattered'! And ... she just came over and gave me a hug ... that's important to me ... it makes her more approachable ... you could express your concerns ... it makes it a lot easier if we have to go up and speak and ask things.* **STB**

## Case Study 9.2   Empathy

Class teacher (CT) mentors and mentees noted empathy, specifically recognition that everyone makes mistakes, as a central element of effective mentoring relationships.

> *I think you have to reassure them that everybody gets it wrong. Certainly, I've already told (participant name) that there are days where sometimes I think 'oh that didn't go very well, I'll not do that again'. And that's something that you have to get used to as a teacher ... sharing ... bad experiences with them makes them feel better cause they realise 'oh right, I'm not the only person who gets it wrong'.* **CTC**

> *I would expect them to say 'do you know what, these days happen, and it happens to us all. But you're a professional. It's what you're paid to do'.* **STC**

## Case Study 9.3   Getting along with each other

> *I think ... she's made it clear that ... she's happy to be with me and ... she's learning a lot from me. And ... that helps towards ... the way that we feel about each other ... if she was ... not happy with what I was doing then I don't suppose we would have such a good relationship with each other.* **CTB**

> *... it can't always be all business and all work ... It is nice to find out more about the person and I think you become more honest with each other as well and you don't hold back and [you] say things you might not have said otherwise ... having an actual friendship with your teacher just makes everything more comfortable. The atmosphere is nicer and you are more willing to just go and say to them 'I have a problem with this, can you help me with that?'.* **STD**

Suggestive of the complexity of mentoring, connectivity between personal and professional dimensions can both assist and impede the mentoring process. Collaborative, dialogic mentoring is facilitated by an effective personal mentor/mentee relationship (Kwan and Lopez-Real, 2005). However, it can cause issues by hampering professional dialogue about mentee development areas because mentors are reticent to risk causing offence to mentees (*ibid.*). This evidences the importance of, but difficulties with, balancing personal and professional dimensions of a mentoring relationship. In this respect, mentor/mentee discussion about the aim of the mentoring process is vital at the outset, namely mentee professional learning about how to teach. It is vital that both parties understand that this aim is founded on relevant professional competency standards (such as those noted in Chapter 1) and that these should be a consistent reference point. This may help avoid situations where mentees conceptualise feedback as personal criticism as opposed to constructive advice about how to improve. In this respect, recognition that mentor professional learning may also occur is helpful. This is reflective of alternative conceptions of traditional hierarchical relationships, where the power lies with the mentor, to more reciprocal, collaborative conceptions of power as 'flux', where both mentor and mentee can be powerful and powerless in the same context (Foucault, 1979).

Based on the aforementioned mentoring aim, mentor and mentee roles should be clearly established and agreed, including practical arrangements to facilitate these roles. As noted in Chapter 1, different approaches to mentoring entail varied associated roles.

## Case Study 9.4   Mentor roles

Based on a dialogic, collaborative mentoring process, joint CT mentor and mentee understandings of the roles of the mentor were:

- *to be reassuring*
- *to be empathetic: recognising all make mistakes*
- *to learn*
- *to observe/be observed*
- *to have a balance of directive and non-directive dialogue*
- *to share ideas*
- *to offer constructive feedback*
- *to encourage self-evaluation*
- *to listen in order to respond*
- *to ask questions*

## Task 9.2   Reflections about mentoring relationships and associated roles

- Review the list of mentor roles made in Chapter 1 (Task 1.3).
- Re-draft this list based on your developing understanding of personal and professional dimensions within a dialogic mentoring relationship.

Mentoring conversations are a significant part of a collaborative mentoring process (Schwille, 2008). The following sections describe and explore salient elements of collaborative, dialogic mentoring, namely communication, constructive dialogue, quality questioning, listening to respond and self-evaluation (Mackie, 2016, 2018, 2020a, 2020b).

## *Communication*

---

### Case Study 9.5    Having good communication

CT mentors and mentees viewed *having good communication* as a key characteristic of their relationship. CTF felt that positivity was important.

> *Certainly positivity ... I think that is the key one ... that comes down to the relationship that the mentor and the mentee have ... I want them to feel comfortable enough to say 'you know what, I am really struggling'. Or 'I feel really down about that today' or 'I am not happy about what is going on'. My role then would be to encourage them, re-highlight all the positive things that they had done. Have a look at how we are going to change what they are going to do so they feel better ...* **CTF**

Being open and honest was noted by STE and STA. STA, in particular, felt that she should not feel constrained in what she talked about for fear of displeasing her CT mentor and that it was important to be open to the opinions of others in order to progress in learning to teach.

> *You shouldn't feel that you are in a tense situation. It should feel like a nice conversation where you can talk about things. You can say good things and bad things. But I don't think it should be tense. I think you should be able to relax and say what you think. And you shouldn't have to think about what you are saying in case 'oh, she might not like that' – you should be able to say everything.* **STA**

---

Reflective of these interpersonal components of mentoring, the attributes of positivity, openness and honesty were viewed as significant in having good communication between mentor and mentee. Mentees are more likely to be receptive and learn if these attributes are present within the relationship (Hyland and Lo, 2006; Jones, 2013).

---

### Case Study 9.6    Having discussions

CT mentors and mentees noted *having discussions* as a central element of the mentor/mentee relationship. Such discussions took place before and after teaching episodes and were both formal and informal.

> *... it's just making sure each time ... she can tell ... me how she's got on ... and I'm giving her ... little bits of advice ... those kinda informal conversations are a form of formative assessment.* **CTC**
>
> *There w[ere] ... times that were definitely set aside ... And then constantly through things, I could seek her advice at any, any point. Every night we got a chance to speak. Even if it was briefly for a few minutes.* **STE**

In respect of conversations taking place both before and after teaching episodes, dialogue can be interpreted as a cyclical, reflective, outside-the-action element of mentoring (Schwille, 2008), where mentors help mentees to make sense of teaching and learning to promote mentee professional learning (Iancu-Haddad and Oplatka, 2014). Although advantageous in this sense, it may also foster substandard quality teachers given that the mentor is on the periphery during mentee teaching practice and can adopt a supervisory, as opposed to educative, role within pre- and post-lesson conversations (*ibid.*).

Dialogue was also noted as both formal and informal. As such, collaboration may be interpreted as both planned and spontaneous (Williams and Prestage, 2002). Both are significant, for example, with regard to addressing challenging situations, and managing anxieties and particular facets of teaching (Hargreaves, 2010). Spontaneous collaboration may be viewed as more effective in promoting mentee professional learning (Patrick, Elliot, Hulme and McPhee, 2010) due to the use of continual professional dialogue as a central support strategy (Williams and Prestage, 2002). However, structured collaboration may also be valuable in enhancing mentoring practices as consistent arrangements are evident (*ibid.*).

## Case Study 9.7   Topics of discussions

CT mentors and mentees noted that topics focused on the mentee learning to teach, with emphasis on aspects such as planning and elements of the mentee's teaching practice. Discussion topics were initiated by both sides.

> *I think they just came about because (participant's name) asked or maybe it was something that had come up if I'd looked at her folder. Or something that I thought of.* **CTD**
>
> *... a kind of mixture between the two of us but it was mostly situations that would arise during teaching or during the class time, even after school. And she would bring things up as well, 'I noticed you did this, you could have done that better by doing ...' or 'how do you think you could have done that better'. So it was both of us really.* **STA**

Joint instigation of discussion topics may be interpreted as mentors occupying an interactive role, which requires both mentor and mentee recognition that each has a distinct and valuable contribution to make (Young Bullough, Draper, Smith and Erickson, 2005). This more equitable conception is reflective of non-directive methods of mentoring concerned with scaffolding mentee understanding through educative strategies to promote responsibility for learning and self-evaluation (Carnell *et al.*, 2006). From a social constructivist perspective, collaboration is central to these practices, where dialogue is significant in both individual and co-constructed learning to shape thinking, re-frame or develop new understandings (Bruner, 1985).

---

### Task 9.3    Reflections about communication

- What do you think are the key elements of good communication between mentor and beginner teacher?
- Identify key points in the day where mentoring conversations may take place. What factors do you think enable/prohibit such conversations?

---

## Constructive dialogue

### Case Study 9.8    Constructive conversations

*Giving feedback* was understood as another key element of mentor/mentee relationships. CT mentors talked about discussing strengths and development points with the mentee using the 'stars and wishes' formative assessment technique that is employed with school pupils as an analogy and then giving feedback on next steps for teaching in future lessons.

> *I tend to do two stars and a wish for individual lessons. They cannot improve every-thing right away. It is a long slow process ... Once they have finished teaching, I try to meet immediately after they have done a direct teach, so that we can get immediate feedback because once you have had time to self-reflect on it you tend to think 'I didnae do that. I could have done that better'.* **CTF**

> *I think quality feedback would be a mixture ... Probably more heavy on the positive comments and maybe just one or two areas to develop. I think too many develop-mental points would not be good for ... confidence.* **CTA**

Mentees noted getting feedback on lesson content and pedagogy. They talked about how CT mentors asked for their perspectives on the strengths and development areas of lessons prior to offering their own views and suggestions.

> *... she would tell me things that I had done well, as well as things that she felt that I needed to improve on. It is always good to start on a positive, either that or end on a positive to make you feel a bit better.* **STA**

> *I think a lot a' that has to be through feedback ... picking up on the positives but also highlighting to you where you could do better. I think a lot a' people are frightened to do that. And that's not beneficial when you need to know in order to get better.* **STC**

Next steps for mentee learning were also identified as part of the dialogue between CT mentors and mentees. CT mentors reported that these were discussed alongside strength and development points; CTD and CTE noted them as specifically linked to the areas identified for development.

> *... these are your strengths and here are your things that maybe next time, look at building on ... your areas for development ... I think that's just a very natural way of how things work in schools now.* **CTD**

> *... she would observe and she would give constructive feedback ... She told me what was good. She said areas to work on which I thought was ... really good.* **STB**

## Case Study 9.9   Being open to constructive criticism

Communication between CT mentor and mentee was seen as essential in facilitating mentees being open to constructive criticism and for mentors to be able to provide it. Mentees maintained that such feedback helped them to identify development areas to foster progression in their learning.

> *I don't think you can develop as a teacher without it. Nobody is going to be able to walk into a classroom and be this great ... I think you need ... the (constructive criticism) or how can you move on from your ideals?* **STC**

CT mentors acknowledged the difficulty in being receptive to constructive criticism.

> *Being able to take on constructive criticism from a mentor ... can sometimes cause ... not friction but [be] stand offish ... It is an openness to take on feedback from someone with more experience and the advice from them ... they have to be able to take constructive criticism, which is difficult for anybody. Nobody likes it.* **CTF**

Dialogue may be interpreted as being based on a feedback process and being constructive in respect of the consideration of strengths, areas for development and next steps in learning (Crasborn, Hennison, Brouwer, Korthagen and Bergen, 2011). CT mentors used the 'stars and wishes' formative assessment technique employed with school pupils as an analogy in their descriptions. These components of mentor feedback are recognised as essential to promote progression in learning (for example, Hennison, Crasborn, Brouwer, Korthagen and Bergen, 2008; Hoffman, Wetzel, Maloch, Greeter, Taylor, DeJulio and Vlach, 2015). This focus on current progression as well as future practice is significant in assisting beginner teachers learning to teach (Schwille, 2008). If such a balance is not evident, beginner teachers may adopt a mainly deficit view of their teaching (Long, Hall, Conway and Murphy, 2012), ignoring their strengths and thus failing to reach their potential (Ulvik and Langorgen, 2012). It may highlight the mentor/mentee power imbalance and lead to mentees feeling exposed (Sewell, Cain, Woodgate-Jones and Srokosz, 2009) or bullied (Maguire, 2001), and relationships breaking down (Kim and Danforth, 2012). Mentees are more likely to be receptive and learn if dialogue is presented in a personable manner (Hyland and Lo, 2006; Jones, 2013), but mentors may not share development points with mentees if they want to preserve existing positive relationships (Timperley, 2001).

Mentees noted that CT mentors asked for their perspectives on the strengths and development areas of lessons prior to offering their own views and suggestions. Indicative of a constructivist perspective, it is suggested that feedback should not consist of one person feeding back to the other but involve individual and shared reflection (Hargreaves, 2007; HMIe, 2011), and both support and challenge the incorporation of self-regulated learning skills (Hargreaves, 2007). These are indicative of mentors adopting non-directive methods of mentoring concerned with scaffolding mentee understanding through educative strategies to promote responsibility for learning and self-evaluation (Carnell *et al.*, 2006). In contrast, mentors may adopt a training role using more directive strategies, such as demonstrating and telling, in which they dominate dialogue (Yeomans and Sampson, 1994; Carnell *et al.*, 2006). This is reflective of more supervisory conceptions of mentoring (O'Brien and Christie, 2005) that are based in traditional expert/novice dualities of power and concerned with the transmission of knowledge rather than encouraging independent thinking. Such approaches are widely acknowledged as not effective in mentoring for understanding (Rogers, 2004). However, it is important to consider the needs of the mentee in terms of the different stages of development in learning to teach. In the early stages of teacher professional learning mentees may require more direction as they begin to develop some degree of understanding of the academic and pedagogical facets of teaching (Schwille, 2008). In addition, telling is a necessary strategy in providing important information about pupils' health and safety, pastoral care issues and academic progression (Hargreaves, 2010).

## Task 9.4 Reflections about constructive dialogue and giving feedback

- Write down in each column of the table examples of feedback that you have offered beginner teachers.
- In what ways are these examples constructive? What amendments might you make based on your reflections about the knowledge, understanding and skills required of an effective mentor?

| Relevant Competency Standard(s) | Mentee Strength | Mentee Area for Development | Mentee Next Steps | Mentor Reflections |
|---|---|---|---|---|
| | | | | |
| | | | | |

*Quality questioning*

## Case Study 9.10   Asking questions

Linked to constructive conversations, *asking questions* was also cited as significant. Mentees noted the importance of being asked questions and asking questions themselves. Mentor questions were mainly literal 'what' and 'how' questions.

> *I'd ask her how do you think that went? What do you think you did well? What do you think the children enjoyed and is there anything that you feel you could improve for your next lesson?* **CTA**

> *So there was an awful lot a', 'hmmm, it was okay … but how would you have made that better … What could you have done? What could you have left out? You know, what other tools were available?'* **STE**

CT mentors viewed mentees asking questions based on self-evaluations about lessons they had taught as important. The majority of mentees focused more on asking lots of fact finding 'how to' questions about classroom practice.

> *… she did say I asked a lot a' questions but she said that was a good thing … I like the fact that she was so knowledgeable and could … tell me like exact answers for things … And obviously by asking her, she'd be able to tell me the way that she finds best.* **STA**

CTF commented on the quantity and types of questions being asked. A vast number of both literal and inferential questions were evident. However, as the placement moved on, the mentee became more independent in putting forward her ideas and asking for an opinion, showing progression in learning.

> *She … asked lots and lots and lots of questions but completely relevant things … A lot of why questions … She was very, very knowledgeable about the theory behind why things … were happening … To begin with it was all 'how should I do this? What should we do next? How should I teach this?' But by the end of it, it was more looking for reassurance of 'this is my idea, what do you think', … which was great because you could really see the progression then.* **CTF**

## Case Study 9.11   Asking for help

Linked to asking questions, CT mentors saw it as important that mentees could go to them and ask for help. CTA acknowledged, as with constructive criticism, that asking for help could be difficult for some mentees for a variety of reasons.

> *I think because you know your mentor's job is [for you] to go to them for help and advice, it makes it easier for people to ask for help and advice … Some people just*

*really hate asking for help ... I think having experience of asking your mentor for advice should help you to ask other people in the future ... probably some people have a bit of ... a pride issue ... they might want to think they can do it on their own, be independent. I think some people sort of feel like a failure if they have to ask for a bit of help.* **CTA**

Mentees also linked asking for help to asking questions generally, and felt it was important to seek assistance in order to have a successful placement experience. Feeling at ease and reassured that the mentor was there to help were noted as significant. STD talked about being proactive before asking for help to show teaching capacity and avoid appearing as expecting to be 'spoon fed'. In formulating these ideas independently, she then sought her CT mentor's approval.

*I was able to ask for help ... I would come up with my own ideas but I would ask her if she thought it was OK. I wouldn't have felt that it was appropriate to just ask for help to be handed to me ... Because you want to show that you are not totally incapable and that although maybe you are not as good as she is, you don't want to seem totally out [of] your depth. I wanted her to know that I could do some things by myself.* **STD**

Quality questioning is a significant aspect of mentoring dialogue. It fosters skills in independent thinking through the use of a variety of different types of open questions, such as simple literal questions based on fact-finding, more complicated inferential ones concerned with more complex ideas and reasoning, and those evaluative in focus about personal opinions and feelings (Brown and Wragg, 1993). Asking questions was cited as an important mentee role. These questions were based on lesson self-evaluations and were perceived as showing that mentees could think for themselves, and as communicating with CT mentors about the sort of advice they required. This perception is indicative of mentees being proactive in their own learning process and of attempts at developing independence. CT mentors viewed mentees as asking both literal questions and inferential ones. As referenced in Chapter 1, mentoring as challenge (Daloz, 1986) may be an appropriate conception here, in that a more metacognitive level of mentee engagement, aimed at promoting their own professional learning, is evident. In contrast, mentees maintained that their questions focused more on literal fact finding 'how to' questions about classroom practice, which is more indicative of the training/supervisory approach to mentoring noted previously.

### Listening to respond

## Case Study 9.12 Listening to respond

Linked to asking questions, CT mentors and mentees cited *listening* as a key role of the mentor within constructive conversations. Responses from the case studies indicate that they are talking particularly about listening in order to respond. This manifested itself in answering questions, giving advice and feedback, and taking account of the views and needs of the mentee.

> *I think if your student … has got questions you need to be able to listen to your student's needs and be able to answer those questions and give help where it's needed.* **CTA**

> *Being a good listener does help when you just want to rant your problems. It is good that, obviously being a good listener, she would think about what I was saying and respond accordingly to try and help me.* **STA**

Listening in this respect is more specific and purposeful because listening, as a general concept, does not necessarily entail offering a response. A constructivist perspective is apposite here. Burleson (2011) conceptualises constructivist listening as a process by which communications are interpreted to foster comprehension of them and associated possible implications. Listening may simply be at surface level: a 'mindless' process accepting facts, ideas or opinions presented (*ibid.*:29). More 'mindful' listening entails listening for more in-depth, underpinning meanings appropriate for the context in which it occurs (*ibid.*:29). 'Mindful' listening was apparent in that a CT mentor was viewed as being a good listener if consideration had been accorded to what the mentee had said and a response offered to try and help. This also entailed listening in order to develop awareness of mentee needs, which suggests the feeling of having a professional responsibility to the beginner teacher.

## Task 9.5   Reflections about quality questioning and listening to respond

- Why do you think the use of questioning is important?
- What kinds of questions have you used/could you use to develop understanding and independent, critical thinking about practice?
- How might you enact listening to respond? What are the challenges to such a strategy?

### *Self-evaluation*

## Case Study 9.13   Self-evaluation

*Being able to engage in self-evaluation* about the strengths and areas for development of teaching episodes was noted as a significant facet of mentee professional learning.

CTE further highlighted the importance of considering the reasons behind certain outcomes and of thinking about next steps in their teaching practice.

> *I think if they can actually really focus on their own practice and actually say, pick out why something didn't go well … So they need to be able to actually look at a lesson or a group of lessons and … evaluate themselves, see if they can come up with a way forward.* **CTE**

*Encouraging self-evaluation* was viewed as a key role of the mentor in getting mentees to think independently, as this is essential to developing reflective practice. Given that mentees tended to be quite harsh in their self-evaluations, it fostered opportunities to encourage mentees to focus on strengths as well as development points. Mentees saw being encouraged to self-evaluate as significant in developing their capacity to think independently in order to foster professional learning. STB recognised that the CT mentor was encouraging her to think about her teaching practice in relation to her own experiences and knowledge.

> *… she would get me to think about it so I came up with an answer and she would say 'yes' or 'no, have you thought about this'. Getting you to enquire and think about your own experience and your own knowledge and how you can put that into practice.* **STB**

Teacher self-evaluation is a key element of dialogic mentoring. Mentee capacity to engage in self-evaluation through consideration of strengths, development areas and next steps in teaching evidences reflection-on-action outwith actual lesson episodes (Schön, 1987). This kind of reflection is significant in developing professional learning as it requires both deconstruction and reconstruction of teaching (Yeomans and Sampsons, 1994). Further, reflection about next steps in teaching may be interpreted as reflection-for-action in order to foster further comprehension of professional learning experiences (Harrison *et al.*, 2005). Both these kinds of reflection require depth of consideration, for example, thinking about why some parts of lessons were successful and some not, as opposed to simple, literal discussions about what happened during lessons (Bleach, 1997). It entails questioning existing beliefs and practices that stem from personal involvement in schooling and teacher education (Harrison *et al.*, 2005; Graham, 1999), and fosters metacognitive levels of thought, including individuals taking responsibility for their own learning.

In encouraging these kinds of reflection mentors inhabit a collaborative, educative role (Schwille, 2008), where the emphasis is on encouraging mentees to transfer knowledge, understanding and skills between a variety of contexts in order to foster transformational changes in practice (Rajuan *et al.*, 2007). Mentees are supported to think about multiple viewpoints (Certo, 2005) and to develop the professional autonomy and responsibility (Harrison, Dymoke and Pell, 2006) necessary to inhabit the requisite teacher academic and pastoral care roles to promote quality learning and teaching (Hudson, 2013). In this respect, mentoring may be interpreted as educative in the sense of challenge (Daloz, 1986) in respect of key elements such as asking questions and encouraging self-evaluation (Certo, 2005). It may be argued that challenge is lacking in the initial stages of teacher education because a foundation level of competence has not been developed (Harrison *et al.*, 2006). However, beginner teachers are able to engage with aspects of challenge even with limited teaching experience (Eraut, 1995). Without challenge the wide-ranging knowledge, understanding and skills required of twenty-first-century teachers may not occur, giving way to compliance to existing practices and therefore inhibiting transformational change (O'Brien and Christie, 2005).

---

### Task 9.6   Reflections about self-evaluation

*   Reflect on your experiences of encouraging beginner teachers to engage in self-evaluation. What enabled/prohibited your attempts to encourage self-evaluation (consider aspects such as mentee stage of development and mentor beliefs about effective mentoring)?

---

## Summary and key points

Collaboration and associated dialogic approaches are central to effective mentoring in the context of a knowledge society where teaching and learning are multifaceted processes requiring broader, more complex knowledge, skill and competence bases (Forde *et al.*, 2006). This chapter has considered:

*   the importance of establishing an appropriate mentoring relationship to foster effective mentor/mentee dialogue;
*   key components of effective dialogue on pre- and post-lesson mentoring discussions;
*   the ways in which dialogue can support the professional learning of teachers; and
*   a range of practical strategies that can be used to enhance the quality of mentor/mentee dialogue.

## Further reading

Ambrosetti, A. & Dekkers, J. (2010) The Interconnectedness of the Roles of Mentors and Mentees in Pre-service Teacher Education Mentoring Relationships, *Australian Journal of Teacher Education*, 35:6, 42–55.

Mackie, L. (2020) Partnership within the Context of Mentoring Initial Teacher Education Students in Scotland: Progress or Maintaining the Status Quo, *Scottish Educational Review*, 52:1, 52–72.

Tillema, H.H. & Smith, K. (2009) Assessment Orientation in Formative Assessment of Learning to Teach, *Teachers and Teaching*, 15:3, 391–405.

## References

Ambrosetti, A. (2010) Mentoring and Learning to Teach: What do Pre-service Teachers Expect to Learn from their Mentor Teachers?, *The International Journal of Learning*, 17:9, 117–132.

Ambrosetti, A., Knight, B.A. & Dekkers, J. (2014) Maximizing the Potential of Mentoring: A Framework for Pre-service Teacher Education, *Mentoring & Tutoring: Partnership in Learning*, 22:3, 224–239.

Bleach, K. (1997) The Importance of Critical Self-reflection in Mentoring Newly Qualified Teachers, *Mentoring and Tutoring*, 4:3, 19-24.

Brown, G. & Wragg, E.C. (1993) *Questioning*, London: Routledge.

Bruner, J. (1985). Models of the Learner. *Educational Researcher*, 14:6, 5-8.

Burleson, B.R. (2011) A Constructivist Approach to Listening, *International Journal of Listening*, 25:1-2, 27-46.

Carnell, E., MacDonald, H. & Askew, S. (2006) *Coaching and mentoring in higher education: A learning-centred approach*, London: Institute of Education.

Certo, J. (2005) Support and Challenge in Mentoring: A Case Study of Beginning Elementary Teachers and Their Mentors, *Journal of Early Childhood Teacher Education*, 26:4, 395-421.

Crasborn, F., Hennison, P., Brouwer, N., Korthagen, F. & Bergen, T. (2011) Exploring a Two-dimensional Model of Mentor Teacher Roles in Mentoring Dialogues, *Teaching and Teacher Education*, 27, 320-331.

Daloz, L. (1986) *Effective teaching and mentoring: Realizing the transformational power of adult learning*, San Francisco: Jossey-Bass.

Eraut, M. (1995) Outcomes and professional knowledge. In Burke, J.W. (Ed.) *Outcomes, learning and the curriculum: Implications for NVQs, GNVQs and other qualifications* (pp. 260-272), London: Falmer Press.

Forde, C., McMahon, M., McPhee, A.D. & Patrick, F. (2006) *Professional development, reflection and enquiry*, London: Paul Chapman Publishing.

Fosnot, C.T. (Ed.) (1996) *Constructivism theory, perspectives and practice*, New York: Teachers College Press.

Foucault, M. (1979). *The history of sexuality, volume one: An introduction*, London: Allen Lane.

Graham, P. (1999) Powerful Influences: A Case of One Student Teacher Renegotiating His Perceptions of Power Relations, *Teaching and Teacher Education*, 15, 523-540.

Hargreaves, A. (2000) Four Ages of Professionalism and Professional Learning. *Teachers and Teaching*, 6:2, 151-182.

Hargreaves, E. (2007) The Validity of Collaborative Assessment for Learning, *Assessment in Education*, 14:2, 185-199.

Hargreaves, E. (2010) Knowledge Construction and Personal Relationship: Insights About a UK University Mentoring and Coaching Service, *Mentoring and Tutoring: Partnership in Learning*, 18:2, 107-120.

Hargreaves, A. & Fullan, M. (2000) Mentoring in the New Millennium, *Theory into Practice*, 39:1, 50-56.

Harrison, J., Dymoke, S. & Pell, T. (2006) Mentoring Beginning Teachers in Secondary Schools: An Analysis of Practice, *Teaching and Teacher Education*, 22, 1055-1067.

Harrison, K., Lawson, T. & Wortley, A. (2005) Mentoring the Beginner Teacher: Developing Professional Autonomy Through Critical Reflection on Practice, *Reflective Practice*, 6:3, 419-441.

Hennison, P., Crasborn, F., Brouwer, N., Korthagen, F. & Bergen, T. (2008) Mapping Mentor Teachers' Roles in Mentoring Dialogues, *Educational Research Review*, 3, 168-186.

HMIe (2011) *Research summary - assessment for learning*, Livingston: HMIe.

Hoffman, J.V., Wetzel, M.M., Maloch, B., Greeter, E., Taylor, L., DeJulio, S. & Vlach, S.K. (2015) What Can We Learn from Studying the Coaching Interactions between Cooperating Teachers and Preservice Teachers? A Literature Review, *Teaching and Teacher Education*, 52, 99-112.

Hudson, P. (2013) Mentoring as Professional Development: 'Growth for Both' Mentor and Mentee, *Professional Development in Education*, 39:5, 771-783.

Hyland, F. & Lo, M.M. (2006) Examining Interaction in Teaching Practicum: Issues of Language, Power and Control, *Mentoring & Tutoring: Partnership in Learning*, 14:2, 163-186.

Iancu-Haddad, D. & Oplatka, I. (2014) Mentoring Novice Teachers: Motives, Process, and Outcomes from the Mentor's Point of View, *The New Educator*, 5, 45-65.

Jones, J. (2013) Factors Influencing Mentees' and Mentors' Learning throughout Formal Mentoring Relationships, *Human Resource Development International*, 16:4, 390-408.

Kim, T. & Danforth, S. (2012) Non-authoritative Approach to Supervision of Student Teachers: Cooperating Teachers' Conceptual Metaphors, *Journal of Education for Teaching: International Research and Pedagogy*, 38:1, 67-82.

Kwan, T. & Lopez-Real, F. (2005) Mentors' Perceptions of Their Roles in Mentoring Student Teachers, *Asia-Pacific Journal of Teacher Education*, 33:3, 275-287.

Laker, A., Laker, J.C. & Lea, S. (2008). Sources of Support for Pre-service Teachers during School Experiences, *Mentoring and Tutoring: Partnership in Learning*, 16:2, 125-140.

Long, F., Hall, K., Conway, P. & Murphy, R. (2012) Novice Teachers as 'Invisible' Learners, *Teachers and Teaching: Theory and Practice*, 18:6, 619-636.

Mackie, L. (2016) Mentoring Primary Education Student Teachers: Understandings of Mentoring and Perceptions of the Use of Formative Assessment within the Mentoring Process, Unpublished Thesis, Edinburgh: University of Edinburgh.

Mackie, L. (2018) Understandings of Mentoring within Initial Teacher Education School Placement Contexts: A Scottish Perspective, *Professional Development in Education*, 44:5, 662-637.

Mackie, L. (2020a) Mentoring Student Teachers within Primary Education School Placement Settings: Dimensions of Collaboration and Power, *Journal of Education for Teaching*, 46:3, 263-280.

Mackie, L. (2020b) Making accurate assessments. In Howells, K. & Lawrence, J. (Eds.) *Mentoring trainee and newly qualified primary school teachers* (pp. 101-111), London: Routledge.

Maguire, M. (2001) Bullying and the Postgraduate Secondary School Trainee Teacher: An English case study, *Journal of Education for Teaching: International Research and Pedagogy*, 27:1, 95-109.

O'Brien, J. & Christie, F. (2005) Characteristics of Support for Beginning Teachers: Evidence from the New Teacher Induction Scheme in Scotland. *Mentoring and Tutoring: Partnership in Learning*, 13:2, 189-203.

Patrick, F., Elliot, D., Hulme, M. & McPhee, A. (2010) The Importance of Collegiality and Reciprocal Learning in the Professional Development of Beginning Teachers, *Journal of Education for Teaching: International Research and Pedagogy*, 36:3, 277-289.

Rajuan, M., Beijaard, D. & Verloop, N. (2007) The Role of the Cooperating Teacher: Bridging the Gap between the Expectations of Cooperating Teachers and Student Teachers, *Mentoring and Tutoring: Partnership in Learning*, 15:3, 223-242.

Rogers, J. (2004) *Coaching skills: A handbook*, Milton Keynes: Open University Press.

Schön, D.A. (1987) *Educating the reflective practitioner*, London: Jossey-Bass.

Schwille, S.A. (2008) The Professional Practice of Mentoring, *American Journal of Education*, 115, 139-167.

Selley, N. (1999) *The art of constructivist teaching in the primary school*, London: David Fulton Publishers.

Sewell, K., Cain, T., Woodgate-Jones, A. & Srokosz, A. (2009) Bullying and the Postgraduate Trainee Teacher: A Comparative Study, *Journal of Education for Teaching: International Research and Pedagogy*, 35:1, 3-18.

Timperley, H. (2001) Mentoring Conversations Designed to Promote Student Teacher Learning, *Asia-Pacific Journal of Teacher Education*, 29:2, 111-123.

Ulvik, M. & Langørgen, K. (2012) What Can Experienced Teachers Learn From Newcomers? Newly Qualified Teachers as a Resource in Schools, *Teachers and Teaching*, 18:1, 43-57.

Vygotsky, L. (1978) *Mind in society: The development of higher psychological processes,* Cambridge: Harvard University Press.

Williams, A. & Prestage, S. (2002) The Induction Tutor: Mentor, manager or both?, *Mentoring & Tutoring: Partnership in Learning,* 10:1, 35-46.

Yeomans, J. & Sampson, R. (Eds.) (1994) *Mentorship in the primary school,* London: The Falmer Press.

Young, J.R., Bullough, Jr R.V., Draper, R.J., Smith, L.K. & Erickson, L.B. (2005) Novice Teacher Growth and Personal Models of Mentoring: Choosing Compassion Over Inquiry, *Mentoring & Tutoring: Partnership in Learning,* 13:2, 169-188.

# 10 Collaborative professional learning through observing practice

*Andrea McIlhatton Cardow*

## Objectives

This chapter examines mentoring approaches to observations of practice, focusing on:

- understanding the importance of the mentoring relationship, as it impacts on the processes involved in completing observations of new teachers teaching;
- knowing how to approach observations of practice to support the professional development of the new teacher and support the professional learning of the observer; and
- understanding the processes involved in completing observations of new teachers' classroom practice in order to know how to effectively manage these.

## Introduction

Observations of new teachers' practice by their mentors are a central component of induction programmes in Scotland. It is essential that, through a series of observations, both the mentor and new teacher work in partnership to explore practice, linking this with theory towards the attainment of the standard required of all teachers, the Professional Standard for Full Registration (SFR) (The General Teaching Council for Scotland (GTCS), n.d.a).

## Observations: Professional learning, relationships and teacher identity

In Scotland, teacher professional development is endorsed through a collaborative culture of individually identified needs (Donaldson, 2010; Scottish Government, 2011, 2016). Teachers, in large part, work in cellular classrooms, which presents the risk of them being cut off from interaction with colleagues, and so from intervention in their thought processes or ways of approaching problem situations. Having methodologies to support those entering the profession to avoid this becoming intrinsic in their work ethic would have advantages. Observations of practice, as a means of collaborative working, offer such opportunity. Through professional interactions between the mentor and the new teacher, practice is shared, stimulating dialogue and discussion of thoughts and ideas. This interaction creates new learning, which in turn, improves practice. It utilises collaboration to deeply engage with practice and focuses on this over a period of time. Interaction with others extends the learning that is possible through individual endeavour alone, with what can be achieved jointly superseding that

DOI: 10.4324/9780429356957-13

which can be achieved independently. Collaborative learning combines the knowledge and skills of those involved. With this, practice is not only shared but new knowledge and skills, arrived at through the synthesis of shared knowledge and skills, are co-constructed. This aligns with the theoretical underpinning of Vygotsky's Zone of Proximal Development (ZPD) (Vygotsky, 1978), which defines the distance between what can be learned independently and what can be learned through collaboration.

---

## Task 10.1  Reflection on collaborative professional learning

Reflect on your school's approach to the professional learning of staff. Is there an ethos of collaboration? What specifically is done that constitutes collaborative learning? Consider how you contribute to this and how you can use such approaches to work collaboratively with new teachers in undertaking observations of their practice. Note down what you can do to approach observations of the new teacher's practice in a collaborative way. You will review this again at the end of this chapter.

---

The importance of the mentor/new teacher relationship cannot be underestimated; the learner's emotional state must be conducive to learning. That is, they must be mentally attuned to learning, which is best arrived at when they feel confident, comfortable and reassured. It stands to reason, therefore, that shared understanding of purpose, to promote a climate of trust, openness and honesty, should be established. It is important to recognise that there are issues of power and control in human interactions (Foucault, 1992), and in the mentoring arrangement itself (Mackie, 2020), in order that these can be defined and, in so doing, be named in such a way that their influence is negated by agreement. Mentoring requires speaking about developing professionalism through partnership, and failing to define this leaves the interpretation open to the politics of control. Naming and defining this control can prevent 'external influence being exerted on the profession' or, in this instance, on new teachers, and instead allows them 'to account for their own professionalism in relation to the principles that they themselves hold dear' (Kennedy and Doherty, 2012: 840). Conducting observations of practice requires an effective mentoring relationship as a prerequisite so that new teachers do not feel daunted or intimidated by the process and the critical analysis of practice and feedback that it involves. This is central to success as it supports 'motivational, contextual and professional aspects' (Flores, 2017: 2) of practice. Observations, with their required need for critical analysis of practice and sharing of feedback, can expose new teachers to a range of complex and negative emotions, which can impact their motivation and affect their abilities (OECD, 2009; Day and Gu, 2010; Voss and Kunter, 2020). Through establishing a sound mentoring relationship, new teachers can trust in their mentor to have their best interests at heart and so fully engage with the mentoring process.

Emotions strongly influence the structuring of teacher identities (Roffey, 2011). That teachers identify positively with who and what they are as professionals is important in supporting their ongoing engagement with their job. This is particularly so for new teachers; as they begin to formulate personal and professional identities, these influence their ways of thinking and learning within their environments. It is therefore important to support positive construction of these identities. Mifsud (2018) draws attention to 'the symbiotic relationship between identity as navigating between experiences and making sense of the same experiences' (Mifsud, 2018: 6). It is precisely the role of the mentor, through carrying out observations, to support the new teacher in reflecting on experiences and understanding them. So, in accordance with what Mifsud states, the mentor is in a pivotal position to support the new teacher's forming identity. Maintaining focus on this, as opposed to 'teachers' effectiveness ... (being) ... implicitly and explicitly equated with measurable performance outcomes' (Hong et al., 2018), is important. It is important in the broader consideration of teacher identity, but it is crucial for beginning teachers, whose beliefs have been identified as being 'formed very early during their schooldays' (Voss and Kunter, 2020: 294). Roffey (2011) emphasises that the perceptions new teachers hold of themselves – their personal emotional literacy – are crucial for increasing positivity and resilience. Supporting positive development of such perceptions is vital in a school environment, which is often fraught with the various emotional challenges presented by 'work overload, a loss of spontaneity and reflective time, an increase in stress and a burgeoning of bureaucracy' (Mackenzie, 2012: 1067). These are factors identified as instrumental in teacher 'burn-out', resulting in teachers leaving the profession (Voss and Kunter, 2020). The need, therefore, to address them from the outset is essential. Observations within teacher induction can, and should, be approached as shared learning experiences that address teachers' emotional awareness, to support belief in self-competence and pedagogic efficacy. Mentors can facilitate this by, for example, inviting the new teacher into their classrooms to see them teaching and to teach collaboratively with them, both prior to the first observation and as an ongoing element of their collaborative engagement.

---

### Task 10.2   Reflection on the role of emotions

Consider the role that emotions can play during an observation. They can be particularly heightened for both the mentor and the new teacher. What can be done to support the emotional development and resilience of the new teacher? What approaches can be taken to ensure accurate feedback with recognition of its impact on the new teacher? Note down any thoughts you have in relation to this and consider them again after reading the next section.

---

## Mentoring through observations

In consideration of a framework for observations, three specific formats are given as valid and reliable when incorporated into a supportive induction programme:

- Formal observations
- Informal observations
- Peer observations

## Formal observations

As a national requirement for new teachers in Scotland obtaining full registration with GTCS, a series of observations of their teaching practice needs to be conducted and evidenced. For those on the Scottish national Teacher Induction Scheme (TIS) (GTCS, n.d.b), a minimum of nine observations across the induction year is specified. Fitting with the democratic philosophy of teacher induction in Scotland, the new teacher and the mentor work in conjunction with one another to plan for and ensure that these observations are completed; the whole process is about working in partnership.

By adopting a mentoring approach to professional discussions, mentors initially agree a set of development priorities with the new teacher. These are linked to the SFR (GTCS, n.d.a) and identify key focuses spanning the three professional capacities: being a teacher in Scotland (encompassing values and commitments); professional knowledge and understanding; and professional skills and abilities. The process of observations should be fully aligned with consideration of and reflection on the SFR. Mentors need to embody the values and commitments that are at the heart of the professional standards, for this is the foundation on which their support should be built. This premise incorporates recognising and challenging unconscious bias (Scottish Government, 2010). Values influence perceptions and actions. A mentor's observation of a new teacher's practice, their subsequent evaluation of this, and the feedback they provide, will be coloured by what they themselves believe about teaching and learning, and what the school's values and principles are and the policies and practices it endorses. This will also affect the way in which the mentor assesses the new teacher against this capacity of the SFR and how they will guide and advise them in meeting it. It is therefore important for mentors to ensure that they actively reflect and evaluate themselves against the central capacity of being a teacher in Scotland. In addition, the values and commitments focus on attitudes to learning and capacity for learning align with Bruner's (1996) statement that:

> Teaching ... is inevitably based on notions about the nature of the learner's mind. Beliefs and assumptions about teaching ... are a direct reflection of the beliefs and assumptions the teacher holds about the learner.
>
> (Bruner, 1996: 46)

It follows that what one believes about learning and teaching will impact on the way in which knowledge is constructed. Through the process of observations, which involve looking, reflecting, discussing, evaluating and implementing change, knowledge in context is understood; intellect is intentionally developed towards the new teacher becoming independent in their practice. Knowledge is built on personal experience, and from engaging in dialogue to explore practice, understanding is achieved.

Knowledge and understanding manifest in skills and abilities. Ryle (1990) identified this as 'know-how' or 'practical' knowledge. Observations give direct access to this. Seeing what the new teacher does and how they do it should open up insights into their values, commitments, knowledge and understanding, as this is reflected in their classroom practice. The SFR provides a structured framework against which these aspects of what it is to be a teacher can be measured. For each capacity, through reflection against the competencies and focuses, the mentor and the new teacher can jointly evaluate the new teacher's practice. GTCS provide various tools for such reflection and evaluation. Their website contains easily accessible materials such as Coaching Wheels and Self-Evaluation templates, along with guides on their use (GTCS, n.d.c).

---

## Task 10.3   Self-evaluation

Have a look at the materials available on the GTCS website and consider how using a Coaching Wheel or Self-Evaluation template could support you to engage with the new teacher in reflecting on their practice.

---

It is from such reflection that development priorities are identified. These then form a set of targets for the new teacher. Around five to six targets (one or two in each of the three professional capacities of the SFR) are set. Progress in these targets is monitored and shared through weekly dialogue. The targets are then reviewed at the end of a block or term and the next set of targets is agreed. The new teacher is instrumental in identifying their own development priorities and in refining these through discussions with their mentor. The agreed targets are formalised in a series of Professional Development Action Plans and form the focus for agreeing key aspects of practice to be addressed through observations. For each observation, one or two of the focuses from the SFR should be identified using the focus codes, for example, focus code 3.1.1 pertains to the teacher's ability to 'Plan effectively to meet learners' needs' (GTCS, n.d.a: 9). These codes should be recorded in the paperwork and the feedback provided should align with them.

The approach to formal observations can be illustrated in three linked stages or iterations, which can be viewed as a spiral, with each of the three stages being interlinked and the third stage informing the first stage of the next cycle. Learning takes place by building knowledge and understanding through professional dialogue and shared practice to improve skills, abilities and professional dispositions, which are then reflected in values and commitments (Figure 10.1).

### 1. Pre-observation (planning)

Observations should be viewed not as tools for critiquing the new teacher's practice but as opportunities to explore that practice while considering the development targets and the SFR more broadly. Starting with a focused mentoring conversation facilitates the process (see Chapter 7). This should support the new teacher by guiding them in identifying key aspects of practice that will form the focus of the observation. If sharing a lesson plan follows, through mentoring dialogue, the new teacher can be guided in realising and addressing any potential issues. Any agreed planning format can be used;

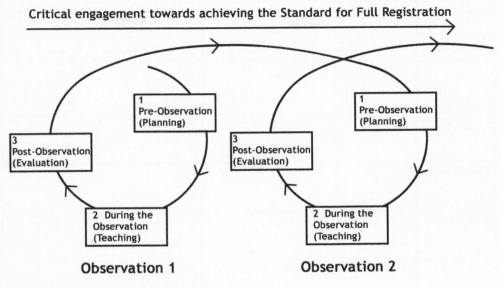

**Critical engagement towards achieving the Standard for Full Registration**

Figure 10.1 Iterative observation cycle

it should not be complex but should outline the key elements of the lesson. See the following example:

| |
|---|
| Probationer: |
| Mentor: |
| Stage/Subject: |
| Focus from SFR: |
| Duration: |
| Comment: |
| Lesson Title: |
| Stage/Year: |
| Date: |
| Prior Knowledge (link to previous learning and Curriculum for Excellence (CFE)): |
| Curricular Area: |
| Learning Intentions: |
| Success Criteria (Link to CfE, Experiences & Outcomes): |
| Assessment: |

| |
|---|
| Resources: |
| Lesson Structure (teaching strategies and activities, including ensuring learning is accessible to all pupils): |
| Extension: |
| Plenary/Evaluation: |
| Next Steps: |

---

## Task 10.4   Sharing a lesson plan

Consider how you could use a plan to support a new teacher in addressing aspects of a proposed lesson that might be identified as *problematic*.

---

In jointly reviewing the lesson plan, the mentor can ask pertinent questions to support the new teacher in thinking through aspects of the proposed lesson, for example, 'What if …? What do you think might happen if …? How will you ensure that …? What could you try in order to …? How will you know '…?' Dialogue such as this can engage the new teacher in critically focusing on a range of important planning considerations. It can, for example, assist by reviewing the lesson aims and objectives to ensure clarity and shared understanding of the lesson purpose. This also helps with building the new teacher's developing curricular knowledge to understand learning progression. It can be used to examine lesson structure and support the development of knowledge and understanding of the important elements of a lesson, and how to pace teaching to address each of them appropriately to meet pupil needs and ensure assessment of learning.

The role of the mentor during the observation should be part of the pre-observation discussion and be agreed so that both the new teacher and mentor are as confident as can be with the way the observation will be conducted. Teacher agency, along with factors that can either promote or discredit this, should be given due consideration (Day and Gu, 2010; Mackenzie, 2012; Flores, 2017; Heikkinen, 2017; Voss and Kunter, 2020). Approaches to mentoring dialogue are outlined in Chapter 7, and are crucial in that they permeate all aspects of mentoring support and have particular relevance in the dialogue required around observations. There is no definitive way of structuring such dialogue, but models such as the GROW model (Whitmore, 2017) and the Mentoring Conversation models, developed by The New Teacher Center (NTC) (NTC, n.d.a.) and endorsed by GTCS and Education Scotland

(ES) (Livingston and Shiach, 2013), prove very worthwhile in framing approaches that can be taken to guide new teachers to their own realisation of their practice and how best to adapt this to meet individual pupil needs. Careful consideration of the language used is important so as to not make decisions for the new teacher or to make them feel discredited but to guide them in identifying solutions themselves. (This is discussed below in '3. Post-observation (evaluation)'.) The dialogue should also establish the key objectives of the observations:

- intended not to be 'show' lessons but to give accurate insight into day-to-day learning and teaching;
- support the new teacher towards autonomy in their practice through realisation of the capacities and competences of the SFR;
- track the new teacher's progress in meeting the SFR;
- provide agreed methodologies and strategies to further the new teacher's progress;
- place the mentor in an informed position to provide supportive feedback that will direct the new teacher to further engagement that can support their practice; and
- facilitate meaningful collaboration within the reciprocal benefits of the mentor/new teacher relationship.

## 2. During the observation (teaching)

Collaboration and collegiate working exist as an inherent part of practice in many schools. Conducting classroom observations as part of a process of collaborative learning links with this ethos. This ensures the new teacher's position with their pupils is not undermined; the pupils do not perceive their new teacher as being monitored or 'checked' by the more experienced mentor, with whom they are likely to be familiar and so could easily perceive as being in a position of authority over the new teacher. Such perceptions can instill negative attitudes in pupils towards the new teacher and, as previously noted, can feed anxieties and stresses identified in new teachers (Day and Gu, 2010; Mackenzie, 2012; Voss and Kunter, 2020).

It is a prerequisite that the mentor gathers evidence of practice and of pupil engagement and learning during the observation; the purpose of which is twofold. It provides concrete evidence with which the unfolding lesson can be discussed in the next stage (outlined below in '3. Post-observation (evaluation)'). Quality evidence is influential in achieving the objectives outlined previously to support new teachers in managing their developing professional identities towards autonomy. Secondly, it provides evidence required by GTCS of the new teacher meeting the SFR. It is essential that, whatever method of recording is used and in whatever format this is stored, the General Data Protection Regulation (GDPR) is adhered to in order to comply fully with legal obligations (The European Parliament and The Council of The European Union, 2016). To record the observation, freehand notes can be taken in a notebook or on a digital device. It is beneficial to agree a format in advance; this provides some reassurance to the new teacher through giving a framework for the aspects of their practice that will be commented on. There are various ways in which to do this. To provide some concrete guidance, two particular methods are presented below, which have been chosen based on the ease with which they can be implemented and due to the rich data that they can provide for the joint analysis of the lesson.

## Method 1: Floor plan (adapted from the New Teacher Center's 'Our Resources', 2021)

Drawing up a simple floor plan of the classroom provides a valuable observation recording format. Lines are drawn on the plan to track the new teacher's position and movement around the classroom. Times can be noted at each position to record how long was spent on each part of the lesson. Codes can be set to indicate important aspects of the lesson and be inserted into the plan as the lesson unfolds. For example, inserting S+ or S– to indicate that the new teacher said something positive or negative or inserting B beside a particular group or pupil's desk to indicate that there was a behaviour issue. The plan can then be used to simply and easily gather a wealth of data that supports analysis of the lesson through exploring the new teacher's positioning in the physical space of the classroom and their interactions with the pupils in terms of teaching and classroom management. Afterwards it should be shared to generate dialogue that can explore, for example:

- the structure of the lesson – How much time was spent on each part of the lesson? How much time was spent with each group? Was this appropriate? Why? Why not?; and
- the levels of engagement with the pupils and their engagement with each other – What type of interaction was there with specific pupils? Was this supportive? Could it have been approached differently? Why were some groups not given teaching input? Should they have been? What was said to pupils? What impact did this have? What could have been done to improve pupil learning? Etc.

## Method 2: Recording dialogue (adapted from the New Teacher Center's 'Our Resources', 2021)

Recording the dialogue between the teacher and the pupils during the observed lesson, and recording the breakdown of the lesson through noting the time frames, provides a useful format for reflective examination of the teaching and learning that took place, as revealed through the communicative interactions of the teacher with their pupils. This can be used to identify where productive changes can be made in spoken communications. The recording of the time frames throughout the lesson, used in conjunction with critical reading of the dialogue, can support exploration of the pace of the lesson and where this was appropriate or could have been improved.

This can promote discussion around, for example:

- the time taken for each part of the lesson (introduction, main learning activity, formative assessment) – Was this appropriate? What might have been a better way to do this?;
- whether questioning could have been improved – What higher order questions could have been used? What questioning strategies could have been used to include all pupils?;
- what could have been done to check pupil understanding – What can be done when it is clear that not all pupils do understand?;
- what resources could have better supported pupils to engage with the lesson; and
- what teaching and learning took place.

If the data gathered is used to feedback in conjunction with the new teacher's own self-reflection on the lesson (see '3. Post-observation (evaluation)'), the feedback is strengthened through engaging the new teacher in their own critical appraisal of their teaching and of pupil learning. It thus supports the meta-cognitive engagement that new teachers need to be effectively self-directing.

While there is no definitive way of conducting the observation, it is beneficial for mentors to utilise a variety of approaches to identify what best suits the individual learning styles and needs of the new teacher. This also allows mentors to be confident in carefully observing and identifying aspects of practice that merit recognition and that require improvement. In essence, these approaches fall into one of two categories:

- Straightforward looking and note taking

Here, the mentor acts in an objective capacity as a removed observer, detached from the learning and teaching; almost as an 'invisible' presence in the classroom. This links to the previous discussion of professional values; mentors need to be conscious of how they interpret what they see and avoid making assumptions based on their own ways of teaching, thus addressing potential issues of unconscious bias (Scottish Government, 2010). It may be argued that this method adheres to a traditionalist paradigm, and while this facilitates close scrutiny to aid ongoing improvement, it can be daunting for the new teacher as it posits the mentor as the knowledge holder in a hierarchical structure, having the privilege to sit and observe. Such a privilege confers certain power over the new teacher as novice, having to impress and meet criteria and expectations. That said, the value of this approach in allowing the mentor to fully focus on the learning and teaching, and so to be in an informed position to provide tailored and supportive feedback, is undoubtedly an important consideration, especially when the focus of the observation has been agreed beforehand. In addition, if a productive mentoring relationship is in place (see earlier section, 'Observations: Professional learning, relationships and teacher identity'), the issues of power and authority can be negated.

- Active participation in the lesson

When the mentor is an active participant in the learning and teaching process, there exists a visible sign of their seeking to balance the issues of power and influence, and the approach can facilitate a social-constructivist partnership (Voss and Kunter, 2020). By working from the ideological basis that both mentor and new teacher are co-constructors of learning and teaching, their interactions structure joint understanding and development of professional and affective knowledge, which translates into mutually agreed practice where ongoing personal and professional development is reciprocal.

### 3. Post-observation (evaluation)

Immediately following the observation, it is appropriate that some verbal feedback be given. It is advisable to keep this brief. If the lesson has gone well, it is usually straightforward to provide such feedback. If, however, the lesson has not gone well, or if concerns have arisen in relation to competence within the SFR through what was observed in relation to the agreed targets, then care needs to be taken to ensure the messages given throughout are clear and consistent. In such cases it might be appropriate for the observer to simply thank the new teacher for sharing their classroom practice and state that the observation will be followed up in the manner agreed.

---

### Task 10.5    Sharing feedback in a productive way

Consider how you can share the feedback you want to give in a way that will be informative and beneficial for the new teacher while ensuring that key points for improvement are understood. How can you support the new teacher in making required changes to their practice to realise these improvements?

---

Bearing in mind the key objective of supporting the new teacher towards independence, within a structure that recognises their central role in guiding their own professional journey and so in having ownership of this, it is beneficial to take a collaborative approach to reviewing the lesson. Adoption of a constructive methodology allows for observations of classroom practice to be conducted in a way that guides the new teacher to their own identification of the principal challenges and understanding of the ways in which these can best be approached. A good way to do this is to encourage written self-reflection following the observation and to use this as part of the data for analysing the lesson.

Having their own reflections recorded in concrete format can be advantageous in supporting new teachers in being instrumental in guiding the post-observation discussion. Bearing in mind the points made previously about power and control (see earlier section, 'Observations: Professional learning, relationships and teacher identity'), it is important to recognize that the new teacher's voice should be central to the discussions. The mentor should guide the dialogue through appropriate questions and with careful consideration of the language used. The dialogue should be reflective, supporting the new teacher's developing meta-cognition. The NTC developed a resource to support such dialogue through classifying specific use of language to aid a mentoring conversation. This is available on the NTC website (NTC, n.d.b) as a chart of Facilitative Coaching Stems. These are fully exemplified in the Mentor Language section of the NTC Toolbox for Mentors and Coaches, which can be accessed from the resources tab on their website. Materials to support mentors in understanding and using language in mentoring conversations are also available on the Education Scotland website. Approaching the post-observation discussion in this way, the mentor can start by focusing on the new teacher's perceptions of their practice and, by sharing their own evidence that was collected during the observation, can guide and direct the new teacher's critical analysis skills.

## Informal observations

While formal observations should not be approached as 'show' lessons, the inclination on the part of new teachers to approach them in this way is difficult to negate as the tendency is to want to demonstrate a polished example of their teaching. Therefore, where there is scope to include what might be termed 'informal observations', which are short (5 to 10 minutes) visits by the mentor to the new teacher's class, outwith the formal observations, there is benefit to be gained as they give an insight into routine practices. Such observations should be agreed in advance of them happening, but the process for completing them does not adhere to that for formal observations. Rather, these are opportunities for the mentor to gain accurate insight into what the new teacher's day-to-day practice is. Having this information allows the mentor to liaise with school management and other colleagues to provide an appropriately tailored programme of in-school support. This support will include opportunities for the new teacher to observe and teach with both their mentor and other colleagues, with a focus on the new teacher's development needs as identified through the observations. This is an invaluable part of the new teacher's professional learning programme. It serves not only to give enriched learning opportunities but works on the principle of collaboration and evidences the benefits of such working, as discussed above. It works on reciprocal learning and engages those involved in processes of meta-cognition (Zepeda et al., 2019).

## Peer observations

Following the changes outlined previously around the conceptions of valuable professional learning and in supporting new teachers in meeting the SFR, which specifies the need for engagement in practitioner enquiry, induction programmes began to be restructured to include an enquiry project. This sees new teachers engage with a structured model to allow them to systematically identify an aspect of their practice and explore the impact of it on pupil learning over time, with the aim of gaining informed insights to improve pupil learning. Practitioner enquiries can be completed independently or collaboratively. The collaborative model allows new teachers to form small working groups with their peers in their own schools (where there is more than one new teacher in a school) and across other schools and sectors in the authority. This, in effect, creates teacher learning communities, or small communities of practice (Wenger, 1998, 2010; Lave and Wenger, 1991). These facilitate inter-school visits, with new teachers having the opportunity to learn from each other within reciprocal classroom visits and/or discussions on practice and reflection. The benefits of this are numerous and the opportunity it presents for peer observations is invaluable.

Conducted in this way, peer observations differ in structure and tone from mentor observations, whether formal or informal. They can be beneficial in a way that mentor observations cannot be as a result of the inherent synergetic relationship existing between peers. Observations are undertaken more as classroom visits between equals, so can completely negate the subtle issues of power play that can interfere with the dynamics of mentor observations. In addition, they facilitate the building of networks for new teachers to support their ongoing professional development.

While there is intrinsic value in this approach, its realisation is not always straightforward. This is down to timetabling. It is relatively simple to structure practitioner enquiry for those on the TIS as they can plan to carry out peer observations during part of their weekly professional learning time (0.2 Full Time Equivalent). However, it is not always so easy to match one new teacher's professional learning time to another's teaching time. Authority-wide appreciation of the value of the model and the benefit of the experiences it provides to new teachers is instrumental in individual school management factoring in flexibility across the weekly timetables to support this.


## Remote observations

In addition to the three main formats of observations specified, there is also an additional format, which brings with it its own advantages. This is remote observation, and the above recommendations can be used to support such observations using communication technologies. This is, of course, subject to the appropriate permissions being in place regarding filming and/or recording of pupils and the use of such media. Such observations would be completed by the new teacher filming their lesson and uploading to a validated platform, from which the mentor can then access the digital file. The teaching can then be reviewed separately and/or jointly by the mentor and the new teacher via an online video meeting, which can take place using any platform agreed by the local authority. Being able to view their teaching in this way can support new teachers in seeing their teaching differently, from a more objective standpoint. It can facilitate identification of aspects of practice where improvements can be made that may not otherwise have been apparent to them. The benefits of remote observations have been identified as:

• supporting new teachers in shifting their evaluation focus from themselves to their pupils, so supports teachers in seeing the lesson from the perspective of the pupils, leading to them better addressing improvements in their practice to benefit pupil learning;
• providing evidence of the teaching and learning, negating the need for the observer to gather evidence themselves;
• facilitating analysis of the lesson by allowing it to be observed more than once and from different perspectives;
• supporting the development of reflective skills, leading to deeper reflection on practice; and
• supporting changes in teachers' beliefs.

(Hamel and Viau-Guay, 2019)

In addition to the benefits given here, in times of social distancing restrictions, such an approach could prove invaluable. It is also a means of engagement that will already be familiar to some new teachers, as a number of Scottish universities that provide teacher education courses utilize this approach for student observations. There are online platforms that support such activity and ensure compliance with the GDPR. Individual authority communications or IT departments should be able to advise and provide support with this.

If there is reticence around filming a taught lesson, then real-time streaming of the lesson is an alternative. Using available online meeting platforms, which are compliant with the GDPR, a meeting link can be used to open up a visual link between a mentor working remotely and the new teacher teaching their lesson in class. While this can address difficulties that might arise in carrying out observations when social distancing measures are in place, it does not include the benefits outlined above that are inherent in having a visual recording of the lesson. Teaching points may be missed and cannot be 'rewound', requiring close observation by the mentor of the unfolding lesson.

## Summary and key points

Teacher induction, with its inherent challenges, certainly brings new teachers to question 'the meanings, values, images and ideals of what it means to be a teacher' (Day and Gu, 2010: 67). Observations of their practice can be viewed by them with apprehension, but reassurance through the approaches outlined here can halt this and, moreover, can support developing identities towards commitment and enjoyment of the job. Observations are a key element of responsive professional development. They can and should support new teachers in reviewing their identities through discussing thoughts, feelings, attitudes and pedagogic positions, and questioning these. The reciprocity of the process should also facilitate this for their mentors. Induction, ultimately, should guide new teachers and their mentors in a renewing of professional identities, frequently challenged by the demands of teaching, to produce a renewed belief in their abilities to make a difference to the lives of their pupils, thus supporting an ongoing desire and commitment to teach.

> ## Task 10.6   Final reflection
>
> Consider your response to Task 10.1. Is there anything that you now think differently about or would change in the way in which you would provide support to a new teacher when undertaking observations of their practice? What are the key learning points for you, as a mentor?

## Further reading

Archer J., Cantrell S., Holtzman L.S., Joe N.J., Tocci M.C. and Wood J. (2016) *Better Feedback for Better Teaching A Practical Guide to Improving Classroom Observations*, San Francisco: Jossey-Bass.
O'Leary M. (2020) *Classroom Observation: A Guide to the Effective Observation of Teaching and Learning*, 2nd edition, London: Routledge.

## References

Bruner J. (1996) *The Culture of Education*, Harvard University Press: Boston.
Day C. and Gu Q. (2010) *The New Lives of Teachers*, Oxford: Routledge.
Donaldson G. (2010) *Teaching Scotland's Future: Report of a Review of Teacher Education in Scotland*. Edinburgh: The Scottish Government. Available online at https://www.webarch ive.org.uk/wayback/archive/20190701211038/https://www2.gov.scot/resource/doc/337 626/0110852.pdf (Accessed 25 June 2020)
Flores M.A. (2017) The complexities and challenges of be(com)ing a teacher and a teacher educator, *European Journal of Teacher Education*, 40 (1) 2-5.
Foucault M. (1992) *Discipline and Punish*, London: Penguin.

Hamel C. and Viau-Guay A. (2019) Using video to support teachers' reflective practice: A literature review, *Cogent Education*, 6 (1) 1-14.

Heikkinen H.L.T. (2017) Mentoring of Newly Qualified Teachers in the Educational Sense. In: Peters M., Cowie B. and Menter I. (eds) *A Companion to Research in Teacher Education*. Singapore: Springer (pp. 813-824).

Hong J., Day C. and Greene B. (2018) The construction of early career teachers' identities: Coping or managing?, *Teacher Development* 22 (2) 249-266.

Kennedy A. and Doherty R. (2012) Professionalism and partnership: Panaceas for teacher education in Scotland?, *Journal of Educational Policy*, 27 (6) 835-848.

Lave J. and Wenger E. (1991) *Situated Learning: Legitimate Peripheral Participation*, Cambridge: Cambridge University Press.

Livingston K. and Shiach, L. (2013) *Teaching Scotland's Future, Mentoring Pilot Partnership Project: Final Report*. Project Report, Livingston, UK: Education Scotland.

Mackenzie S. (2012) 'It's been a bit of a rollercoaster': Special educational needs, emotional labour and emotion work, *International Journal of Inclusive Education*, 16 (10) 1067-1082.

Mackie L. (2020) Understandings of mentoring in school placement settings within the context of initial teacher education in Scotland: Dimensions of collaboration and power, *Journal of Education for Teaching*, 46 (3) 263-280.

Mifsud D. (2018) Setting the Stage for Student Teacher Identities in Initial Teacher Education. In: Mifsud, D. (ed.) *Professional Identities in Initial Teacher Education: The Narratives and Questions of Teacher Agency*, London: Palgrave Macmillan (pp 1-20).

Organisation for Economic Development (OECD) (2009) Teaching Practices, Teachers' Beliefs and Attitudes. In: OECD, *Creating Effective Teaching and Learning Environments: First Results From TALIS*, OECD Publishing. Available online at http://www.oecd.org/berlin/43541655.pdf (Accessed 17 February 2021)

Roffey S. (2011) *The New Teacher's Survival Guide to Behaviour*, 2nd edition, London: Sage.

Ryle G. (1990) *The Concept of Mind*, Chicago: Chicago University Press.

Scottish Government (2010) *Equality Act 2010*. Available online at https://www.legislation.gov.uk/ukpga/2010/15/contents (Accessed 2 July 2021)

Scottish Government (2011) *Advancing Professionalism in Teaching: The Report of the review of Teacher Employment in Scotland*. Edinburgh: Scottish Government. Available online at https://dera.ioe.ac.uk/10421/7/the-report-of-the-review-of-teacher-employment-in-scotland-0911_Redacted.pdf (Accessed 16 December 2021)

Scottish Government (2016) *Evaluation of the Impact of the Implementation of Teaching Scotland's Future*. Edinburgh: Scottish Government. Available online at https://www.gov.scot/publications/evaluation-impact-implementation-teaching-scotlands-future/ (Accessed 16 December 2021)

The European Parliament and The Council of The European Union (2016) Regulation (EU) 2016/679 of The European Parliament and The Council of 27 April 2016 on the protection of natural persons with regard to the processing of personal data and on the free movement of such data, and repealing Directive 95/46/EC (General Data Protection Regulation), *Official Journal of The European Union*. Available online at https://eur-lex.europa.eu/legal-content/EN/TXT/PDF/?uri=CELEX:32016R0679 (Accessed 25 June 2020)

The General Teaching Council for Scotland (GTCS) (n.d.a) *The Standard for Full Registration Mandatory Requirements for Registration with the General Teaching Council for Scotland Formal Enactment 2 August 2021*. Available online at https://www.gtcs.org.uk/wp-content/uploads/2021/09/standard-for-full-registration.pdf (Accessed 17 February 2021)

The General Teaching Council for Scotland (GTCS) (n.d.b) *Teacher Induction Scheme*. Available online at http://in2teaching.org.uk/teacher-induction-scheme/teacher-induction-scheme.aspx (Accessed 25 June 2020)

The General Teaching council for Scotland (GTCS) (n.d.c) *Professional Standards Self-Evaluation?* Available online at https://www.gtcs.org.uk/professional-standards/self-evaluation/ (Accessed 28 January 2022)

The New Teacher Centre (NTC) (n.d.a) Available online at https://newteachercenter.org/ (Accessed 17 February 2021)

The New Teacher Centre (NTC) (n.d.b) Facilitative Coaching Stems: Quick Chart https://newteachercenter.org/wp-content/uploads/2021/07/Facilitative-Coaching-Stems-Chart-Quick-Chart_RB21.pdf

The New Teacher Center (NTC) (2021) *Our Resources*. Available online at https://newteachercenter.org/resources/ (Accessed 5 July 2021)

Voss T. and Kunter M. (2020) 'Reality shock' of beginning teachers? Changes in teacher candidates' emotional exhaustion and constructivist-oriented beliefs, *Journal of Teacher Education*, 7 (3) 292–306.

Vygotsky L. (1978) *Mind in Society: The Development of Higher Psychological Processes*, Cambridge: Harvard University Press.

Wenger E. (1998) *Communities of Practice: Learning, Meaning and Identity*, Cambridge: Cambridge University Press.

Wenger E. (2010) Communities of Practice and Social Learning Systems: The Career of a Concept. In: Blackmore C. (ed.) *Social Learning Systems and Communities of Practice*, London: Springer and the Open University. Available online at http://wenger-trayner.com/wp-content/uploads/2012/01/09-10-27-CoPs-and-systems-v2.01.pdf (Accessed 28 January 2022)

Whitmore J. (2017) *The Principles and Practice of Coaching and Leadership*, 5th edition, Boston: Nicholas Brealey.

Zepeda C.D., Hlutkowsky C.O., Partika A.C. and Nokes-Malach T.J. (2019) Identifying teachers' supports of metacognition through classroom talk and its relation to growth in conceptual learning, *Journal of Educational Psychology*, 111 (3) 522–541.

# 11 Giving feedback that feeds forward

*Sandra Eady*

## Objectives

At the end of this chapter, you should be able to:

- identify practical ways to organise meaningful weekly debriefs;
- use a framework of feed up, feedback and feed forward to structure debrief meetings;
- engage in productive, evidence-informed learning conversations; and
- access research and make use of research findings.

## Introduction

This chapter will consider practical ways to structure longer, sustained feedback through weekly debriefs, enabling teachers to move beyond individual lessons. An effective weekly debrief provides greater scope for reflection and professional dialogue than post-lesson feedback. It is where productive conversations include structured feed up, feedback and feed forward, enabling the mentee to always leave a mentoring conversation knowing what to do next. This chapter specifically looks at how the mentor might manage this process with students and beginning teachers, although many of the approaches are relevant across all stages of teaching. The chapter uses Hattie and Timperley's (2007) feedback framework, together with Earl and Timperley's (2009) model of productive learning conversations, and considers practical ways for mentors to make learning visible through effective use of weekly debrief meetings.

First, the chapter will consider the practicalities of setting up weekly debriefs. Without a dedicated time and place to meet, it is difficult to provide consistent support for the student/beginning teacher and, ultimately, a structure for early professional development.

Weekly debrief meetings tend to be more productive when there is a dedicated time set aside each week. This may be best done on a Friday, enabling a reflection back on the week, or on a Monday, allowing for some reflection on the previous week in order to agree a focus for the next meeting. In other instances, a mid-week meeting might work well. The crucial aspect is finding a day that works best for both of you. When arranging a suitable time, it is also important to try to pick a time when there will be the least disruptions. Often this is at the end of the school day, although there might be opportunities to identify some non-teaching time during the week. Again, each school and context will be different, but the

DOI: 10.4324/9780429356957-14

key point is to identify a weekly time to which you can both commit. A meeting of 30 to 40 minutes is usually long enough to keep the debrief focused, allowing you to engage in meaningful dialogue.

Another important consideration is the meeting place. The ideal would be somewhere the mentee and mentor feel comfortable to engage in discussions freely without the threat of interruption from other colleagues or pupils. If meetings take place at the end of the day, this could be an empty classroom or the head teacher's office. However, in some cases, the likelihood of interruptions may mean this is not always the best place. In some settings, conducting a virtual, online meeting may be preferable and more productive (see Chapter 13 for detailed discussion about digital mentoring). Having access to the internet, to video clips or other data could also be an important consideration. A meeting on school premises might be more realistic than one outside of the premises, especially if either of you are scheduled to teach before or after the meeting.

It is a good idea to set an agenda prior to each meeting and agree a focus or any advanced preparation, although it is important to be flexible and bear in mind that things can unexpectedly arise that will need to be discussed. Finally, confirm how many meetings will take place. This might be straightforward for a student on a block of school experience, but for a teacher in the probationary year, this might need greater discussion, as weekly debriefs might be appropriate in the first term but could become fortnightly or monthly debriefs as the induction year progresses and depending on the probationary teacher's progress.

An obvious point, but one that is perhaps easily overlooked, is to agree the purpose of the weekly debriefs. At the first meeting it would be advisable to negotiate the boundaries of what can and cannot be discussed and if particular topics are considered off limits. For example, sometimes a mentee's performance in the work context could be affected by personal issues or events and the mentee may or may not wish to discuss these. Similarly, some conversations could lead to a disclosure of misconduct, incompetence or the poor practice of other colleagues or a subject department that either directly or indirectly affects the student or beginning teacher. Such disclosure of information, and depending on the status of the mentor, could also have other implications in terms of a wider management responsibility within the educational setting, especially so if the mentor has a managerial role within the school. For more information on role boundaries see Chapter 1.

Another important and related consideration is how the power balance between mentor and mentee might influence who sets the agenda, decides the focus for the meeting and leads the discussion. Mentor and mentee might have differing assumptions about the agenda of weekly debriefs or how open or structured the meetings should be. Much of the literature suggests that the mentee should identify the focus and content, and lead or direct the discussion, if they are to have ownership or progress their teaching. If the mentee is reluctant to take the lead, it might be appropriate to take it in turns to lead alternative weekly debriefings, or to mutually agree the focus in advance of each meeting. However, it is important for the mentee to increasingly self-evaluate and identify areas for development as the placement or probationary year progresses. It is worth bearing in mind that if it is the mentor who is also making judgments about the quality of teaching, or whether the school placement or induction year is satisfactory, then it is likely this could affect how honest the mentee might be during the weekly debrief. If the mentor is not directly involved in the assessment process, then it is likely that the mentee may discuss strengths and issues more openly. This can be dependent on the development of a trusting relationship. Chapter 1 provides further discussion on the importance of co-mentoring/learning.

Hattie (2015) suggests that for students in Higher Education, learning is as much about identity, reputational enhancement and growth as it is about becoming knowledgeable critics and problem solvers. This is particularly the case for teachers in the early career phase. Rose and Eriksson (2017) suggest that perceived priorities and concerns for student and beginning teachers can be categorised under two broad headings of relationship building with pupils and managing excessive workload related to learning and teaching (see Table 11.1). These are often seen as key priorities in the early career phase and students and beginning teachers indirectly relate this to how they see themselves as 'credible' teachers. This, in turn, can impact on self-efficacy, and whether a student or beginning teacher continues in or leaves the profession. It would seem logical that the content for weekly debriefings might focus on the intersection of managing relationships and learning and teaching linked to relevant teaching standards. If there is an issue with subject content, for example, this may be the focus for three weeks until the issue is resolved, then another challenge or standard could be addressed, for example, relationships with pupils, differentiated teaching and so on, according to the specific areas for development of the mentee. The General Teaching Council for Scotland (GTCS) suggest selecting two or three standards to focus on in meetings. However, it is important to note that individual needs of mentees are so variable that it might sometimes be difficult to specify the focus of weekly debriefs. The key thing is flexibility so that weekly debriefs are always as meaningful as possible for the mentee.

*Table 11.1* Student/beginning teachers' perceived priorities

| Managing relationships | Learning and teaching |
| --- | --- |
| • On task learning | • Marking and assessment of learning |
| • Understanding behaviour | • Planning |
| • Motivating pupils | • Differentiation |
| • Setting ground rules | • Classroom organisation and management |
| • Managing challenging behaviour | • Teaching strategies and responsive teaching |
| • Knowledge of learners' additional support needs | • Managing and prioritising work load |
| | • Teacher explanations and questions |
| | • Subject knowledge |

Adapted from Rose and Eriksson (2017)

---

### Task 11.1   Weekly debriefs

As a mentor, consider the following:

• How will you structure weekly briefings in terms of day/time/place?
• Who will set the focus/agenda and lead/guide the discussion during weekly debriefs?
• Are there any topics that are off limits?

- To what extent do you envisage weekly debriefs to be concerned with practical matters, for example, of building relationships/teaching and learning?
- Will the meetings reference relevant theory and research, teaching standards or school priorities?

## Structuring weekly debrief meetings

It is easy for weekly debriefs to become a platform for the mentee to offload everything that has happened during the previous week and for the mentor to provide emotional support, a listening ear or sympathy. Without any focus or structure to the meetings, this can take up most of the time, leaving little space for productive dialogue or deeper probing of some of the issues or opportunities to make connections between practical learning and relevant theory. Weekly debriefs can be considered as ongoing professional development for the student/beginning teacher, where classroom incidents and practices can be reflected upon in more depth and in relation to relevant theory and research. Thus, there needs to be some structure or preparation beforehand so that such debriefings are valuable for both mentee and mentor.

A measure of a good weekly debrief is when the mentee leaves feeling positive and knowing what to do next. This implies there will be some reflection of overall goals in relation to professional values, current practice and the steps needed to get there. At the beginning teacher stage there also needs to be reflection and discussion about one or two of the teaching standards, as they are mandatory for students and probationers. Hattie and Timperley's (2007) model, which illustrates the powerful effect of feedback on pupil learning, could provide an effective framework for getting the mentee to think more deeply about their practice. What makes the model distinctive is that the three feedback questions can be focused at four different levels, meaning it can help make all teachers more effective in their teaching and in the way they motivate and encourage children to learn (see Figure 11.1).

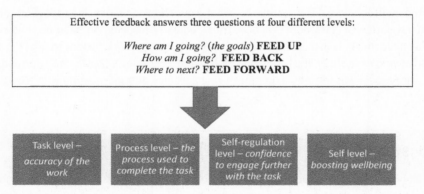

*Figure 11.1* A framework for structuring dialogue about learning and teaching
Adapted from Hattie and Timperley (2007)

*Table 11.2* Using the feedback questions with student or beginning teachers

---

**FEED UP** Where am I going? (What are the goals?)

For student/beginning teachers it is important to help identify goals – the ideal situation. What would be their underlying values? Where would they see their current practice in relation to this?

**FEEDBACK** How am I going? (What progress is being made towards the goal?)

For student/beginning teachers it is important to reflect on the effectiveness of particular (sequences of) lessons, strategies and resources employed, and how particular actions, framing of teacher questions and the use of inclusive pedagogies lead to positive behaviour and relationships in relation to moving towards the main goal.

**FEED FORWARD** Where to next? (What activities need to be undertaken to make better progress?)

For student/beginning teachers it is important to identify the likely steps they need to take to reach the goal. Also, to consider if the goal is realistic in light of current practice. For example, is it too broad or general, and thus needs to be more focused? Does the goal still relate to underlying values?

---

Adapted from Hattie and Timperley (2007)

The model proposes that feedback can be most effective where there is a difference between what a pupil knows and understands already and what they need to know and understand in order to learn. To help reduce this discrepancy, Hattie and Timperley (2007) suggest that teachers should consider how the three feedback questions can increase a pupil's effort, motivation or engagement to ultimately close the gap between what they currently know, what they need to know and the steps to get there (Hattie & Timperley 2007). In the same way, mentors can use the model to structure weekly debriefs with mentees. All too often there is a tendency to focus on 'feedback' and sometimes offer advice in the form of 'feed forward'. The initial weekly debrief offers the mentor opportunities to start with the broader 'feed up' question and return to this at other times (see Table 11.2).

This approach can be used in two ways. First, it can be used by the mentor to encourage the mentee to critically reflect on and evaluate how they engage pupils during lessons in terms of teaching, learning and managing relationships. Secondly, it can be a powerful way to structure and focus reflection and discussion on their developing values and identity as a teacher, as well as their ability to build and sustain professional relationships with other colleagues. A key role for the mentor is to get the mentee to adopt a questioning stance and reflect on relevant research in relation to classroom practice. Thus, regularly focusing on 'feed up' – where am I going (as a teacher) – is just as important as 'how am I going?' and 'where to next?'

The following case study illustrates how Hattie and Timperley's (2007) feed up/feedback/feed forward model was used by a mentor during a weekly debrief meeting with a beginning teacher.

## Case Study 11.1

A beginning teacher in a primary school wanted to be the kind of teacher that gave pupils autonomy over their learning (feed up). They believed that pupils reviewing their learning and setting their own goals was key to this but often found that their maths lessons lacked pace, with some pupils frequently off-task and needing much direction to keep focused. The problem seemed to be around the ability to provide a fast-paced lesson that enabled children to review their previous learning and then move them on in their learning (feedback). In discussion with the mentor, they decided to watch a clip from a maths mastery lesson together, which is freely available from The National Centre for Excellence in the Teaching of Mathematics (NCETM): https://www.ncetm.org.uk

The mentor knew that the lesson in the video focused on the addition of fractions by breaking down the lesson into small steps (feed forward). The lesson begins with a review of unit and non-unit fractions, and then progresses to the new learning of adding fractions with the same denominator. The lesson concludes with the generalisation that 'when adding fractions with the same denominator, the denominator remains the same and the numerators are added'.

By jointly reviewing the lesson clip, both mentee and mentor were able to open up a dialogue about how the structure, pace and timing of the lesson might sustain pupil interest. They focused on how the teacher achieved a good pace to the lesson in the video by breaking the lesson down into smaller sections. This allowed the beginning teacher to compare it with the way their lessons were structured, highlighting similarities and differences. An unexpected outcome from the discussion was also the need for securer subject knowledge regarding the mathematical concepts in order to achieve the goal (feed forward).

Thus, by applying Hattie and Timperley's feed up/feedback/feed forward model at different task levels over the following weeks, the mentor and beginning teacher agreed they would place a key focus on the following:

* structuring and breaking down the learning within maths lessons (task knowledge);
* revisiting subject knowledge and conceptual understanding on the teaching of fractions (process knowledge); and
* watching the video clip several times so that the beginning teacher could familiarise herself with strategies used in the clip before trying them out, and then evaluating how effective these strategies had been in her own lessons (self-regulation).

Talking through the dilemma and practicing the strategies enabled the beginning teacher to gradually increase their confidence in their ability to improve the pace of maths lessons and, ultimately, the interest of pupils in their learning (boosting wellbeing).

Implications for the mentor included knowing about a resource bank of video clips to use with the mentee and developing an operational understanding of accessing journals through the EBSCO database, which is accessible through the GTCS website for registered teachers. The mentor also needed to be skilled in asking open questions that prompted reflection on practice and the beginning teacher to consider ways in which they could research (self-regulation and process).

## Task 11.2   Identifying personal goals

Ahead of the first weekly debrief, ask the mentee to consider the 'feed up' question in Table 11.2 to identify personal goals relating to their current practice. For student teachers this could be where they want to be by the end of a block of school experience. For beginning teachers in their induction year this might focus on goals for the end of the probationary year or for the first school term. In the initial meeting there may be some need for discussion about broader goals about becoming a teacher, such as developing teacher identity/credibility, and breaking these down into shorter term goals that are more focused on day-to-day priorities.

## Evidence-informed conversations

Often students and beginning teachers base their perceptions of 'excellent' learning and teaching and 'effective' management of relationships on anecdotal evidence or hearsay, 'hunches' or 'one-off' experiences in the classroom. Thus, it is a key role of the mentor to engage the mentee in productive learning conversations (Earl & Timperley 2009) at task, process, self-regulation and self level (see Hattie & Timperley 2007 and Figure 11.1). Weekly debrief meetings offer the opportunity to analyse perceptions and reflections more deeply, by identifying and examining the claims and the underlying values, and to explore data and research that may provide alternative interpretations and explanations. Thus, building a robust understanding of the evidence and exploring competing or alternative perspectives (also based on reliable evidence) can lead to more informed ways of making sense of experiences and actions within the classroom. For example, building stronger relationships with individual children might lead to a greater understanding of the underlying reasons as to why a child lacks focus or doesn't hand in homework. This might include a deeper knowledge of external contexts as well as academic abilities, for example, knowing they are a young carer, have no computer or internet access, or no space to work at home.

Earl and Timperley's (2009) notion of evidence-informed learning conversations could provide a foundation for mentor discussions about relationship building, as well as teaching and learning (see also Chapter 7). The basis of a learning conversation is the mutual understanding of each contributor's claims and the values, together with the reasoning and evidence, on which these are based. These processes relate to each aspect of improving practice, whether identifying the current situation and its merits and difficulties, or deciding the goals of improvement and how best to get there.

The notion of evidence-informed conversations provides mentors with a way to structure conversations with their mentees. These learning conversations are a combination of three elements, as illustrated in Figure 11.2, which can be applied to the task/process/self-regulation level of Hattie and Timperley's (2007) model. The three elements to learning conversations are discussed next.

| Using relevant data | Inquiry habit of mind | Relationships of respect and challenge |
|---|---|---|
| - *What other data could we draw upon?*<br><br>- *Is there another way of interpreting this evidence?* | - *What does the data show us?*<br><br>- *How does it benefit the learners?* | - *Do we both share the same understanding?* |

*Figure 11.2* Evidence-informed learning conversations
Adapted from Earl and Timperley (2009)

## Using relevant data

As already mentioned, sometimes we find local anecdotal knowledge more powerful than knowledge developed through research because it is more personal and is perceived to relate directly to the context in which improvement is sought (Earl & Timperley 2009). As a mentor it is important to resist drawing on anecdotal knowledge and to recognise when a mentee is doing so. Earl and Timperley (2009) suggest that all too often educational decisions are made using data that are available rather than data that are appropriate. Data might include external and contextual evidence, as well as numerical data about a pupil and local and national contexts (academic and social). Data might also include information from other professionals and from relevant research. Thus, it is important to become knowledgeable in judging the origins and value of the evidence, and for both mentor and beginning teacher to feel able to clarify the purpose of any data and mutually agree the criteria on which to judge its quality.

Weekly debriefings can provide an opportunity to engage in learning conversations where mentees identify and evaluate the quality of the evidence they have identified (Earl & Timperley 2009). This might also mean developing some knowledge about statistical and measurement concepts and how these can be or have been interpreted. If educators are going to be active in interpreting and using data, as well as challenging and disputing interpretations or uses that they believe are contestable, they must become knowledgeable in judging the value and quality of the evidence.

## Inquiry habit of mind

Earl and Timperley (2009) use the notion of an inquiry habit of mind to refer to an ongoing process of using evidence to make decisions. Inquiry is, very simply, a way of finding things out – collecting data and interpreting evidence in ways that enhance and advance understanding (Earl & Timperley 2009). Weekly debriefs can provide a space in which mentor and mentee can practice developing an inquiry habit of mind. The mentor can support by encouraging the mentee to adopt a questioning stance, either at task, process or self-regulation level (Hattie & Timperley 2007), when discussing aspects of relationship building or learning and teaching. See also the section in Chapter 1 on co-mentoring, whereby the mentor and the mentee engage in problem-solving together and use evidence during their discussion to identify next steps.

### Relationships of respect and challenge

In this context, 'respect' is not just about taking the time for the mentor and mentee to understand each other's viewpoints but is also about probing meanings, and challenging interpretations of the evidence and the reasoning on which the different viewpoints are based. Considering this at task, process and self-regulation level enables knowledge to become generic and socially constructed by both the mentor and mentee, with the merits debated and the potential flaws exposed. This is as much about challenge as it is about support, and thus, mutual trust and respect need to be key elements of a learning conversation. Chapter 1 also highlights the importance of both support and challenge within a mentoring relationship.

## Using research and developing professional scepticism

The focus, through learning conversations, should be at task, process and self-regulation level in order for mentors to support student/beginning teachers to intelligently make connections between evidence from their classrooms and high-quality research. This is summed up by the following quote:

> It is less what teachers do in their teaching, but more how they think about their role. It is their mind frames, or ways of thinking about teaching and learning, that are most critical.

(Hattie 2015:81)

Whilst this suggests that mentors need to encourage mentees to adopt a questioning attitude and willingness to interrogate claims, it also assumes that both parties will have a certain degree of background knowledge to inform this critical stance and have the skills to apply these to their practice in order to be 'intelligent consumers of research' (Rose & Eriksson 2017). In other words, mentees need to know how to select and 'read' relevant data, and make use of relevant research, to challenge meanings in order to adopt an inquiry habit of mind.

Rose and Eriksson (2017) argue that the process of becoming an 'intelligent consumer of research' can take a teacher many years, and therefore advise caution around what this actually means in relation to supporting new teachers. For example, it might be more productive for a mentor to support the mentee to intelligently use a piece of high-quality research, which the mentor or mentee has selected or sign-posted, to inform teaching and learning. In other words, discussion during the weekly debrief can then be used to support mentees to:

- make sense of specific research they encounter;
- reflect on complex ideas and concepts involved in research methods and statistics; and

- use the research evidence to help them solve the sorts of problems and challenges they encounter as novice teachers.

(Adapted from Rose and Eriksson, 2017, p.9)

However, the assumption here is that mentors and mentees know where they can access relevant research, or reviews of the latest research, and have time to read, reflect on this and embed it in their practice. Asking student/beginning teachers to recall a particular piece of research or theory from their initial teacher education (ITE) course could be a useful starting point. Some examples of how to access research and user reviews of research findings are now given.

## GTCS EBSCO Resources

The GTCS provides all fully registered teachers with free access to a range of peer reviewed education journals through EBSCO Resources (education journals, ebooks and online resources): https://www.gtcs.org.uk/professional-update/research.aspx. Scottish teachers also have access to the EducationHUB, an interactive online platform enabling education practitioners to share, discuss and review unpublished practitioner research and enquiry: https://www.gtcs.org.uk. This also supports the notion of teacher as 'enquiring professional' that sits at the heart of the Professional Standards in Scotland.

## Education Endowment Foundation (EEF)

Mentors and mentees can also make use of freely available user reviews such as those compiled by the EEF, who provide evidence-based resources designed to support a teacher's practice in the classroom and enhance pupil learning. On the EEF website the Teaching and Learning Toolkit evaluates the latest research and interventions in terms of impact and cost: https://educationendowmentfoundation.org.uk/evidence-summaries/teaching-learning-toolkit/. The Big Picture pulls together evidence from the Teaching and Learning Toolkit and EEF-funded projects, focusing on 14 high-priority issues, or themes, for schools: https://educationendowmentfoundation.org.uk/school-themes/.

## National Foundation for Educational Research (NFER)

The NFER is still a leading independent provider of educational research and insights. The 'Schools' tab on the drop-down menu provides a link to the latest publications and research. There is also a link to 'Research in Schools: "How to" Guides', which give advice on how to run your own in-school research project. The 'Assessment Hub' link provides access to a collection of short-read articles on assessment: https://www.nfer.ac.uk.

## Evidence for Policy and Practice Information and Co-ordinating (EPPI) Centre

The EPPI Centre provides evidence-based systematic reviews of research evidence to inform policy and practice. The 'Publications' tab provides a comprehensive chronological index of systematic reviews on aspects of education, health promotion, public health, social welfare and international development: https://eppi.ioe.ac.uk/cms/.

## Practical ways mentors can 'make learning visible'

Mentors can help mentees to develop a mindset whereby they perceive themselves as teachers 'coming to the class to evaluate the impact of their teaching' rather than a mindset of 'pupils coming to the class to be taught' (Hattie 2015).

From this perspective, mentors can encourage mentees to share and think more deeply about how they differentiate challenging goals of learning for certain pupils, and what might be the most appropriate teaching strategy. Mentors can support mentees to question whether a preferred approach to teaching and assessment is always the most appropriate one for particular pupils. Through evidence-informed conversations structured around the three feedback questions outlined earlier in this chapter, the mentor can encourage a mentee to reflect on the purpose of assessment, as well as the current use and interpretations of assessments in their educational setting, and consider:

- how much is relevant to feedback on pupil learning?
- how much provides a benchmark or comparative data at class, school, local or national level?

Using relevant research on assessment will help develop greater criticality regarding the purpose of assessment and who is benefiting from it. This can enable the mentee to distinguish between different forms of assessment and how these align with underlying values. Student/beginning teachers can also evaluate when assessment provides learning that is of value to pupils and when it closes down learning, as can sometimes be the case in terms of pupils' responses to tests. By adopting a questioning stance in this way, mentees are more likely to become more aware of the importance of embedding teaching interventions that enable their pupils to adopt self-assessment and evaluation strategies, and develop error detection procedures and heightened self-efficacy, to enable them to tackle more challenging tasks, so leading to mastery and understanding (Hattie 2015).

## Relation between feedback and instruction

Once mentees develop a mindset of evaluating the impact of their teaching, mentors can help them see how the relationship between combining feedback/feed forward with effective instruction in classrooms can be very powerful in enhancing pupil learning. Drawing on evidence from practice and research, mentors can help mentees reflect on when instruction is more effective than feedback. Mentors may find Hattie's (2015) acronym helpful: "Teachers are to DIE for", in that they participate in

- *Di*agnosing the status of students as they begin lessons;
- selecting from multiple *I*nterventions if their current intervention is not having the desired impact; and
- *E*valuating the students' responses to their interventions.

---

## Task 11.3 Adopting a critical stance

Consider the following questions (adapted from Hattie 2015) to enable student/ beginning teachers to adopt a critical stance and reflect more deeply about their lessons:

- How did you inform pupils of success criteria near the beginning of the lesson?
- Did you modify your teaching in light of a clear understanding of pupils' prior achievement?
- What teaching methods did you use that focused on moving pupils from surface to deeper understanding?
- How did you vary your teaching methods according to individual learners?
- How did you ensure that the topic/lesson was sufficiently challenging to encourage all learners to aim for mastery of the desired content, skills and understandings?
- How did you maximise feedback about where to go next?
- How did you ensure the assessment was aligned with the success criteria and that appropriate proportions of surface and deep learning were taking place?

---

## Summary and key points

In summary, this chapter introduced readers to:

- the logistics of organising meaningful weekly debriefs;
- a feed up, feedback and feed forward framework (Hattie & Timperley 2007);
- a model of productive, evidence-informed learning conversations based on trust and respect, and support and challenge (Earl & Timperley 2009);
- accessing research and user reviews of research findings; and
- practical ways in which mentors can support mentees to make learning more visible.

## Further Reading

Education Endowment Foundation (EEF). https://educationendowmentfoundation.org.uk Accessed 4/01/2021.
National Foundation for Educational Research (NFER) https://www.nfer.ac.uk Accessed 4/01/2021.
The Evidence for Policy and Practice Information (EPPI) Centre, University of Central London. https://eppi.ioe.ac.uk/cms/ Accessed 4/01/2021.

The General Teaching Council Scotland (GTCS). https://www.gtcs.org.uk/professional-upd ate/research.aspx Accessed 4/01/2021

## References

Earl, L. & Timperley, H. (2009) *Professional Learning Conversations: Challenges in Using Evidence for Improvement*. Springer.

Hattie, J. (2015) Teacher-ready research review: The applicability of visible learning to higher education, *Scholarship of Teaching and Learning in Psychology*, Vol. 1, No. 1, 79–91.

Hattie, J. & Timperley, H. (2007) The power of feedback. *Review of Educational Research*, Vol. 77, No. 1, 81–112.

Rose, N. & Eriksson, S. (2017) Putting evidence to work: How can we help new teachers use research evidence to inform their teaching? TeachFirst. https://www.teachfirst.org.uk/ sites/default/files/2017-10/Putting_Evidence_to_work_2017.pdf Accessed 4/01/2021.

# 12 Much more than results: towards a fluidity of practice

*Jane Essex*

## Objectives

At the end of this chapter, you should be able to:

- understand the difference between success based on a competency model and a 'fluent' professional teacher;
- recognise the difficulties that a teacher is likely to experience in implementing inclusive practice; and
- evaluate potential strategies for mentors to enhance teachers' development of their capacity to teach inclusively.

## Introduction

As teachers' careers progress, their work is characterised by an increasing ability to integrate knowledge and experience into a confident and versatile practice. They have an increasingly complete understanding of the multi-faceted nature of teaching and after several years demonstrate the quality of 'fluency' in their work. The process by which a teacher becomes 'mature', that is, able to apply principles flexibly in response to multiple different contexts and do so apparently effortlessly, is considered in this chapter. It considers this development as a continuum of professional growth, and describes how a mentor can support the development of the high levels of versatility that can be acquired as a teacher gains, and reflects on, experience. This process will be exemplified by looking at how teachers can be helped to teach in an increasingly inclusive manner. Inclusion can be defined, and enacted, in various ways but will be used here to denote teaching that enables all pupils to achieve their full potential in an environment that is equally supportive for all learners. It is an attitude that does not problematise diversity in pupils but recognises it and seeks to offer all learners an experience of equivalent value, though not necessarily the same experience. Very importantly, inclusion requires teachers to recognise that all their pupils differ in their capacity and developmental needs and to teach them accordingly. Although inclusion is a requirement for teachers, it is something that many, especially beginning teachers, struggle to do effectively or even to understand securely (Essex, Alexiadou and Zwozdiak-Myers, 2019).

DOI: 10.4324/9780429356957-15

This chapter will describe the implications of a distinctly Scottish model of mentoring, as described in Chapter 1, on the development of complex skills, exemplified by inclusive teaching. The Scottish Government's explicit expectation that professional learning, supported and stimulated by mentors, will be an ongoing and cyclical undertaking is captured in the Standards for career-long professional learning (see also Chapter 6). The ethos associated with career-long mentoring is precisely the sort in which complex skills, and the ability to make nuanced judgements, can be developed over time. Moreover, such skills can be exercised and honed in the confident knowledge that the teacher will be supported in deploying their growing skills. The emphasis is on mentoring as a strategic intervention that permeates all levels of a school's hierarchy, and which brings a multiplicity of benefits, meaning that mentors can be important in the development of the most demanding teaching skills, such as being an inclusive teacher.

### Task 12.1    Auditing career-long mentoring in your school

Reflect on the extent to which a culture of career-long mentoring exists in your school, as recommended in the Donaldson (2011) Report. What formal mentoring mechanisms are you aware of? Are these formal mechanisms supplemented by additional informal systems? How well do you feel that the mentoring systems enable teachers at every stage of their career to be supported in dealing with developing the 'hard to achieve' skills, such as teaching inclusively?

## What are the likely development needs of teachers?

The Scottish model of becoming a teacher is a gradualised one, in which the early career teacher is recognised as having distinctive developmental needs. This is in line with research evidence that shows qualitative differences in their work when compared to more experienced teachers (Berliner, 2004). They have less experience upon which to draw and fewer ideas about how they might manage complex situations, whereas experienced teachers are able to inform their selection of strategies using a wealth of previous experience (Doqaruni, 2017). This situation will be familiar to Initial Teacher Educators, who frequently find that, until pupil teachers have encountered problems with their lessons, they find it hard to envisage what might go wrong. Experienced teachers, by contrast, are better at envisaging multiple possible outcomes during a lesson, and have a raft of contingency plans ready. They also focus on individual pupil's attainment rather than on the entire class (Berliner, 2004). Berliner's earlier (1988) account of teacher maturation says that novices learn what he describes as 'context-free rules' or, as we might call them, generalisations. These can be very unhelpful when considering inclusion as they may prevent the teacher from getting to know the individual's needs and capacities. Teacher maturation leads to an understanding of the basis of the rules, so that when contexts in which rules should be applied differently occur, the teacher has a transferable insight into the boundaries of generalisability and can make context-sensitive exceptions. Shulman (1986) terms this ability to apply rules flexibly as 'contextual knowledge', and this is a key factor in being able to teach diverse learners in a way that affords each learner equitable opportunities. This account of the growth in understanding points to the ways in which a mentor can promote the sort of adaptive professional flexibility that Berliner (2001) describes as the hallmark of an expert teacher.

---

## Case Study 12.1

Fiona is a teacher in her induction year, whom you are mentoring. She says she wants to move into pastoral care because she doesn't feel confident about her subject knowledge, especially teaching her subject with high achieving and very confident Nat 5 pupils. She describes herself as 'not a high flier' and as 'kindly, good with children who are having problems'. After this conversation, you wonder whether she is meeting the educational needs of the high attaining pupils as well as she offers support to those known to be having pastoral difficulties.

---

## Case Study 12.2

Graham is in his third year after his PGDE and is new in the department where you are Principal Teacher. You are responsible for his induction into the department. He came to you with a reputation for being a creative and very effective teacher who kept his classes entranced, but he has found settling into the new school more difficult than you had anticipated at his appointment. He was previously working in a school in an affluent area, whereas your school has a high proportion of children who live in poverty. He is having some minor issues with classroom management, mainly with low attaining pupils, some of whom could be described as disaffected. Nevertheless, he has contributed some very high-quality resources and teaching ideas to colleagues.

---

## Task 12.2   Identifying individual development needs

On the basis of the descriptions given in Case Study 12.1 and 12.2, identify the development needs for each of these mentees, considering both the groups that they are including effectively in lessons and those that they may not be. Think about how a mentor could support them in meeting these needs more effectively. What aspects of inclusion are they currently focusing on, and what mechanisms for achieving inclusion are they deploying? In what ways might you wish to see their current understanding of inclusion developing as they gain further experience?

## How can mentoring promote progression towards teaching maturity?

Mentoring is a mechanism for promoting professional development through a mixture of dialogue, advice and support for professional and personal issues that impact on a mentee's teaching. In addition, mentors commonly act as assessors and evaluate development. Mentors are typically experienced colleagues who can share their knowledge and insights to the benefit of their colleague, thereby offering a role model to their mentee. The potential limitation of that is that the mentor's own areas of inexperience or uncertainty can limit the scope of the work they do. Mentoring is, however, far more than the transmission of practice to an unquestioning recipient who, in turn, duplicates the mentor's practices, in what Maynard and Furlong (1998) describe as the 'apprenticeship model'. Mentoring should be a holistic process, addressing the diverse personal and professional needs of a teacher at this pivotal point of their career (CIDP, 2012). The expectation that both members of the mentoring partnership will share the same goals (GTCS, n.d.) can only be realised if the aims encompass outcomes that are valued by both parties. The implication of this is that the teacher would wish to become a better teacher not solely for their own benefit but to benefit the wider school community, including those with additional support needs. If mentor and mentee both have a clear grasp of how their individual development is contributing to the attainment of institutional goals, the work acquires a motivating strategic importance for them both. It is, therefore, essential that these goals are articulated, especially when the goal is diversely understood, or not well defined, as is often the case with inclusion. These conversations will need to encompass both ideals and practicalities of specific pupils and classes.

An analytical approach is a common starting point, with the mentor asking questions to probe what the mentee understands of their current practice and future development needs. Such questions might, for example, include how to implement differentiation for specific groups of learners, or approaches to subject pedagogy that facilitate access for all pupils. The mentor themselves may, where appropriate, broker relationships with other knowledgeable colleagues; in the case of inclusion, this should include the school's Additional Support Needs (ASN) co-ordinator, staff who liaise with external agencies and colleagues who focus on provision for other 'vulnerable learners', such as pupils living in poverty.

Although mentoring is considered important at all stages at which a significant career transition is undertaken, mentoring of early career teachers has distinctive features. Early teachers may be wrestling with fundamental issues of their teacher 'persona' and how to balance the multiple demands on their time with the need to maintain their well-being (Essex, Alexiadou and Zwozdiak-Myers, 2019). This is commonly reported as a reason for not engaging more fully with inclusion, despite positive feelings about it as an aspiration, because it is seen as extra work rather than core to effective teaching. These practical difficulties may prevent teachers from becoming inclusive practitioners. Less experienced teachers tend to focus on the immediate difficulties that they perceive in their classroom, such as students who can't read instructions, and this results in them finding short-term 'workarounds' rather than looking critically and holistically at how lessons can be made meaningful and rewarding for all learners. The understanding that inclusive teaching involves the use of strategies that will enable all pupils to participate and succeed may develop later, after much reflection.

Although many beginning teachers are highly committed to inclusion, they do not understand how to implement it in practice (Essex, Alexiadou and Zwozdiak-Myers, 2019). The mentee may still be having to consciously grapple with some of the many capabilities that are required of them in an environment of high-stakes assessments, along with the unwavering expectation of the highest professional standards (Pollard, 2014). A mentor should be supporting the early career teacher in attaining the different professional standards, which will, inevitably, involve adhering, to some extent, to the competence model of mentoring that is described by Maynard and Furlong (1995).

Although interventions commonly focus on the observable behaviours of mentees, and the subsequent responses of their pupils, the most effective form of mentoring is that which instils deep understanding and a critical insight into the mentees' practice. For this to happen we must look to more collaborative and reflective approaches to mentoring (for example, Le Cornu, 2005, described in more detail in Chapter 1). Such probing dialogue will be especially helpful to beginning teachers who are still formulating their ideas about complex concepts, such as inclusion and how to enact their notion of inclusion. Many beginning teachers will hold a medical model of diversity, focusing on the 'deficiencies' and needs associated with an ASN 'diagnosis rather than their capabilities' (Essex, Alexiadou and Zwozdiak-Myers, 2019). A mentor will be able to develop their thinking by discussing alternative ideas, such as how school processes may unintentionally present barriers to some learners (the so-called 'social model' of disability). A mentor may model inclusive practice, or reflect on their own experiences, in order to give the mentee a framework of ideas and approaches to develop their practice. The mentor will also need to model their own reflective thought processes very explicitly to help develop similar reflective responses by the mentee. The basis of deeply held beliefs about teaching, for example of diverse pupils, may be explored, and evidence from previous lessons and developing trends in practice will be considered in new ways as the result of the mentor's questioning. Such discussion is clearly sensitive and it is with this aspect of mentoring in mind that the mentor is expected to treat conversations as confidential, unless serious safeguarding issues come to light.

Most models of mentoring describe it primarily in terms of support. One notable exception is Daloz's model (2012, described further in Chapter 1), which considers that challenge, provided in conjunction with support, is required for optimal development. For the mentee, appropriate challenge will vary with the stage of development and context but, at the beginning, is likely to be found in the day-to-day practical demands of the job. For example, the need to differentiate learning is inherently challenging for teachers with limited classroom experience. A compounding difficulty is that of the need to develop knowledge of approaches to teaching subject content, so-called pedagogic content knowledge, which is needed for effective differentiation of content. These two challenges together provide substantial challenge, and one for which commensurately high levels of support will be required. As the teacher's experience grows, challenge may be provided by critical reflection on experience, for instance on what didn't go well in a lesson for specific learners and why. Such reflections can be a useful way of helping the mentee to understand the limitations of practising mechanistically through the use of an 'inclusion by checklist' (see Chapter 7 on reflection). It should be noted, incidentally, that Daloz's model also provides a powerful framework for considering inclusive teaching; evaluating both the challenge and support that different learners will face within a lesson is a powerful auditing tool for checking that the lesson will promote the development of all pupils.

The 'competence' approach to teaching, described in Chapter 1, is liable to fail when complex skills are being developed because even if all the expected component skills are used, they may not be integrated in the way that is needed for an inclusive lesson. For example, if a teacher is focusing on classroom management, their mentor could suggest reprimanding poor behaviour, but it would be far more effective to explore the underlying causes and how these could be mitigated. For example, is a pupil disruptive because they are bored or frustrated by the difficulty of their work? In conjunction with analysis, it might be helpful to evaluate the impact of purposive challenge, for example, using differentiated resources, trying out different ways of grouping pupils for discussion or changing the duration of the different sections of a lesson. In line with the reflective model of mentoring (see Chapter 8), a longer-term aspiration would be for the early career teacher to be able to identify suitable challenges and implement them independently.

---

**Task 12.3    Analysing the development needs of an early career teacher**

Consider an early career teacher known to you. It might be someone you have been, or are currently, mentoring, or it might be what you remember of yourself.

How well does the account of early career teachers' needs for constructive challenge as well as support describe the teacher you are thinking of? Did they view teaching as a compilation of constituent skills, such as classroom management, teacher input, assessment and inclusion, or were they starting to understand the interplay of all these elements?

---

## Recognising the sequential phases of development

There are several models of development, some of which are described in Chapter 1, which seek to characterise the successive stages through which a teacher might be expected to pass. These are collated and summarised in Figure 12.1. Progression will occur over very variable timescales, and different aspects of the teacher's work may mature at very different rates, so the stages can only be indicative. It is also important to recognise that different stages will recur in different developmental contexts and with respect to different professional skills. For instance, a teacher who has learned how to enhance engagement with pupils living in poverty is likely to find that adjustments in approaches are needed when they move to a school with a high level of ethnic or linguistic diversity. Moreover, mentees may regress to previous stages or 'skip' stages in the frameworks, so the description is also only indicative. Nevertheless, a general account of progression, with six stages, follows, and can be a useful guide for mentors wanting to assess the stage of development of their mentee and can help mentors identify suitable approaches through which to provide support and challenge.

| Stage | Indicative timing | Katz (1995) | Maynard and Furlong (1995) | Berliner (1988) |
|---|---|---|---|---|
| 1 | Initial Teacher Education year | | Early idealism | |
| 2 | ITE and induction year | Survival | Survival | Novice |
| 3 | Second and third year of teaching | Consolidation | | Advanced beginner |
| 4 | Between 3 and 5 years of teaching | | Recognising difficulties (Plateau) | Competent |
| 5 | Around 5 years of teaching | Renewal | Moving on | Proficient |
| 6 | Around 7 years of teaching | Maturity | | Expert |
| 7 | Many years of teaching | | | Adaptive expert |

*Figure 12.1* How the different models of development correspond

1. Maynard and Furlong (1995) describe teachers at the start of their Initial Teacher Education as being in a phase of 'early idealism'. At this point, they tend to identify with pupils and view their behaviour sympathetically. They have a strong sense of the sort of teacher they aspire to become and, equally, can give examples of the sort of teacher they would emphatically not like to turn into! With respect to inclusion, this phase is associated with a very positive, and highly principled, stance on the desirability of inclusion in education coupled with the ability to recognise some of the reasons for a pupil having additional support needs. At this stage, mentors can encourage mentees to reflect on the multiple demands and opportunities that exist in any classroom situation, such as assessment pressures, balancing the needs of specific individuals with those of the whole class, and the teacher's own well-being.

2. The second stage is characterised by a focus is on achieving basic tasks successfully, such as routine administration, reliable forward planning and knowing something of each of their pupils. In terms of inclusion, it is commonly marked by the subjugation of the earlier good intentions to teach inclusively to more immediate pressures around performativity, such as classroom management or ensuring that pupils' attainment is in line with expectations. Challenge often comes in the form of the vast amount of new information to be assimilated and the fact that beginning teachers may lack understanding of how their work fits into the wider strategic context of the whole school (Berliner, 2004). They are likely to understand their lessons in terms of a 'checklist' of required elements rather than a holistic view of the lesson. In terms of inclusion, they may attend to a 'checklist' of categories of pupil vulnerability, such as disability, low Scottish Index of Multiple Deprivation (SIMD) background, black and minority ethnic pupils, being in care or using English as an additional language. At this stage, their knowledge is commonly inflexible and based on 'rules', for instance, 'I should praise correct answers' or 'All children should get the same opportunities in the classroom'.

   The mentor will need to provide a high level of support corresponding to the high levels of perceived challenge. This may be in the form of guidance on the relative import-ance of different components of the job so that work can be prioritised. Alternatively, support may be provided by signposting the novice teacher to the wealth of information intended to make their job manageable and meaningful. However, above all else, the thing that will help the novice to move on is direct experience coupled with reflection, rather than advice, and this cannot be 'fast tracked' (Berliner, 2004).

3. The third stage corresponds to what Katz (1995) calls 'consolidation', whilst Berliner (1988) calls it the stage of an 'advanced beginner'. By now, the mentee may have established a routine for themselves and be managing their workload successfully, providing that nothing very untoward happens. They may have built up a series of context-specific experiences to the point where they understand how context can impact upon their teaching and pupils' learning, for example, 'My S3 pupils are always difficult to settle when they come in from P.E. lessons'. They may also be able to identify similarities in different events in school, and to analyse what circumstantial factors might unite apparently disparate incidents. This helps them to predict events and to take pre-emptive actions, although they may not always be able to articulate the reasons for the actions they choose in the light of experience. This awareness starts to inform them when working with diverse pupils, for example, pupils on the autistic spectrum generally cope better with changes in routine if they have advance warning of them or that a pupil with literacy difficulties feels more confident when they have their Aurally Coded English dictionary to hand. The knowledge that they are building is from multiple routine experiences rather than mentor input, and it is orientated towards action rather than deeper understanding. As their body of experience grows, strategic knowledge is built up about when to break the rules that were previously stuck to rigidly. For example, 'Always praise correct answers' is now qualified with, 'If you keep praising correct answers from the same pupil, they may not value the praise anymore'. This corresponds to Shulman's (1986) 'contextual knowledge'. Despite their increased knowledge through experience, the 'good enough teacher' may not yet believe in their agency in the classroom but, instead, see themselves as effective responders to circumstance.

   At this stage, a mentor can helpfully provide the stimulus for ongoing reflection so that the mentee can develop a deeper understanding of their experience. The mentor can also help the mentee to gain a more holistic understanding, which will be applicable to a wide range of situations. Asking questions that require them to reflect and be analytical will help the mentee to develop a broader understanding of context and, crucially, their role in the events of the classroom. For example, 'Can you think of ways to help them make the transition between two very contrasting styles of lesson?', 'Why do you think that a pupil responds so differently to the activity that you introduced to the rest of the class?' and 'Have you noticed anything about the way that you speak to that pupil as they enter the classroom, and how it affects their subsequent conduct in the lesson?' At this stage of development, support from the mentor may also take the form of re-connecting them to their first phase early idealism, and helping them to see how the practical demands of the job are the fabric through which high aspirations can be delivered. This is a point at which a mentor can have a huge effect by enhancing the mentored teachers' satisfaction with their job and, ultimately, increasing retention rates in the profession.

4. The next stage of development might be described as the 'realist' stage. The mentee is able to reliably demonstrate all the competences required, and they now take

responsibility for their actions, and the impact of these upon all learners, rather than simply mimicking existing practice. Such teachers make conscious choices, select teaching goals rationally and can make strategic decisions in the moment when unanticipated events occur. A related development is the competent teacher's ability to avoid 'targeting errors', such as choosing pupils to answer questions, choosing teaching materials that will appeal to marginalised pupils or offering support with a specific task. This capacity to make such choices is especially important when dealing with potentially sensitive issues, such as inclusion practice. The ability to work effectively in a range of situations and to make informed decisions about practice, such as which examples to choose to illustrate a concept that is being taught or when to move on to a new topic, enables teachers to make context-based decisions. In summary, the 'realist' teacher is characterised by being insightful, competent and rational about their teaching. It is, therefore, the earliest stage of their development when they can strategically choose suitable responses to learner diversity rather than making purely pragmatic choices. This could include when to intervene and offer additional support and when to give pupils the space to resolve a difficulty with their work independently. Alternatively, this might involve grouping pupils on the basis of their complementary skills rather than their friendship groups.

At this stage, the mentor can assist by facilitating deliberative and repeated reflection on lessons, for example though a series of 'lesson studies' or peer observations, or through the co-planning of lessons. The other important role of the mentor is to support the creation of 'communities of practice' through formal and informal networks and the sponsorship of the mentee within the school community.

5.  This phase marks the greatest apparent divergence in the various frameworks, which testifies to the very multi-faceted nature of effective teaching and the processes that underpin it. Both Katz's (1995) term 'renewal' and Maynard and Furlong's (1995) 'moving on' indicate the dynamic processes that accompany the attainment of what Berliner (1988) terms 'proficiency'.

Teachers at this stage are now able to dedicate more time to making nuanced responses to diverse learners, such as planning differentiated, or even individualised, learning experiences. With respect to inclusion, they will now be critically evaluating some of the simpler models of diversity, such as the medical model, that they found helpful earlier in their development. They will now understand the complexity of factors that intersect to create individual learners' profiles and will question whether simple fixes can address complex educational situations.

At this stage, the teacher is re-engaging with higher level teaching and strategic challenges. They can do this because routine teaching has become deeply embedded in their understanding, leaving them with processing capacity for other matters. Teachers working at this level are likely to be working in, or aspiring to work in, leadership and management and to be receiving mentoring as they work to meet the GTCS Professional Standards for Leadership and Management. The classroom practice of such teachers is underpinned by intuition (or 'know how'). They make micro-adjustments without much conscious thought, identify patterns intuitively and draw on prior experiences from a range of contexts to make very accurate predictions about the consequences of classroom decisions without conscious effort. However, they are consciously analytical and deliberative when forward planning.

6.  Teachers who reach the final stage of development (and many teachers never do) are now fast at planning and reacting in the classroom because they no longer need to consciously think about routine teaching or decisions. Berliner (2004) describes them as 'arational', meaning 'without reason'. They possess and apply extensive tacit knowledge about their subject and classroom context when they are problem solving, though, paradoxically, they may struggle to articulate the way in which they do their job. They are thus able to respond to a huge range of situations, and are described as 'fluid' and 'flexible' in their practice (Berliner, 2004). They introduce more challenge into the curriculum and provide very skilful monitoring and feedback, thereby engendering deep learning and promoting higher attainment in their pupils. These teachers draw on a deep knowledge of individual pupils, which lets them minimise routine bureaucracy and maximise pupil-centred adjustments to teaching and classroom procedures (Berliner, 2004). As in Stage 5, the needs of exceptional pupils can be given ample conscious consideration, and such teachers are likely to be very good at making adjustments for individual pupils. These teachers are likely to be able to respond rapidly and positively to high levels of pupil diversity, and find doing so both interesting and professionally rewarding.

Mentoring a teacher at this stage is likely to entail two elements. One is to provide a critical friend with whom ideas can be shared and considered; the other is to provide support for the development of specific skills or knowledge, as identified by the mentee.

## Task 12.4

Think about the mentees described in Case Study 12.1 and 12.2. At which stage, of the six stages outlined, would you place them? What support and challenge does their stage suggest that they would benefit from to develop their ability to teach better and more inclusively? Now carry out a similar analysis of a mentee who is known to you, or with whom you have worked in the past. Finally, consider what stage you would place yourself at presently and consider what the implications of this are for your own mentoring needs.

## Task 12.5

Berliner (2004) noted that expert teachers did no better than advanced beginners when they moved to a new school. Can you think of reasons why this might be and suggest what support could be given to these teachers to help them regain their expert teacher persona as quickly as possible?

## Summary and key points

In this chapter, you have considered the different ways in which you, as a mentor, will be required to support and challenge teachers at all the different developmental stages. The characteristics of teachers at six successive stages of development have been described, along with the corresponding role of the mentor. The development of inclusive teaching practices has been considered as an example of skills that cannot be fully realised through the use of a 'competence model'. Instead, with growing experience and support, teachers can demonstrate the expected competences and demonstrate proficiency. With still greater experience, they need to think less about routine classroom matters and can increasingly attend to complex issues, such as inclusion, in a holistic way. At every stage of development, mentors have a crucial role to play in challenging teachers to undertake deep reflection and analysis whilst providing support in the form of reassurance and social sponsorship.

Having worked through this chapter, you should now be able to:

- recognise the professional pressures and personal factors that may shape early career teachers' aspirations;
- understand the difference between success based on a competency model and a fluent professional teacher;
- understand the role of the mentor in helping early career teachers to develop towards fluency of practice;
- evaluate potential strategies for enhancing early career teachers' understanding of what inclusive teaching means.

## Further reading

Allen, R. and Sims, S. (2018). *The Teacher Gap*. London: Routledge.

## References

Berliner, D.C. (1988). *The Development of Expertise in Pedagogy*. Washington, D.C.: American Association of Colleges for Teacher Education.

Berliner, D.C. (2001). Learning about and learning from expert teachers. *International Journal of Educational Research*, 35: 463-482.

Berliner, D.C. (2004). Expert teachers: Their characteristics, development and accomplishments. In R. Batllori i Obiols, A.E. Gomez Martinez, M. Oller i Freixa and J. Pages i Blanch (eds.), *De la teoria ... a l'aula: Formacio del professorat ensenyament de las ciències socials* (pp. 13-28). Barcelona, Spain: Departament de Didàctica de la Llengua de la Literatura I de les Ciències Socials, Universitat Autònoma de Barcelona.

CIDP (Chartered Institute of Personnel and Development). (2021). *Coaching and Mentoring Factsheet*. Available online at: https://www.cipd.co.uk/knowledge/fundamentals/people/development/coaching-mentoring-factsheet

Daloz, L.A. (2012). *Mentor: Guiding the Journey of Adult Learners*. New York: Wiley.

Donaldson, G. (2011). *Teaching Scotland's Future: Report of a review of teacher education in Scotland*. Edinburgh, UK: The Scottish Government.

Doqaruni, V.R. (2017). Communication strategies in experienced vs. inexperienced teachers' talk: A sign of transformation in teacher cognition. *Innovation in Language Learning and Teaching*, 11 (1): 17-31.

Essex, J., Alexiadou, N. and Zwozdiak-Myers, P. (2019). Understanding inclusion in teacher education – A view from pupil teachers in England. *International Journal of Inclusive Education*, https://doi.org/10.1080/13603116.2019.1614232

Furlong, J. and Maynard, T. (1998). *Mentoring Student Teachers: The Growth of Professional Knowledge*. Abingdon, UK: Routledge.

GTCS (n.d.) *Coaching and Mentoring*. Available online at: https://www.gtcs.org.uk/professional-update/coaching-and-mentoring.aspx

Katz, L. (1995). *The Developmental Stages of Teachers in Talks with Teachers of Young Children: A Collection*. Stamford, CT: Ablex.

Le Cornu, R. (2005). Peer mentoring: Engaging pre-service teachers in mentoring one another. *Mentoring & Tutoring: Partnership in Learning*, 13 (3): 355–366.

Maynard, T. and Furlong, J. (1995). Learning to teach and models of mentoring. In T. Kerry and A. Shelton-Mayes (eds.), *Issues in Mentoring* (pp. 10–14). London: Routledge.

Pollard, A. (2014). *Reflective Teaching*. London: Bloomsbury.

Shulman, L.S. (1986). Those who understand: Knowledge growth in teaching. *Educational Researcher*, 15 (2): 4–31.

# 13 Digital and remote models of mentoring

*Geetha Marcus*

## Objectives

At the end of this chapter, you should be able to:

- recognise three main criteria for appraising innovative and effective mentoring via digital and remote models;
- reflect on three innovative and effective digital and remote models of mentoring; and
- reflect on the impact of vision, values and attitudes of mentors on styles, strategies and practices when mentoring in the digital realm.

## Introduction

This chapter identifies some guiding principles and models of mentoring that challenge us to reflect on what is best practice in a digital and remote post-COVID world. Building on the work in previous chapters, and in particular Chapter 4, which explored the vision, values and attitudes of mentors, this section considers how a mentor's own experiences of being supported might impact their digital mentoring styles, strategies and practices. The chapter will then draw on both national and international literature from a range of disciplines to recommend three key innovative and effective digital models of mentoring employed in the professional learning of 21st-century teachers, highlighting how common guiding principles and key mentoring strategies can be adapted digitally.

## The new context

The common objectives for professional learning across all levels for teachers in Scotland are essentially to improve the effectiveness of learning, teaching and leadership; to encourage reflection on good practice; and, of course, to improve attainment, achievement and participation of children and young people. Recently "SARS-CoV-2, more commonly known as COVID-19, has acted as a severe disruptor for communities across the globe, not least for educational institutions" (Nordmann et al., 2020: 4). Compelled to close their doors completely or partially, educational institutions saw a "pivot towards online learning and teaching" (Nordmann et al., 2020: 4). Many traditional on-campus programmes had no option but to be delivered fully online, resulting in digital interactions with students.

DOI: 10.4324/9780429356957-16

The COVID global pandemic enabled us to consider how the digital can be used to enhance the mentoring experience remotely, while acknowledging the potential challenges. This chapter considers how a mentor might integrate the use of digital and remote mentoring in an accessible and fair way for teachers at all stages in their career and create a humanised and empathic online learning experience for mentees. Clearly, the level of support, resource and expertise will, as usual, vary depending on the individual being mentored and, at the same time, the availability of compatible hardware and a suitable home or school environment will need to be taken into account. There are aspects to the mentoring that will stay the same, and aspects that will need to be altered. But first, what exactly do we mean by the terms "digital" and "remote"?

## Digital and remote

The term digital as used in this chapter encompasses any method of communication that occurs online through the use of a range of technologies, tools and resources – ranging from the use of the internet, mobile phones, email, social media platforms, e-books, virtual reality, augmented reality and so on. It is not direct face-to-face communication or interaction.

Digital interactions for learning, teaching and mentoring have several benefits for teacher professionals. These include flexibility, being able to balance work with personal commitments, and studying at one's own pace and at times and places that suit oneself. We can meet and engage with fellow colleagues in online sessions. We can easily access, revise and review up-to-date materials, and have informed discussions about cutting-edge research and its impact on practice. Digital platforms can provide us with access to specialised knowledge in a comfortable, friendly, community-based online environment. As we transition more and more to the online world, these benefits will become increasingly important in the future. As technology continues to transform the way we live, so it will continue to change the way we learn, develop and engage with others.

The digital can offer many opportunities for enhancing the mentoring process in remote and rural areas. New forms of learning and working are developing fast, giving us the freedom to live, work, travel and pursue leisure without being confined to the traditional physical "office space". Learners can access seminars, conferences, talks, exercise classes, counselling and a myriad range of activities online and from a distance, cutting down on the need to travel and, in turn, time spent travelling. Mentors, mentees and mentoring no longer have to be confined to local or national boundaries, and a whole world of possibilities, skills and experiences is now available online, no matter where one resides or how remotely. It can be a truly inclusive process because of its reach. Materials can be shared virtually on-screen, and discussed and edited in real time, making the learning experience more meaningful and immediate. Studies have also shown that digital mentoring can have a positive impact on the "quality and duration" of mentoring relationships (Schwartz et al., 2014).

However, digital participation has implications for social and economic equality (White, 2016). Globally, there is often a digital divide between urban and rural areas, with consequences for Wi-Fi availability and connectivity. The situation in Scotland is no different. Rural living is pitted against urban living, but the rurality is further categorised into that which is accessible and that which is remote or very remote (The Scottish Government, 2018).

The conditions of rurality and remoteness are determined by the size of a settlement and its distance from an urban centre (The Scottish Government, 2018). Areas that have less than 3,000 people and that have a drive time of over 30 minutes to a settlement of 10,000 or more are considered "rural and remote" (as opposed to rural and accessible). Furthermore, "areas with a population of less than 3,000 people, and with a drive time of over 60 minutes to a settlement of 10,000 or more" are labelled "very remote rural". Of the 32 Local Authorities in Scotland, 18 have populations that live in remote rural areas based on a six-fold Urban Rural category (The Scottish Government, 2018). This is a significant number. Of the total population of Scotland, approximately 6% live in remote rural areas and are dispersed across 70% of the land mass. In contrast, the rest of Scotland accounts for approximately 83% of the total population of Scotland but only 2% of the land mass. Despite this, with the aid of European Union funds, "the digital infra-structure [in remote areas] has significantly improved in the last few years" (Coker, 2019). One could argue that the terms "rural" and "remote" are contested terms, as it depends on who is defining it, how it is defined and the underlying socio-political discourses at play (Frouws, 1998).

Technology and education have the potential to be transformative factors for rural devel-opment (Odero and Chinapah, 2016). However, the COVID-19 pandemic has highlighted another type of digital divide that challenges our understanding of the term "remote" – poverty and other social inequalities that impact on the availability of technological devices, the ability to afford effective Wi-Fi access if available, and the suitability of the "work from home" environment of sections of the population. The prospect of learning, teaching, and being supported and mentored online have underscored considerable challenges and redefined the term "remote" for student and probationary teachers across Initial Teacher Education (ITE) programmes in Scotland. Remoteness is no longer just a geographical phe-nomenon but a socio-economic one. Digital accessibility and remoteness now cut across geographical divides.

In pre-COVID days, professionals who lived and chose to work in rural communities created and engaged with alternative forms of professional learning and connected to pro-fessional communities who were previously geographically distanced and therefore challen-ging to engage with. Therefore, probationers and early career teachers in smaller and/or rural schools have engaged with various digital platforms to widen their circle of connections and support, for example, via peer networking on various social media sites, attending resi-dential courses, and engagement with educational sites like Argyll and Bute's: "SALi is where all educators can share information, resources and ideas. It is visible to everyone and is also shared via the National Glow Site" (Argyll and Bute Council, 2020). There are several areas of interest that one can choose from on the Argyll and Bute Council site, such as information on the Curriculum for Excellence, Education Scotland, a GIRFEC e-learning module and teacher resources for learning.

---

**Task 13.1    Mentoring digitally**

- What are your experiences of digital and remote mentoring or of being mentored digitally and remotely?
- What is your attitude to digital models of working? How comfortable or skilled are you when interacting, learning, teaching or mentoring online?

---

The COVID-19 pandemic forced nearly all interactions online, and this in itself can frustrate professional connections (Nordmann et al., 2020). Reports of increased anxiety, loneliness, relationship problems and a deterioration in mental health are some examples of the psychological toll the pandemic has taken on individuals across the country. Whilst some practices may move online, others will continue to be face to face. Nevertheless, a more blended approach will have implications for all educators, not least the manner in which mentors mentor mentees online. Initially this is likely to be more demanding and intense than face-to-face communication, for both mentors and mentees. However, there are a range of support mechanisms available to mitigate against these anxieties. For example, The National Improvement Hub (https://education.gov.scot/improvement/) have some useful videos that might be good for mentors/mentees to share with each other. Education Scotland also has a YouTube video channel, which hosts good resources for mentoring remotely (www.youtube.com/user/educationscotland/featured). Mentors can direct their mentees to these websites. Both could watch a video clip together online and discuss or assess a learning resource and how it might be implemented in the classroom context. Mentors and mentees can co-create lesson plans or small projects together, with the mentor acting as facilitator and guide. BBC Bitesize have Scottish curriculum resources (www.bbc.co.uk/bitesize/levels/zgckjxs). TED Talks, GLOW or curriculum sites to support subject knowledge, for example, in instances where rural secondary teachers have to teach other subject areas, such as a biology teacher having to teach physics or chemistry, can also be helpful and are widely available online.

---

**Task 13.2    Mentoring resources**

Take some time to explore the resources listed above, and others, and consider how you might use these to support learning and dialogue with a mentee online.

---

## Vision and values

Chapter 3 highlighted the importance of critical reflection on how our personal values are embedded in mentoring, especially in relation to the General Teaching Council for Scotland's (GTCS) Professional Standards. These values apply just as much, if not more, when mentoring digitally and remotely. Senge (2006) defines vision as what you would like to build for yourself and the world around you, and argues that having awareness of one's "personal vision and genuine aspirations" are necessary elements of long-term personal, professional and organisational change, as it is the first step to a shared vision with others: "It is the essential cornerstone of the learning organisation, the learning organisation's spiritual foundation" (Senge, 2006: 7). Healthy and positive digital and remote mentoring occurs when mentors are aware of personal visions and can translate those visions into a "[negotiated and] shared vision" between mentor and mentee. A starting point for a mentor, therefore, is to be cognisant of not just their expert professional knowledge and skills but, crucially, their own vision and values, especially with regard to the nuances of interactions online and the use of resources to expand the knowledge and skills of their mentees. Personal visions can translate to shared visions, which in turn aid personal mastery and growth. For example, a mentor might consider it important to work on building a meaningful connection or partnership with their mentee, share core content and resources, and encourage creative thinking.

According to Clutterbuck (2004), "Mentoring involves primarily listening with empathy, sharing experience, professional friendship, developing insight through reflection, being a sounding board, encouraging." Each of these descriptors is dependent on the personal vision and values of the mentor, as emphasised earlier in the chapter. "Every mentoring relationship is unique, just as every individual is unique" (Clutterbuck, 2004: 117). A mentor's vision and values influence their attitudes to mentoring and the styles, strategies and practices they employ.

---

### Task 13.3   Digital vision statement

In earlier chapters you would have reflected on your own values as a mentor. In 100 words or less, list three fundamental aspects that you would embed into your personal vision of digital and remote mentoring.

---

## Criteria for appraising innovative and effective mentoring

There are many criteria for appraising innovative and effective mentoring, and much of these depend on the discipline within which these criteria develop – philosophy, psychology and education to name a few. For the purposes of this chapter, and given that the focus of this book is on mentoring within the Scottish educational context, the GTCS' (2020) criteria, as highlighted in Chapter 3, seem a good starting point for managing mentoring virtually:

- A prerequisite for effective mentoring is a "climate of trust".
- There is a culture of "openness" within and between people.
- People at all levels "feel valued" and demonstrate that they value others.
- A personal commitment to the process, and a positive relationship between the mentor and mentee is key.

In addition, there is general agreement (Cloke and Goldsmith, 2003; Covey and Covey, 2020; Senge, 2006; Stanier, 2016) that:

- clear objectives and boundaries ought to be set;
- clear communication is important;

- there needs to be an agreed reason for change;
- there needs to be time to affect change; and
- mentees need to feel heard and have a voice.

Some aspects of mentoring are the same whether the approach is in-person or digital, but there are extra conditions that a mentor ought to be mindful of when collaborating with a mentee online.

Interactions in digital spaces operate differently to face-to-face interactions (Cetina, 2008; Conole, 2009). In a virtual mentoring platform, communication becomes more challenging as the space for interaction is artificial and time is slightly delayed. Thus, it is paramount that the following points are managed well by a mentor and extra attention is placed on:

- a balance between the need for interaction and the need for space;
- greater intentionality in communication (i.e., clear plans for why, when, how often, and the need to communicate);
- a negotiated balance between the need for structure and flexibility (low structure, high structure or no structure);
- the creative use of technologies; and
- paying attention to a mentee's wellbeing.

In addition, mentoring professionals from rural areas requires an understanding of the "supports and constraints available in these communities", and mentors ought to be aware of the complexities of such contexts (Brook et al., 2015). Mentors ought to ensure that as barriers to progress and change are managed and removed, new problems, which may previously have seemed unimportant or were not previously considered, don't inadvertently become major barriers (Senge, 2006). This cognisance can be camouflaged in the virtual arena where human interaction, body language and eye contact can be challenging to read. There is an urgent need to create a more humanised and empathic online learning experience to relieve some of the tensions of remote contact for both parties.

## Task 13.4   Mentoring digitally

Consider how digital and remote mentoring might be similar to or different from face-to-face mentoring.

## Case Study 13.1   A lesson from undergraduate student teachers

Since March 2020, nearly all learning at universities in Scotland has seen a shift to a mixture of online and on-campus delivery, especially for teacher education courses. Claire, a lecturer and educator with many years' experience teaching and mentoring face to face within a physically designated space, had to adjust quickly to online teaching, learning and mentoring. She learned about various systems of education online and that the three giants, Google, Apple and Microsoft, all offered sophisticated online platforms, tools and training, in addition to the Blackboard system her university was already using. Claire attended a dozen training courses to improve her digital skills and learned to record lectures using Panopto, adding captions and ensuring that the material she was producing met the legal requirement to support students with additional visual and auditory needs. Each lecture took hours to create and upload for students to view at their leisure before online seminars took place. Lectures were run asynchronously and seminars were timetabled (synchronous). However, Claire was not prepared for what she experienced in seminars with 30 or more undergraduate student teachers online, or even when having individual mentoring conversations with students for whom she was a Personal Academic Tutor (PAT). During online seminars, she found herself talking to a dark screen carved up into individual squares of initials. The student teachers were not comfortable revealing themselves on screen, and neither were they willing to talk, ask or answer questions without much artful prompting. In other words, they were visually absent and auditorily muted. The debates and discussions they would have had in a physical classroom setting were minimised. Similarly, mentoring conversations with students on school experience were often constrained by the student's awareness of others in the school staff room or other family disruptions if at home.

Claire was frustrated with the situation and tried to find out what students were thinking. Students explained that they did not feel safe or comfortable to reveal themselves online unless it was through the filter of their Facebook or Instagram photo, where they could present a certain image of themselves. Some students did not want to reveal their home setting, some were learning in the midst of small busy households or in their personal bedroom space. They also explained that they were afraid of sounding stupid or being ridiculed if they gave the wrong answer in class, with the added risk of it being recorded and going viral. These were genuine fears, anxieties and concerns.

After negotiation with students, Claire and her students co-created a system that would support safe dialogue and interaction. In online classes the use of break-out groups of three or four students helped them to engage with each other, with one representative in each group then taking a turn to share their discussion and answer. Others used the chat box facility to expand on their notes and answers. In some classes, she formed teams of three or four students who met online in advance of the seminar to prepare answers to activities, again with members taking it in turns to present points of note from their discussions. Whilst Claire still could not "see" them, they would at the very least see each other in small groups, talk to one another, make connections and build relationships with their peers. Also, Claire could join the break-out groups to aid discussion and she found that, within this small setting, students had their videos and microphones turned on. When mentoring students on school experience, Claire became more aware of the importance of encouraging the student to agree a time that was appropriate for their discussion and feedback in a place where the student felt able to talk freely and turn on their camera.

As a teacher, facilitator and mentor, Claire had to provide a high level of structure in order to aid communication and learning. In paying attention to students' wellbeing, there had to be, as mentioned earlier, greater intentionality in her communication with them (and in theirs with her), allowing for a balance between the need for interaction and the need for personal safety and space. Claire also used various online creative tools offered by Blackboard Collaborate or Microsoft Teams to encourage participation, such as the use of the chat box, break-out groups, polls, sharing of prepared word documents, TED Talks and YouTube videos to aid understanding of the material being covered and provoke discussion. Providing no or little structure and expecting a free flow of sophisticated debate and discussion was not going to be possible without careful, organised intervention.

Claire's experience also made her reflect on how this situation would influence mentoring conversations, when the best time would be for such conversations to take place, and how pre-prepared word documents and teaching videos could be used prior to or during mentoring sessions.

---

### Task 13.5    Different structures for a mentoring relationship

- How could Claire's experience from Case Study 13.1 influence how you might conduct digital mentoring conversations?
- Based on the difference between Claire's face-to-face teaching and digital teaching, what difference can you identify between face-to-face and online digital mentoring?
- What type of mentoring structure do you prefer (low, high, no structure)?
- What are the merits/drawbacks of your preference?
- Which structure best encourages the growth of the individual through the digital realm?

Use this iMentoring (2020) guide to help you: https://mentoringgroup.com/types-of-mentoring.html

---

## Three innovative and effective digital and "remote" models

Based on the criteria highlighted earlier, this section recommends three innovative and effective digital models of mentoring that are interactive, solutions focussed and mentee-centric. It is useful for both mentor and mentee to agree before each mentoring conversation whether it can be recorded and, if so, by whom. If it is agreed that they can be recorded, it enables the mentee to replay and listen again to a mentoring conversation and use this for further reflection. The three models to be discussed are:

- GROW
- Active questioning and listening for understanding
- BIFF feedback model and reverse mentoring

## Issues to consider

There are several issues to consider and work through with the mentee in a digital and remote context, and this is part of an early initiation phase, which builds rapport and sets direction (Clutterbuck, 2004: 110). Issues may include the following:

- **Digital boundaries and limitations**
  What boundaries of time, access and space do you need to negotiate?
  What obstacles to digital working does the mentee face (hardware, software, connectivity issues, home environment, availability, caring responsibilities, personal issues).
- **Contracting**
  A contract between mentor and mentee creates clarity, transparency and agreed expectations regarding how mentoring processes are managed. For example, a contract allows mentor and mentee to be upfront about how any unanticipated issues of confidentiality might be processed, agree procedures and timescales for meetings and reviews, and outlines how these expectations might differ when using a digital, online platform compared to face-to-face meetings.
- **Commitment and accountability**
  It is important that both parties discuss and clarify each other's commitment to the enterprise, reasons why the mentor is mentoring and what the mentee hopes to gain from the mentoring. The sharing of personal experiences helps to humanise the individuals involved, and the process of mentoring itself. It helps to "mediate" against the artificiality of digital interaction (Coker, 2016, 2019).

## The GROW model (Whitmore, 1992)

*GROW* is a widely used coaching model from the 1980s and stands for *Goals*, *Reality*, *Options*, *Way Forward*, which is a simple but highly effective approach to structuring a coaching or mentoring dialogue. Typically, the GROW model assumes that the mentor is not an expert in the client's situation, and therefore acts as a professional facilitator, helping the mentee select the best options for growth and development. The GROW model is very much at the non-directive end of mentoring conversations and is recommended by the GTCS (2020).

As the acronym indicates, there are four stages to using GROW in a mentoring session:

Stage 1: Establish the *Goal*
At the start of the session, it is vital to define and agree the goal or outcome to be achieved for that session – one that is specific, measurable and realistic. This is where learning needs are established.
To achieve this, it may be useful to ask questions like:

- "How will you be able to tell that you have achieved that goal?"
- "How will you know that the issue is solved?"

Stage 2: Examine present *Reality*

In discussing the mentee's current reality, a solution may start to emerge. This is where the mentee is encouraged to become an independent learner and take responsibility.

Useful questions include:

- "What is the result of that?"
- "What is happening at the moment?"

Stage 3: Explore *Options*

At this point, it is appropriate to explore what is possible, generating as many useful options as possible and discussing these. In a digital setting it's useful to ask questions, but mentors should be conscious of the virtual space and should mediate for opportunities to enable the mentee to do most of the talking. This is where the mentor can help the mentee to evaluate the success of the options.

Questions used to generate ideas may include:

- "What else could you do?"
- "What if this or that barrier was removed?"
- "What are the pros and cons of each option?"
- "What criteria will you use to weigh up the options?"

Stage 4: Establish the *Way Forward* (or *What Next*)

The mentee should now have a better idea of how he or she can achieve their goal. At this final stage, your role as mentor is to encourage the mentee to commit to action points to facilitate the achievement of objectives set earlier in the process. This is also where the mentor can help the mentee to evaluate the success of their relationship (see BIFF feedback model and reverse mentoring).

Useful questions include:

- "What will you do now?"
- "What could get in the way?"
- "How will you overcome it?"
- "Will this address your goal?"

The stages as described here seem linear and formal, however in reality, as collaborative dialogue occurs, these stages may intersect or develop cyclically, and this is desirable to encourage a humanistic, empathetic digital relationship. It is the mentor's role to be cognisant of these processes and manage them effectively.

## Active questioning and listening for understanding

Questioning and listening are two vital models for a successful mentoring relationship, not just in face-to-face interactions but also online. It is worth pointing out the importance of being able to see the other person when working remotely, meaning when both parties have their cameras switched on. As educators we are familiar with the role that closed and open questions play, and the need for higher order questions (Bloom, 1956). Hypothesising questions and probing questions help the mentee to reflect or imagine different scenarios. Hypothetical questions are "What if's" – questions that challenge and present options and alternatives. Probing questions include "What else ...?", "What happens when ...?", "Why did you say that ...?" and "Why did you do that ...?"

Mentors ought to avoid leading questions because they encourage mentees to guess what a mentor would like to hear or the right answer. Multiple questions at once should also be avoided, as are simply confusing and could hamper reflection or produce garbled answers. And when a mentor has asked a question, listening just enough to then come in briskly with a prepared answer is counter-productive.

Listening with understanding involves suspending judgement and hearing what the mentee is actually trying to convey. During online interactions we are tempted to multi-task – texting, reading and answering emails – but this inevitably means we are not focussing on exactly what is being said. Listening with understanding helps to humanise online interactions, which in turn builds positive relationships and, as mentioned earlier, bridges the slight delay and ethereal gap when communicating virtually. The attentive and empathic listener is of course what mentors (and indeed mentees) ought to aim for. Mentoring online has its advantages in that material and resources can be shared efficiently and instantly. For example, mentor and mentee can share and engage simultaneously with texts, video clips, pupils' work, lesson plans, reflective journals and portfolios. Additionally, the mentoring experience is not time-lagged, and comments and advice can be recorded verbally in the "chat box" or the session can be audio-recorded for both parties to refer to again. See Table 13.1 for four levels of listening (Covey, 2004):

*Table 13.1* Four levels of listening

| Level | Characteristics |
| --- | --- |
| 1) Ignoring the speaker or pretending to listen | Not really listening to the speaker |
| | Really just waiting for your turn to speak |
| | Already decided what you are going to say |
| | Nodding but not really paying attention |
| | Doing other things at the same time |
| | Can't replay back what the person said |
| 2) Selective listening | Picking out the parts you are interested in or the parts that impact you |
| | Not getting the whole message or meaning |
| 3) Attentive listening | Focusing only on the speaker |
| | Concentrating on what they have to say |
| | Allowing them to finish what they have to say |
| | Asking follow-up questions |
| 4) Empathic listening | Focusing only on the speaker |
| | Listening carefully to the words used |
| | Understanding the feelings behind the words |
| | Recognising the emotions expressed |
| | Talking less and listening more |

## 1)  *The BIFF feedback model (Roberts, 2020) and reverse mentoring*

There are several effective feedback models that support structured, affirmative feedback to allow dynamic change to take place in the mentee – AID (Action, Impact, Development), CEDAR (Context, Examples, Diagnosis, Action, Review) and BOOST (Balanced, Observed, Objective, Specific, Timely) to name a few. The Behaviour, Impact, Future and Feelings (BIFF) model, however, asks the mentee to share their feelings about the feedback they have received. It can be challenging to receive feedback, so this model gives the mentee space to voice their reaction and the mentor the opportunity to support the mentee through this. The BIFF model is as follows:

B    Behaviour: Specific description of what the person receiving the feedback has done.
I     Impact: What effect this behaviour has had on you, other people or their performance.
F    Future: What you expect in terms of behaviour or performance.
F    Feelings: How do you feel about this?

Equally, it is important that the mentor gets feedback from the mentee, not just at the end of the mentoring contract but throughout the process, asking for suggestions in order that they, too, may improve. This is also known as reverse mentoring. A digital mentoring session could be structured in such a way that feedback is sought from the mentee after a particular topic or theme has been covered in the discussion, rather than waiting to the end of the entire mentoring project before getting an evaluation. "Reverse mentoring is situated in the mentoring literature as an alternative form of mentoring" and has become "best practice" in many global organisations (Marcinkus Murphy, 2012: 550). At a formal level, "it involves the pairing of a junior employee acting as mentor to share expertise with a senior colleague as mentee … in addition, there is an emphasis on the leadership development of the mentors" (Marcinkus Murphy, 2012: 550). Knowledge is exchanged, the mentoring relationship becomes a symbiotic partnership, and both parties benefit.

At a basic informal level, reverse mentoring takes place when the mentor asks their mentee what aspects worked well and what could have been better. The mentee, for example, could be encouraged to answer three evaluative questions: What did I like about the session?; What did I not like about the session?; and what would I like to change? It is about being consciously competent (Gullander, 1974). Did the mentee change for the better and progress *because* of the support they received? Determining what exact part of the mentoring contributed to changes is not easy when working digitally and remotely, but it is a crucial exercise for evaluation and growth. One of the biggest errors that mentors make is not to collect feedback from their mentees. Moreover, mentors should not assume that their style and support of mentoring given online was a good match for the mentee just because their face-to-face mentoring style would have been a good match (Covey and Covey, 2020; Phillips-Jones, 2020). Feedback is a fundamental tool for building relationships online, and for developing ourselves and others (see Case Study 13.1 and 13.2). Given the importance of humanising the mentoring experience in the digital realm, reverse mentoring in the form of evaluative feedback helps to build the "virtual" relationship between mentor and mentee.

## Case Study 13.2  The use of remote mentoring to support students on school placements

A class of secondary postgraduate student teachers are out on placement during the COVID-19 outbreak. It is deemed unsafe and impractical for university-based tutors to visit their students in school, and so the usual observed lesson by the university tutor cannot take place. Neither can school-based mentors join the university for a twilight session to find out how the placement for that year is going to be run, meet each other and have any concerns answered.

The university tutors set up a series of initiatives to counter this. 1) Every student teacher has an *e-portfolio*, called a *Professional Development Portfolio (PDP)*. Lesson plans, resources, videos, audio recordings, reflective logs, formative feedback and summative reports against the GTCS' SPR standards are filed in this e-portfolio that is stored within platforms such as *One Drive* or *PebblePad*. These can be shared with the university tutor and the school mentor at any time, material can be downloaded for tutors and mentors to check progress, and, crucially, students can take this PDP with them when they leave the university. The e-portfolio of work replaces the traditional paper teaching folder, which saves on paper and is environmentally sound. Students are also set up with *GLOW accounts* so that they can access the Wi-Fi and resources in the school. 2) To counter the fact that students, university tutors and school mentors are unable to meet face to face, *weekly feedback sessions* are held in which there is a three-way, structured, reflective dialogue and active listening. In these weekly sessions, lesson plans, video clips, examples of good practice and university documentation can be shared, explained and discussed.

The weekly sessions are effective in building positive relationships and understanding between university tutors and school mentors, and the university decides to do away with the face-to-face twilight sessions in the future. The formal summative observation is either carried out by the school mentor and a member of the senior management team or, if classroom video technology, like *IRIS Connect*, is available, observations can be done remotely. IRIS Connect allows students to record their lessons, quickly and easily, using a mobile camera system. After a recording has taken place, the video is uploaded directly to the student's personal, password-protected, account in a secure online platform where they can watch it back for their own personal reflection or share it with a mentor for feedback.

Using the GROW model, as recommended by the GTCS (2020), and active listening, as described above, the university tutors and school mentors work together with the student teacher/mentee. The weekly three-way dialogic approach together with evidence from the student's e-portfolio of work is an effective way of mentoring student teachers/mentees online and remotely.

---

**Task 13.6   Models of mentoring digitally**

What barriers might you and your mentee face when meeting online and how might you go about addressing these challenges, considering the various models, structures and suggestions given in this chapter?

---

## Summary and key points

Mentoring is fundamental to professional learning and development through all stages of an educator's career in Scotland, and is closely aligned to the Professional Standards set out by the GTCS. Mentoring is a highly challenging and complex process and the main responsibility for ensuring its success lies with the mentor. A successful mentoring relationship requires an investment of time along with an understanding of the process. However, as a result of the COVID-19 pandemic, the challenges for communication and interaction need to be reframed to take account of the benefits and challenges of remote mentoring. Maintaining positive relationships and personal wellbeing digitally means that many of the choices we make as mentors will be far from simple. Mentoring success online and remotely does not only depend on a mentor's and mentee's digital capabilities. There are aspects to the mentoring that will stay the same and aspects that will need to be altered. This chapter identified some guiding principles and models of mentoring that invite us to reflect on how we can build on best practice in the digital and remote post-COVID world.

This chapter has considered:

- three main criteria for appraising innovative and effective mentoring via digital and remote models;
- three innovative and effective digital and remote models of mentoring; and
- the need for mentors to clarify their personal vision, values and attitudes, and to understand the consequent impact of these on their style, strategies and practices when mentoring in an increasingly digital realm.

## Further reading

Coker, H. (2018). Purpose, pedagogy and philosophy: "Being" an online lecturer. *International Review of Research in Open and Distributed Learning*, 19(5), 128–144.
Kanatouri, S. (2020). *The digital coach*. London: Routledge.
Lemov, D. (2020). *Teaching in the online classroom: Surviving and thriving in the new normal*. New Jersey: Jossey-Bass.

## References

Argyll and Bute Council (2020). SALi: Sharing Argyll Learning Ideas. https://blogs.glowscotland.org.uk/ab/sali/
Bloom, B. S. (1956). *Taxonomy of educational objectives. Vol. 1: Cognitive domain*. New York: McKay.

Brook, J., Hobbs, N., Neumann-Fuhr, D., O'Riordan, A., Paterson, M. and Johnston, J. (2015). Preparing students in professional programs for rural practice: A case study. *Canadian Journal of Higher Education*, 45(2), 23-40.

Cetina, K. K. (2008). Objectual practice. In: Mazzotti, M. (ed). *Knowledge as social order: Rethinking the sociology of Barry Barnes* (pp. 83-98). Hampshire, UK: Ashgate Publishing.

Cloke, K. and Goldsmith, J. (2003). *The art of waking people up: Cultivating awareness and authenticity at work* (J-B Warren Bennis Series). San Francisco, CA: Jossey-Bass.

Clutterbuck, D. (2004). *Everyone needs a mentor: Fostering talent in your organisation.* Fourth Edition. Chartered Institute of Personnel and Development (CIPD). London: McGraw-Hill Education.

Coker, H. (2016). Understanding Pedagogic Collaboration in the Online Environment. PhD Thesis, University of Aberdeen.

Coker, H. (2019). Mediating the flow of professional capital: The potential of technology for rural teachers professional learning in Scotland. *Australian and International Journal of Rural Education*, 29(3), 39-55.

Conole, G. (2009). The role of mediating artefacts in learning design. In: Lockyer, L., Bennett, S., Agostinho, S. and Harper, B. (eds). *Handbook of research on learning design and learning objects: Issues, applications, and technologies* (pp. 188-208). New York: IGI Global.

Covey, S. (2004). *Seven habits of highly effective people.* London: Simon & Schuster.

Covey, S. R. and Covey, S. (2020). *The 7 habits of highly effective people.* London: Simon & Schuster.

Frouws, J. (1998). The contested redefinition of the countryside. An analysis of rural discourses in the Netherlands. *Sociologia ruralis*, 38(1), 54-68.

GTCS (2020) Coaching and Mentoring. https://www.gtcs.org.uk/professional-update/coaching-and-mentoring.aspx

Gullander, O. E. (1974). Conscious competency: The mark of a competent instructor. *Canadian Training Methods*, 7(1), 20-21.

iMentoring (2020). Different Types of Mentoring Relationships. https://mentoringgroup.com/types-of-mentoring.html

Marcinkus Murphy, W. (2012). Reverse mentoring at work: Fostering cross-generational learning and developing millennial leaders. *Human Resource Management*, 51(4), 549-573.

Megginson, D. (2005). *Mentoring in action: A practical guide.* London: Kogan.

Nordmann, E., Horlin, C., Hutchison, J., Murray, J. A., Robson, L., Seery, M. and MacKay, J. (2020). 10 simple rules for supporting a temporary online pivot in higher education. https://doi.org/10.31234/osf.io/qdh25

Odero, J. O. and Chinapah, V. (2016). Towards inclusive, quality ICT-based learning for rural transformation. *Journal of Education and Research*, 5(5.2 and 6.1), 107-125.

Phillips-Jones, L. (2020). Creating or Revising Your Personal Vision. https://mentoringgroup.com/personal-vision-statement.html

Roberts, A. (2020). The BIFF Feedback Model. https://andiroberts.com/feedback-models-hub/>

Schwartz, S. E., Rhodes, J. E., Liang, B., Sánchez, B., Spencer, R., Kremer, S. and Kanchewa, S. (2014). Mentoring in the digital age: Social media use in adult-youth relationships. *Children and Youth Services Review*, 47, 205-213.

Senge, P. M. (2006). *The fifth discipline: The art and practice of the learning organization.* London: Random House.

Stanier, M. B. (2016). *The coaching habit: Say less, ask more & change the way you lead forever.* Toronto, Canada: Box of Crayons Press.

The Scottish Government (2018). Scottish Government Urban Rural Classification 2016. https://www.gov.scot/publications/scottish-government-urban-rural-classification-2016/pages/5/

White, D. (2016). *Digital participation and social justice in Scotland*. Dunfermline: Carnegie UK Trust.

Whitmore, J. (1992). *Coaching for performance: A practical guide to growing your own skills*. London: Nicholas Brealey Publishing.

# INDEX